Best Homes *of the* 1920s

STANDARD HOMES COMPANY

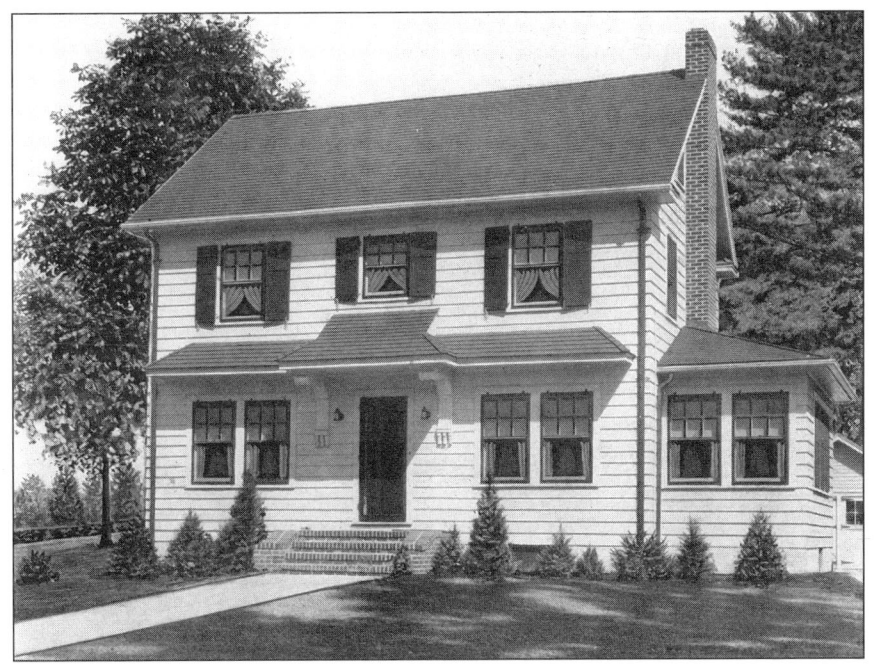

DOVER PUBLICATIONS, INC.
Mineola, New York

Bibliographical Note

This Dover edition, first published in 2008, is an unabridged republication of the work originally published in 1928 as *Better Homes at Lower Cost* by Standard Homes Company, Washington, D. C. The only significant alteration consists in omitting the index for space considerations.

Library of Congress Cataloging-in-Publication Data

Best homes of the 1920s.
    p. cm.
   Originally published: Washington, D. C. : Standard Homes Co., 1928.
   ISBN-13: 978-0-486-45430-6
   ISBN-10: 0-486-45430-4
    1. Architecture, Domestic—United States—Designs and plans. 2. Architecture—United States—20th century—Designs and plans. I. Standard Homes Company. II. Title: Best homes of the 1920s.

NA7208.S73 2007
728'.370222—dc22

2007027555

Manufactured in the United States of America
Dover Publications, Inc., 31 East 2nd Street, Mineola, N.Y. 11501

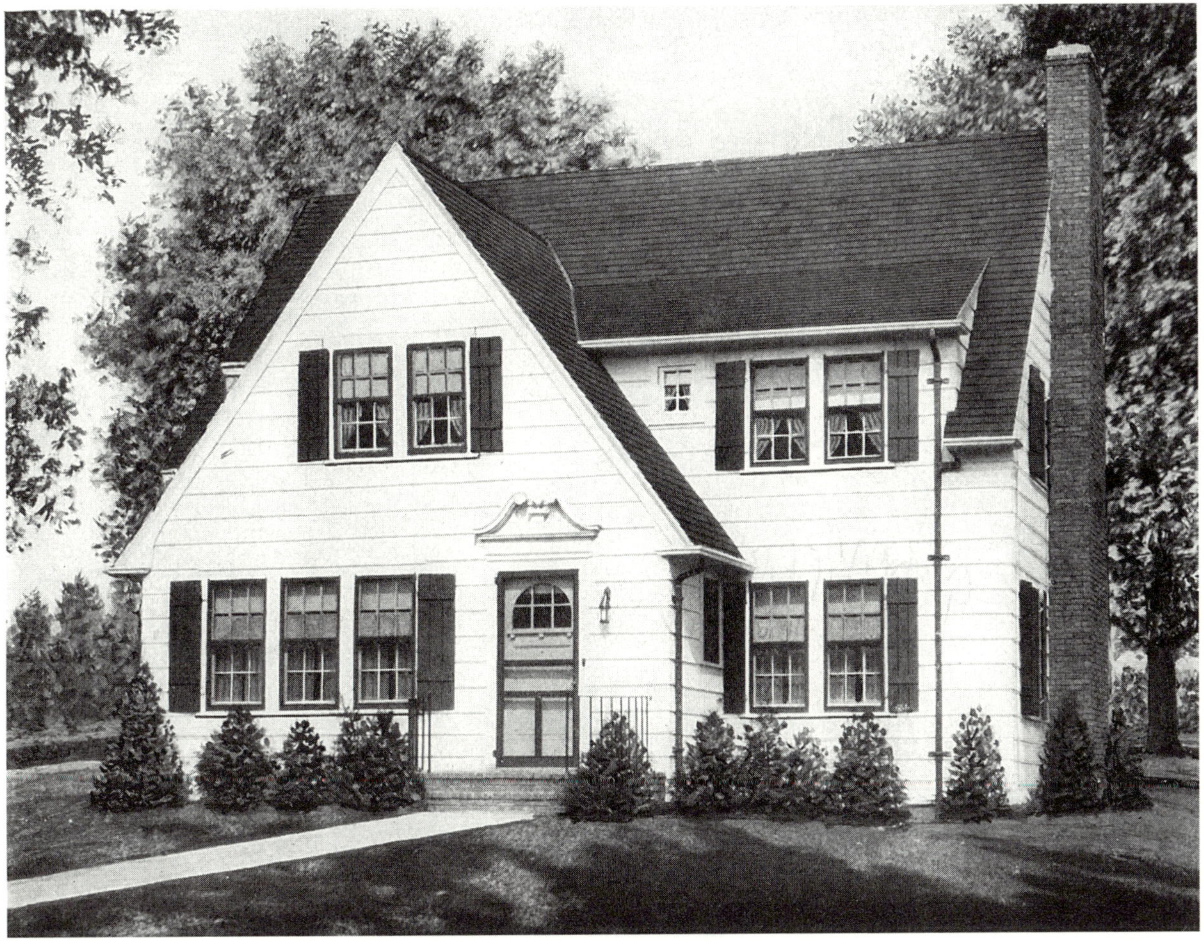

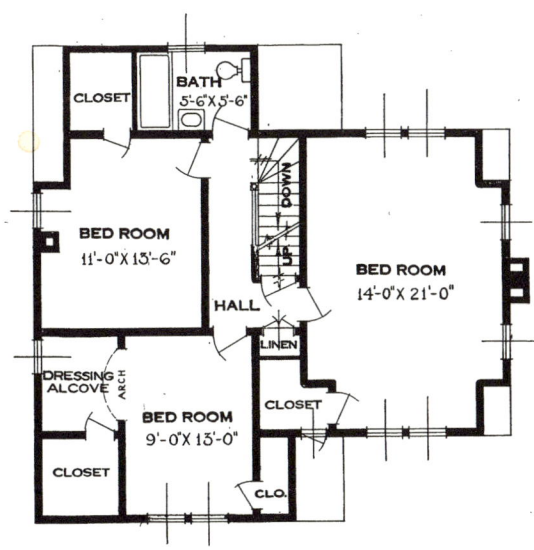
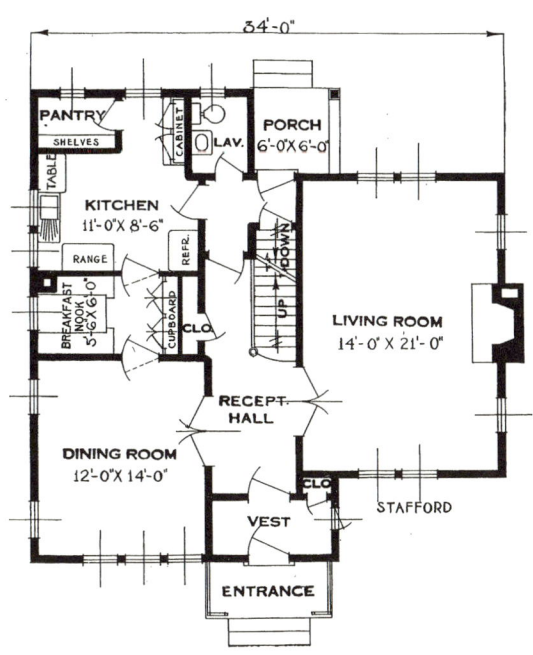

The STAFFORD (Size 34x34')

Humanity's earnest call is for kindness and good cheer. Those best fitted to do their bit toward human betterment are those who practice in their homes the principles which they endeavor to demonstrate abroad. Living up to one's moral standards is not a great risk if the surroundings are satisfying and the arrangement of the home is as ideal as The Stafford.

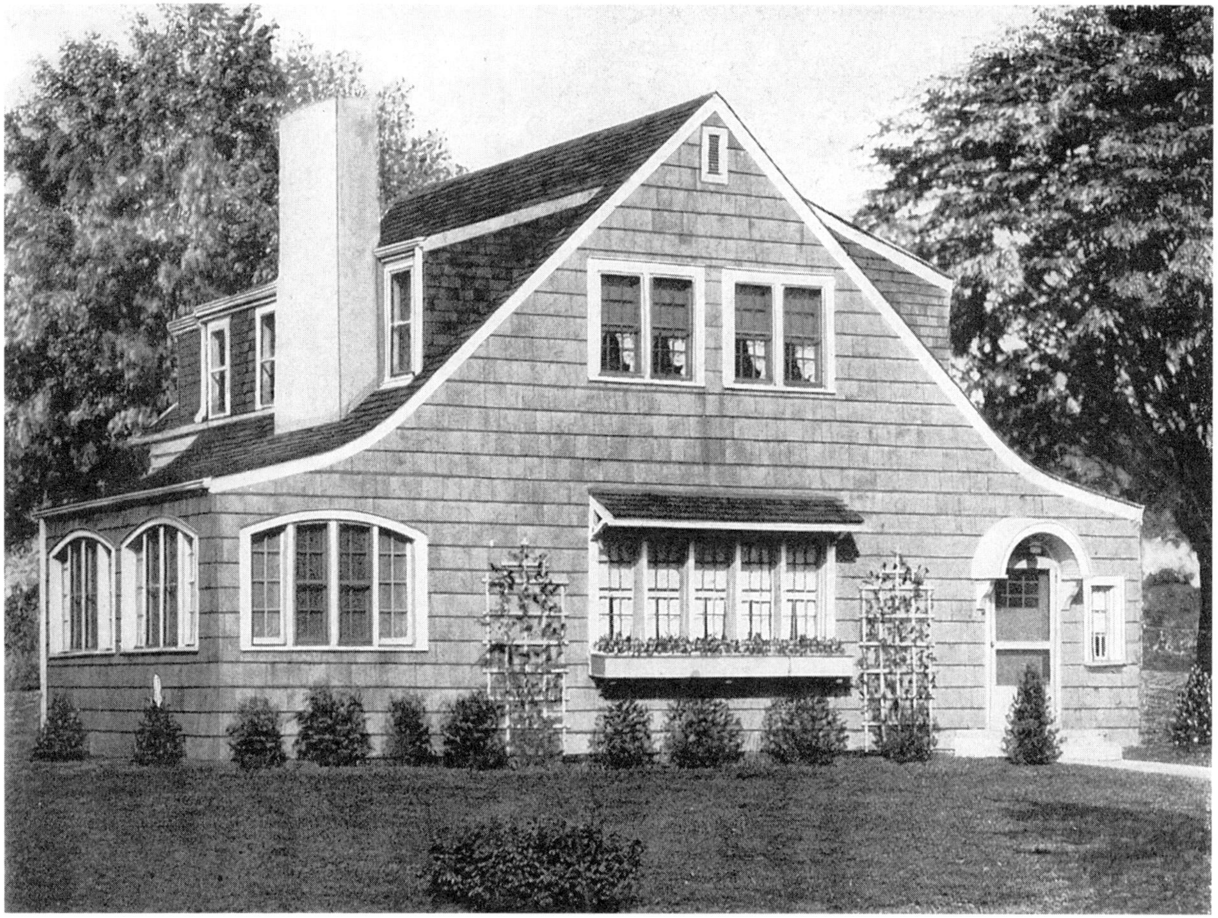

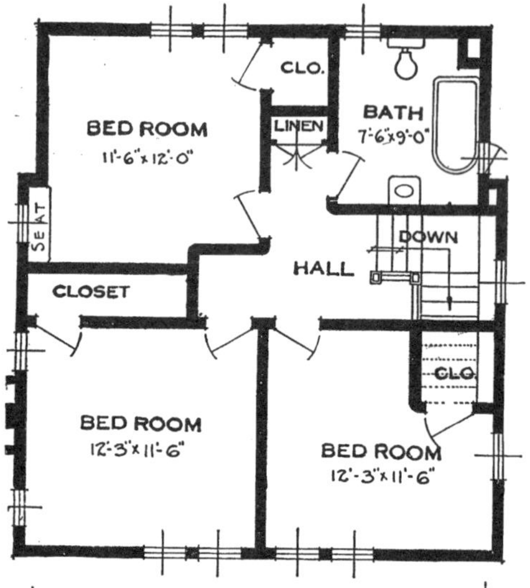

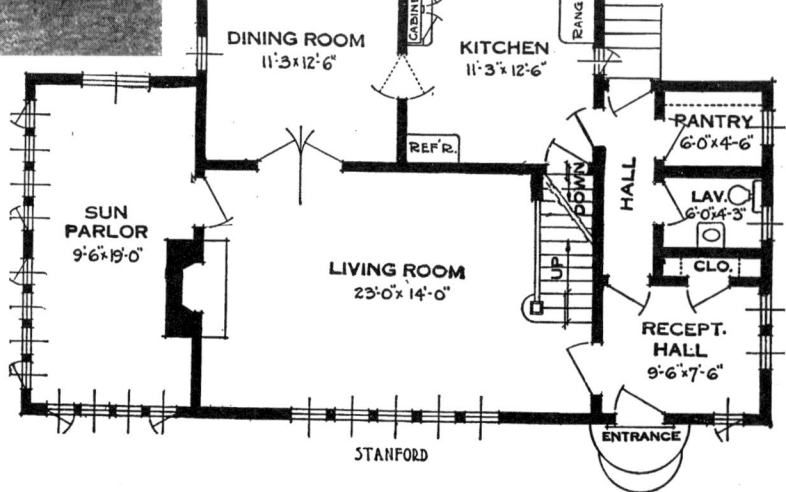

The STANFORD (Size 24x28')

Man's strength can easily be gauged by his faith in the strength of woman. Woman's intuition has always equalled, and in many instances surpassed, man's reason. Strong men know this vital principle of life and strive daily to keep harmonious the home in which dwells the heart and source of their strength. This is an easy task in beautiful new homes like The Stanford.

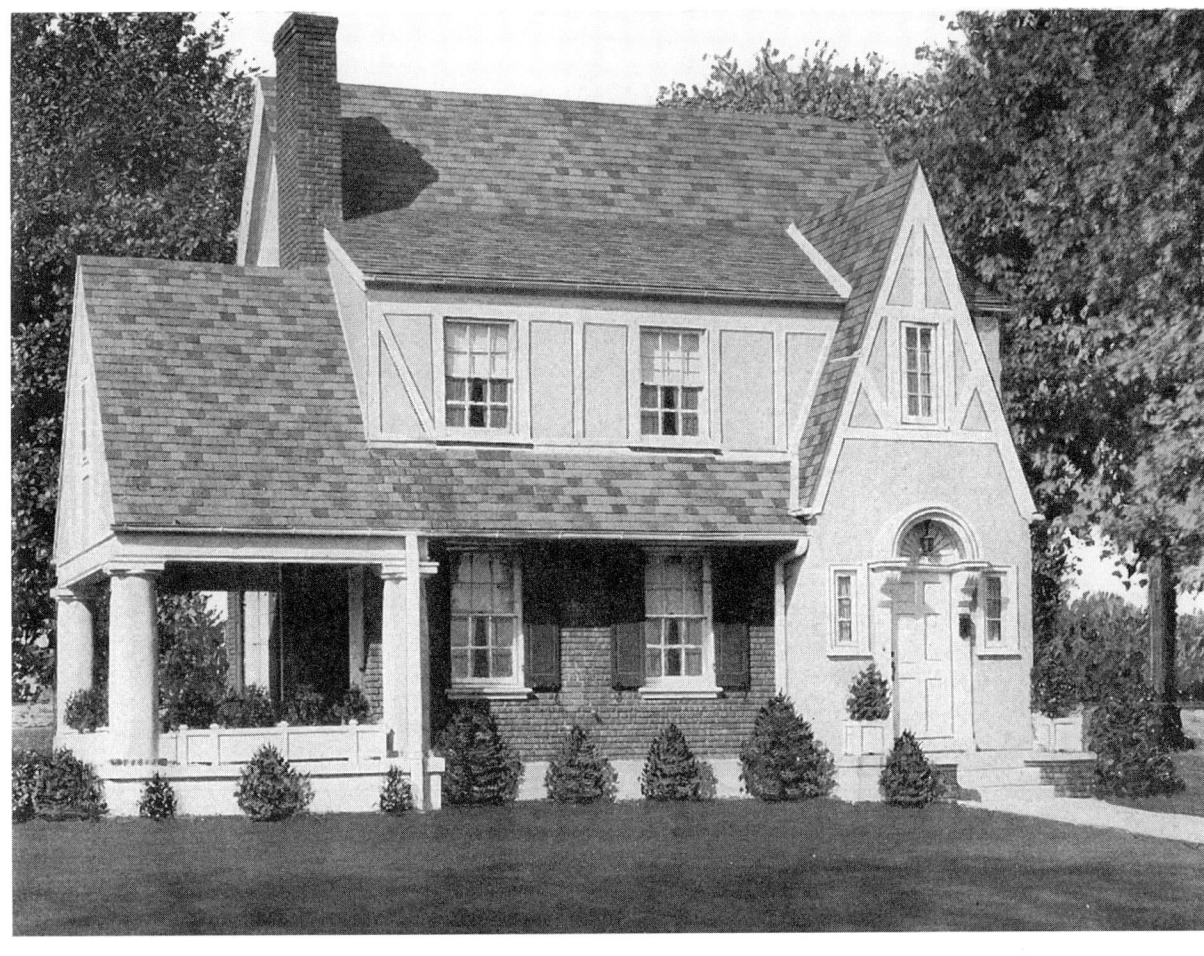
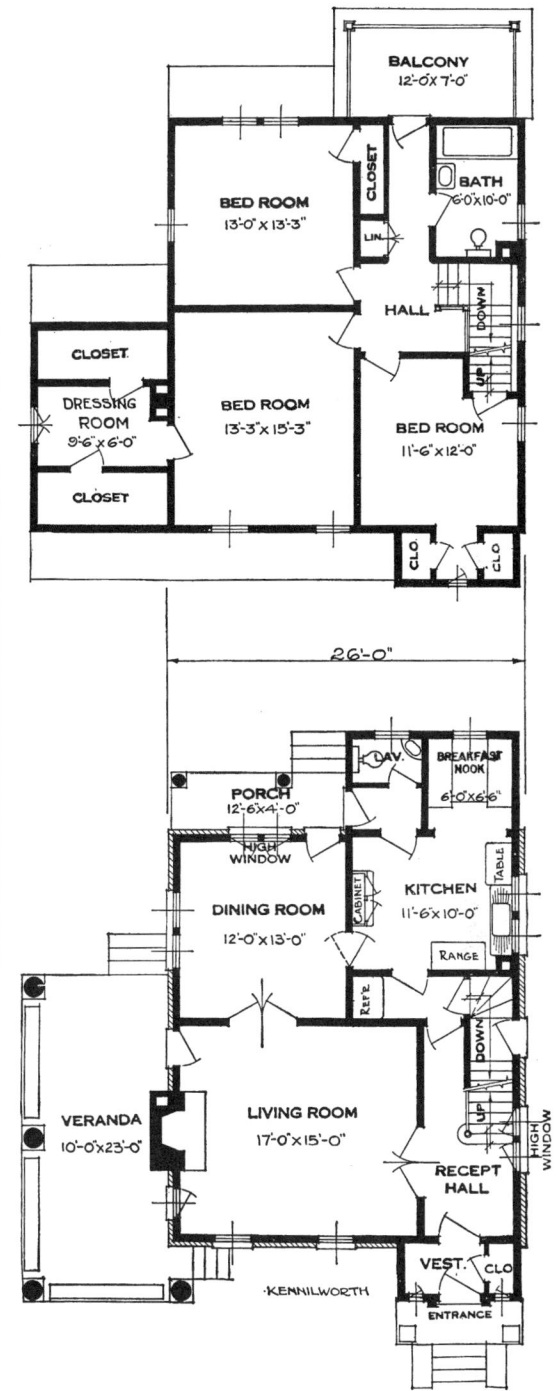

The KENNILWORTH (Size 26x30′)

Every movement for human betterment first finds expression in the home. There is something in the inner beings of optimistic men and women which prompts them to lend a hand to the helpless and give a word of cheer to the cheerless. Those who make The Kennilworth their home will be prompted daily to radiate the sunshine its comforts will bring.

All plans are so prepared as to permit frame, stucco, brick or tile construction.

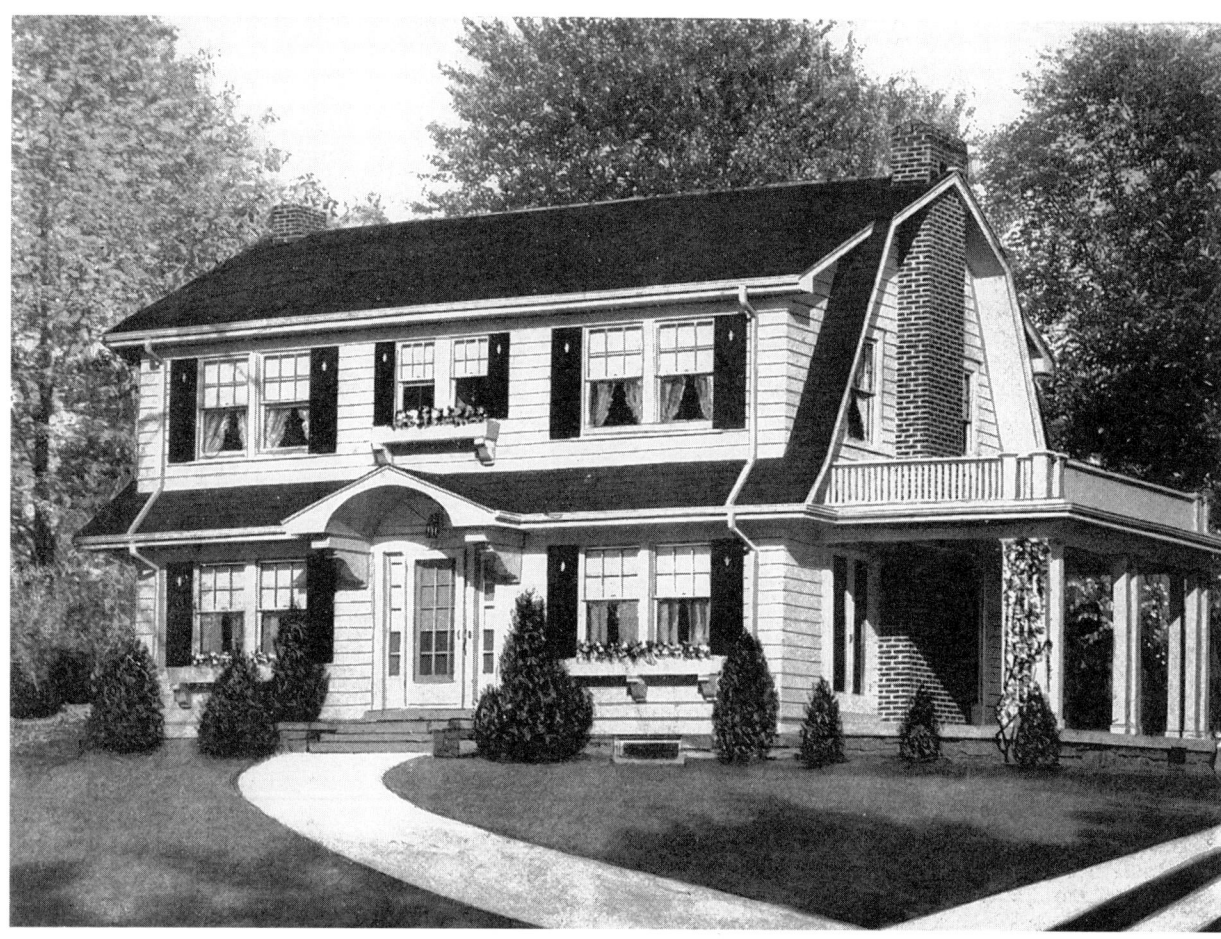
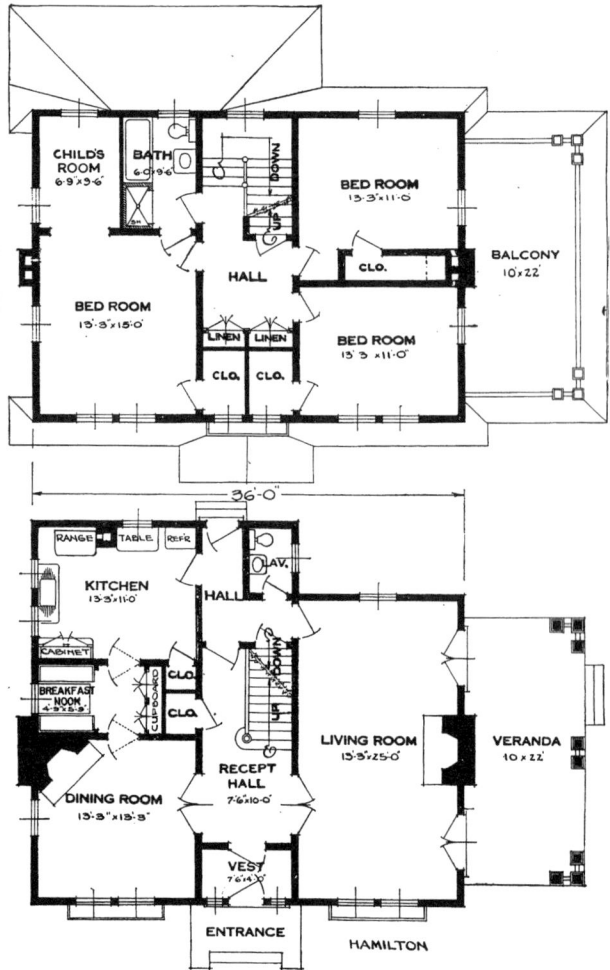

> It cannot be estimated what civilization owes to pure-minded women who love their homes.

The HAMILTON (Size 36x26')

Nothing so stimulates and elevates a man as for his life companion to believe in him, and in no other way can a man show his appreciation of such confidence and trust as in the earnest endeavor to build her a home of her own. Any woman who has tact, forethought, and patience with her husband need not despair of owning eventually just such a home as The Hamilton.

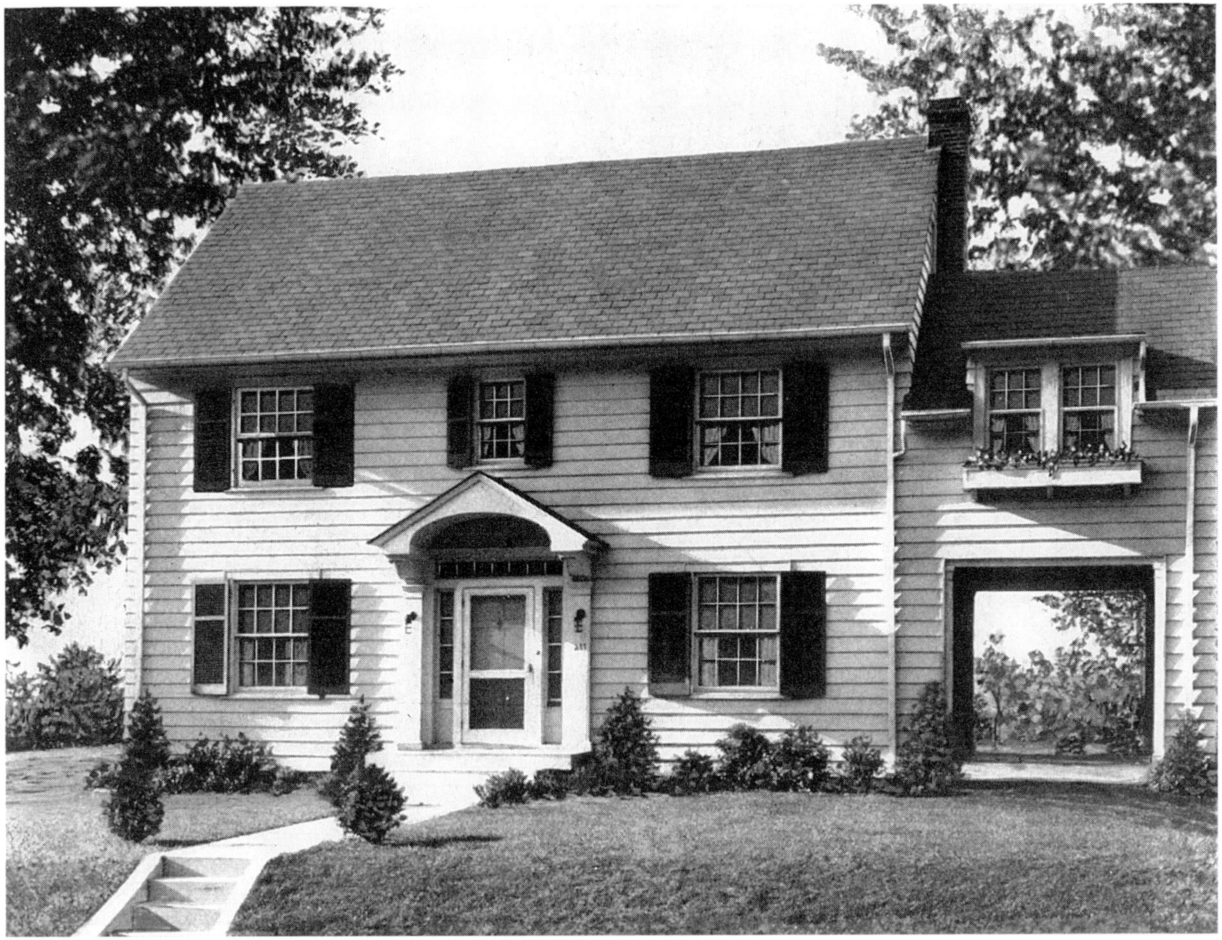

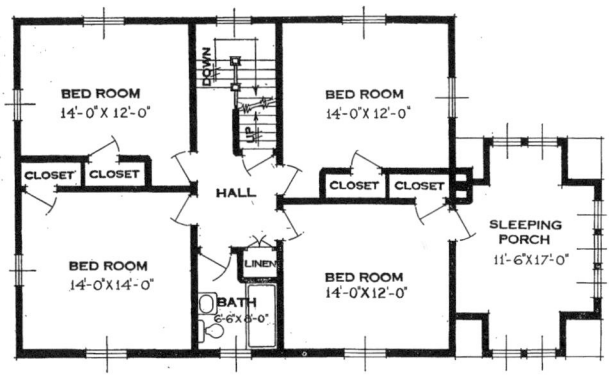

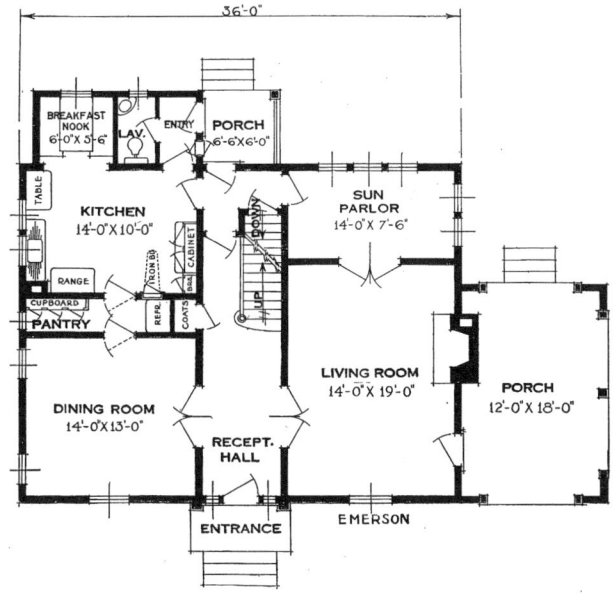

The EMERSON (Size 36x28')

The life that would be complete, that would be sweet and sane as well as strong must be softened and enriched by the love of all things beautiful. In no other way has man proven his onward and upward march as in the creation of beautiful homes like The Emerson. Such homes are civilization's guide posts on the path of progress.

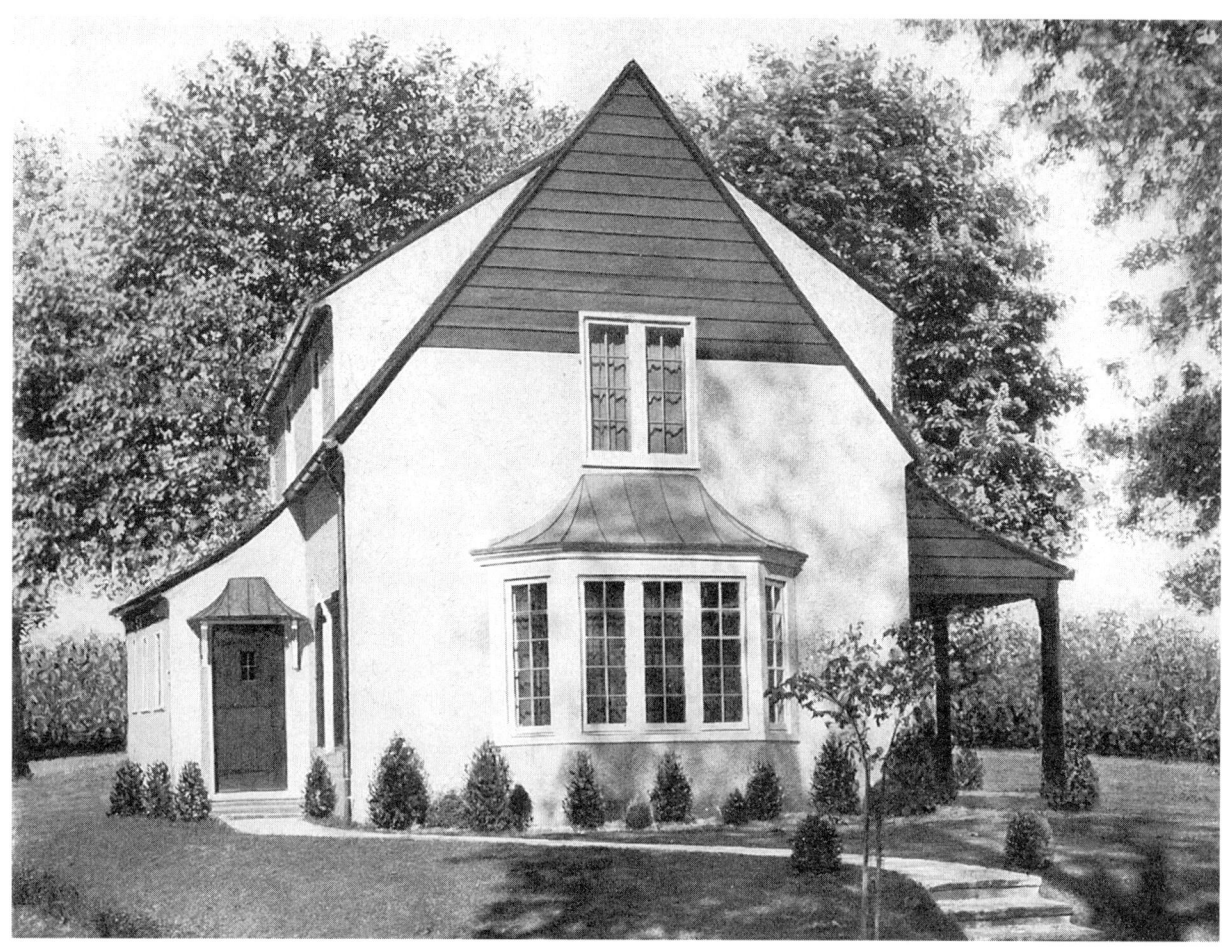
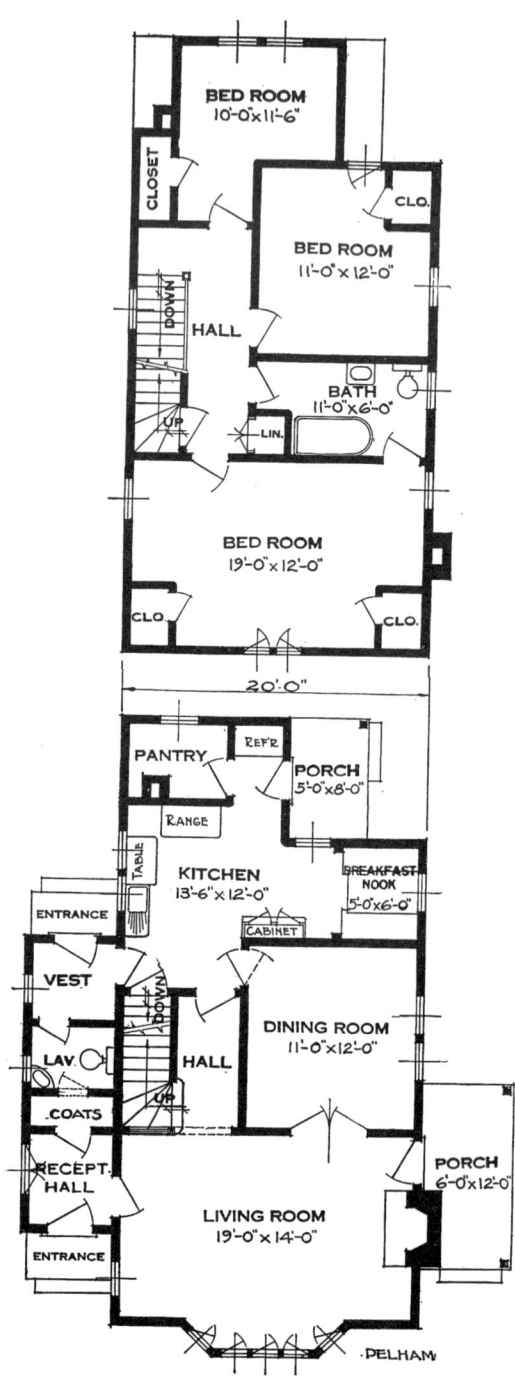

The PELHAM (Size 20x32′)

All mothers should be free from those things which disturb and distress. They should at all times feel a sense of restfulness, serenity, peace and poise. Conditions for such a state of mind cannot be found in crowded districts, but rather in ideal private homes, where only those influences are permitted which tend to satisfy the maternal senses.

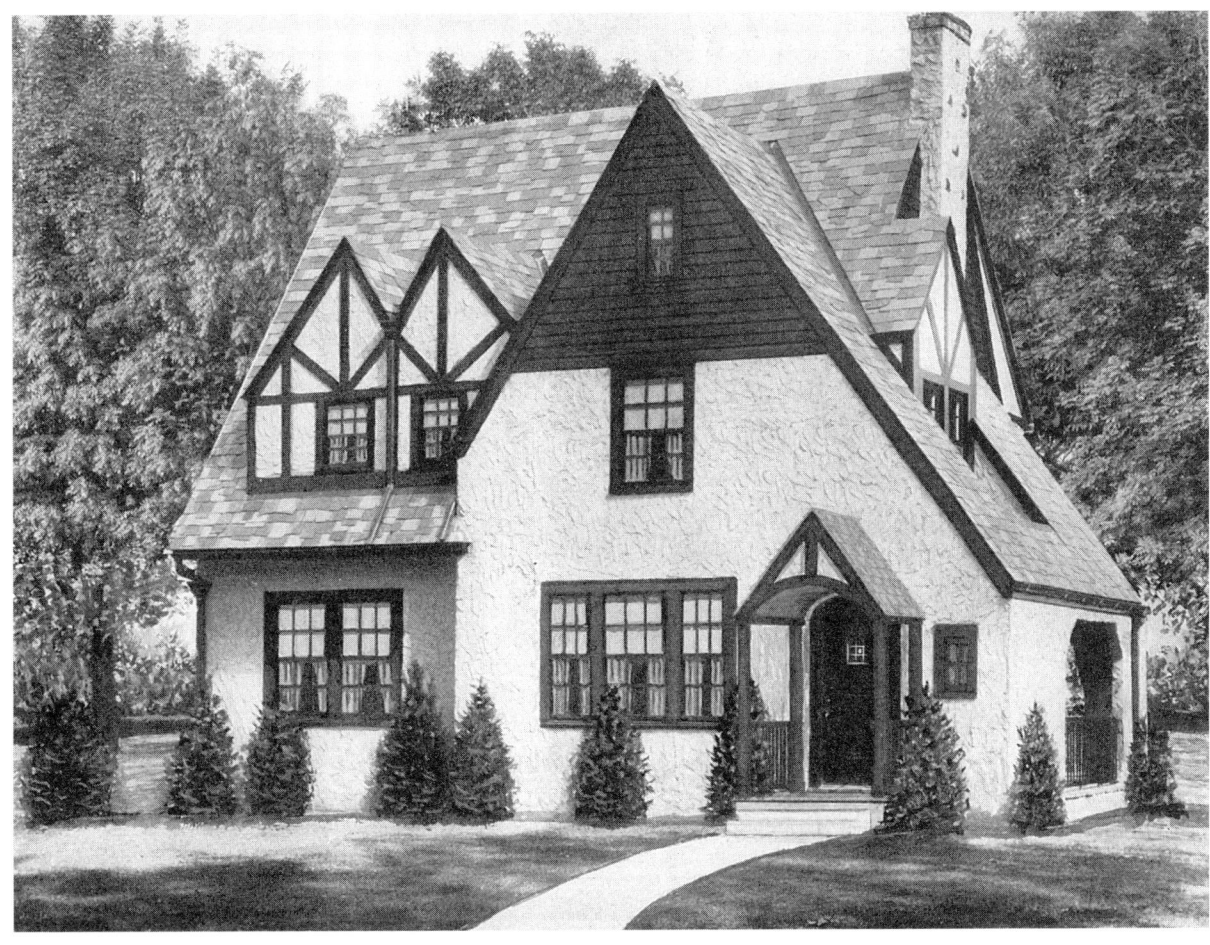
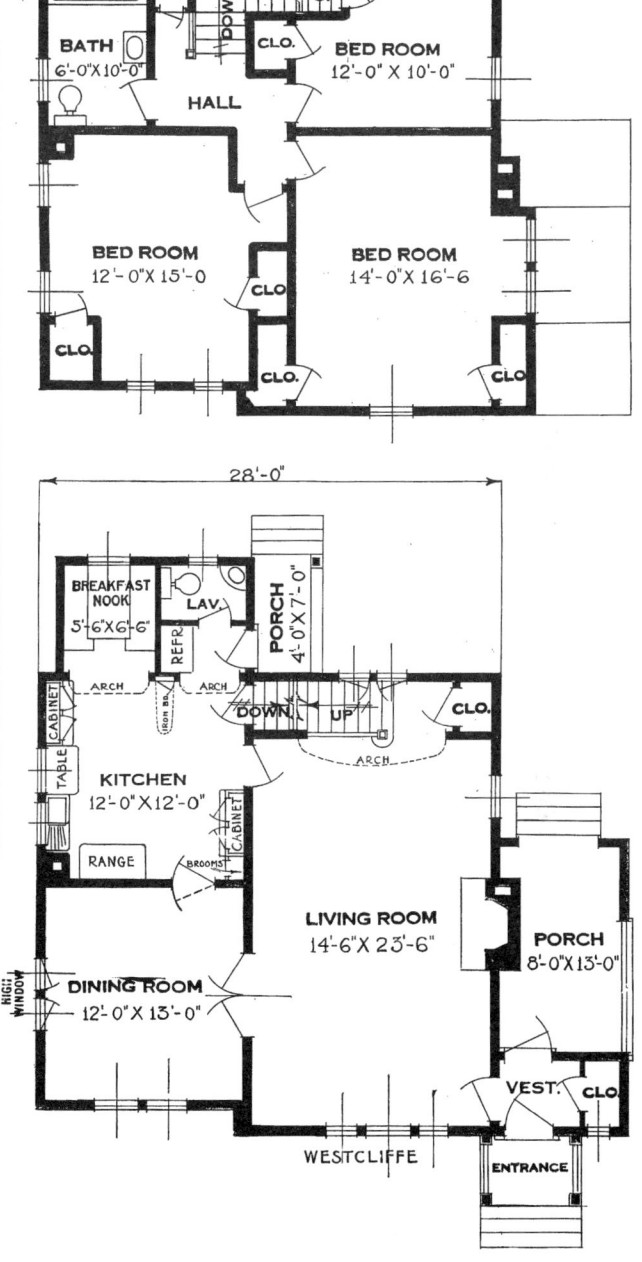

The WESTCLIFFE (Size 28x28')

It is never the size nor monetary value of a home that grips and holds the heart of a child as the years lead him into manhood. Instead it is the sympathy, companionship and love demonstrated by contented parents who have early learned that life is fuller and more abundant in a convenient home of their own.

All plans are so prepared as to permit frame, stucco, brick or tile construction.

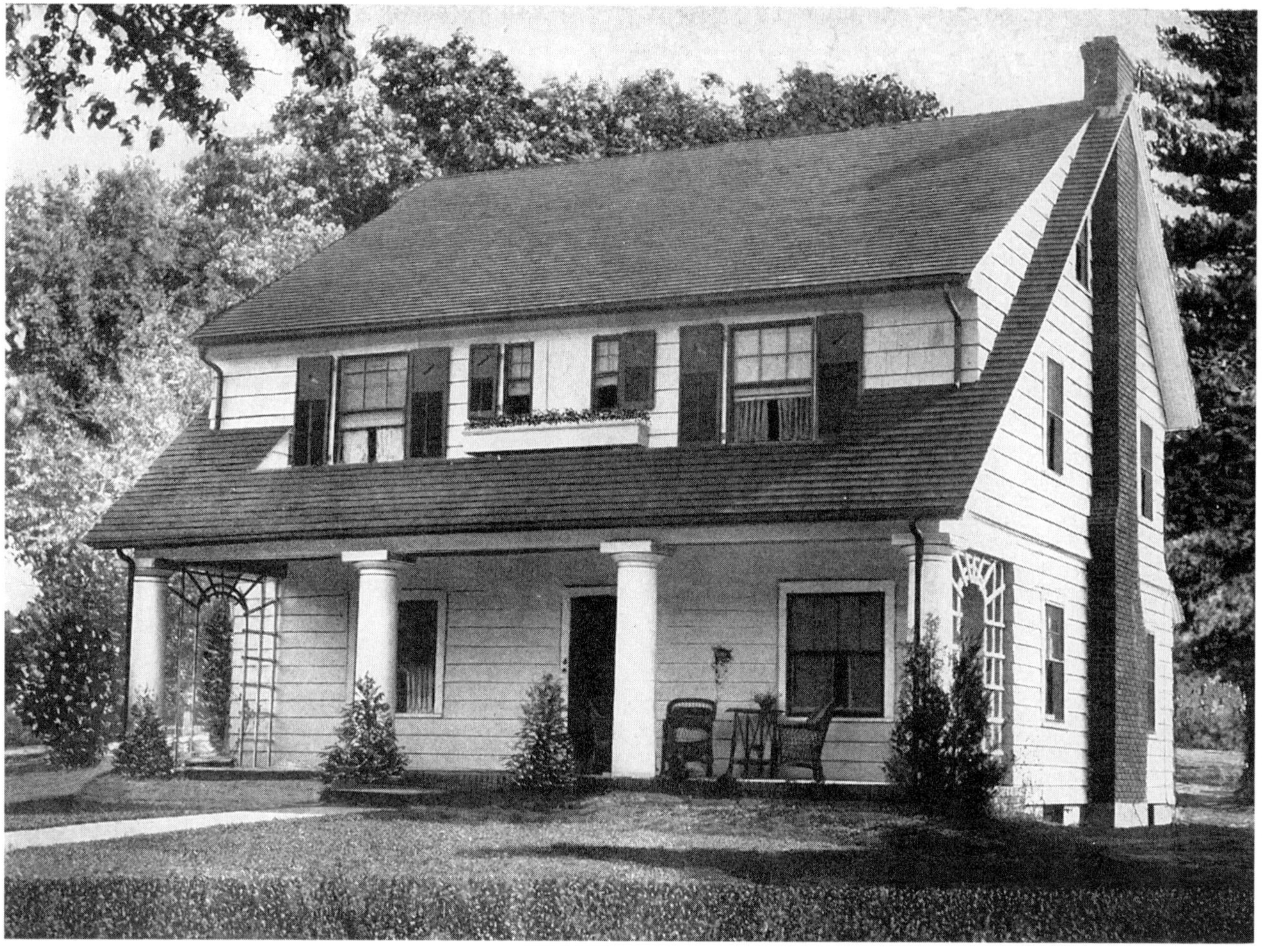

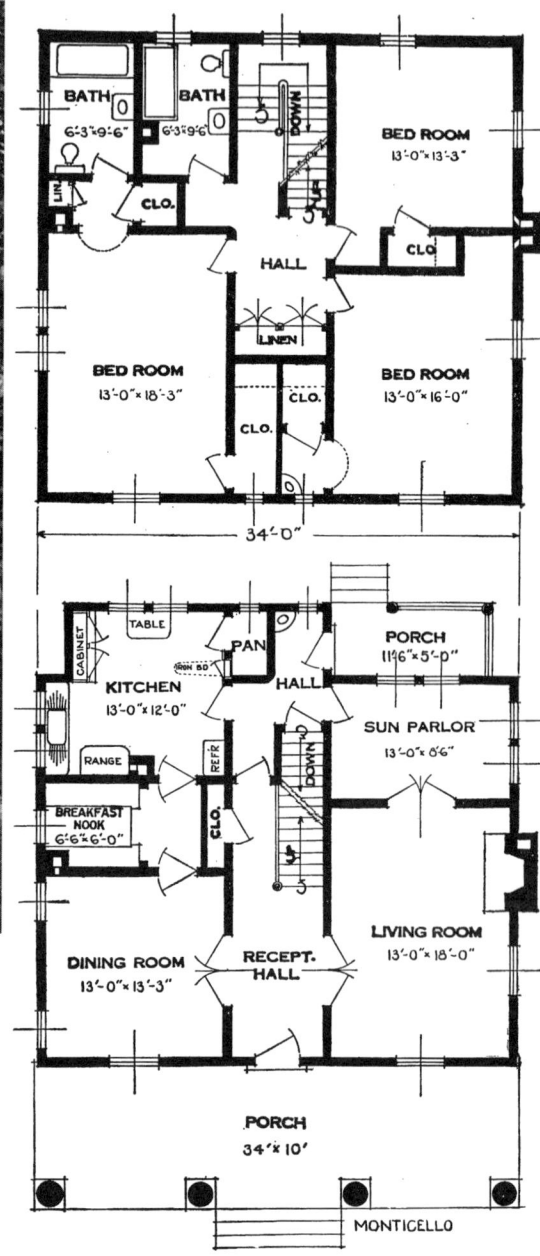

The MONTICELLO (Size 34x28′)

If those who occupy homes like The Monticello are not happy it is because they have violated some natural law, or are not conscious of the fact that happiness is a condition of the mind and comes as the result of the mastery of one's moods. It is not a thing to be purchased at a price, but rather a fact to be recognized or accepted, regardless.

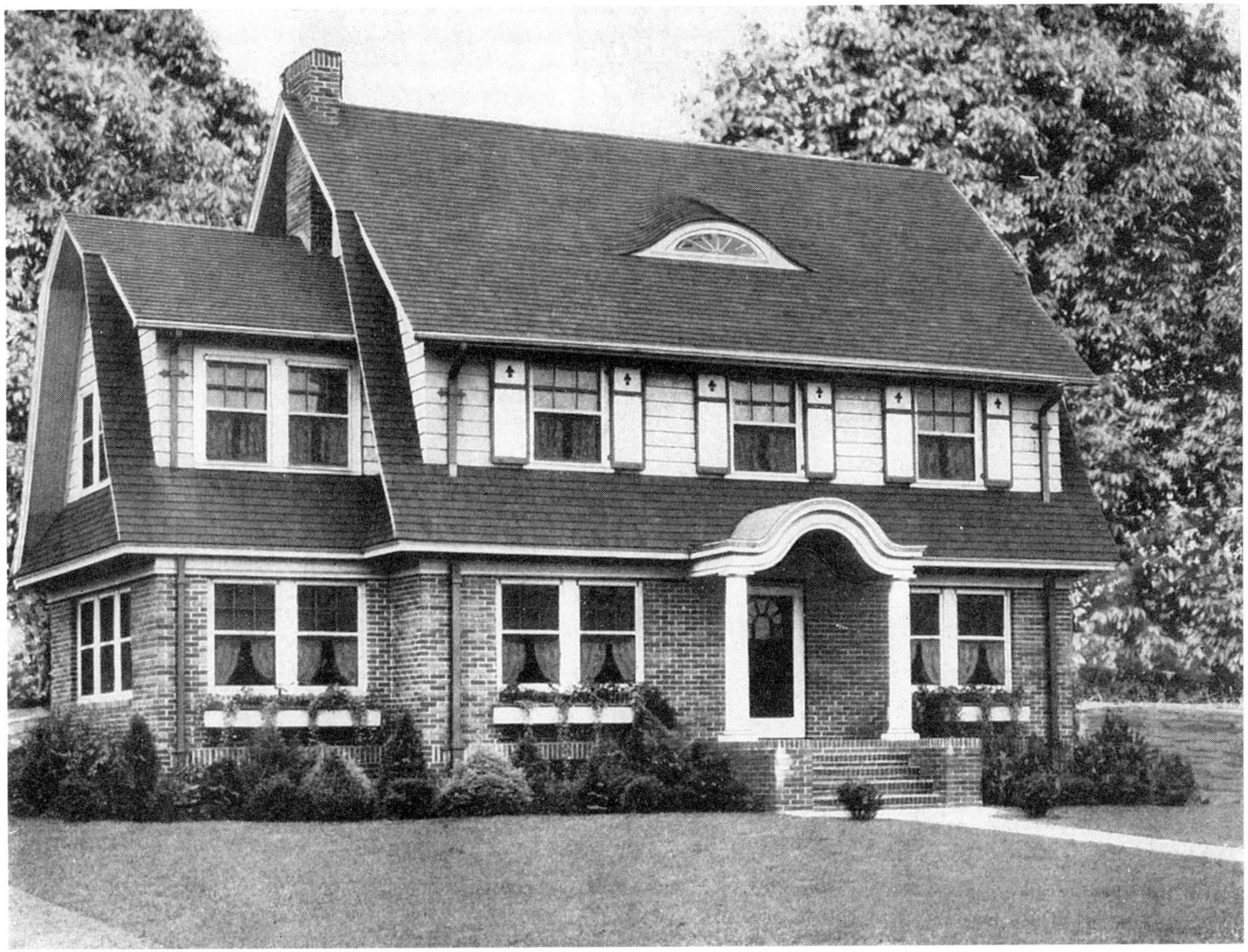

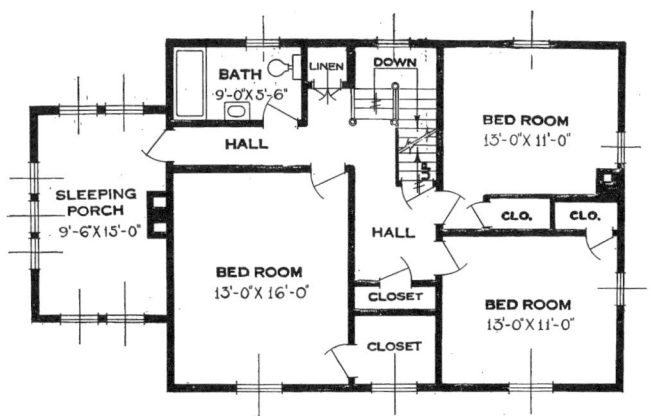

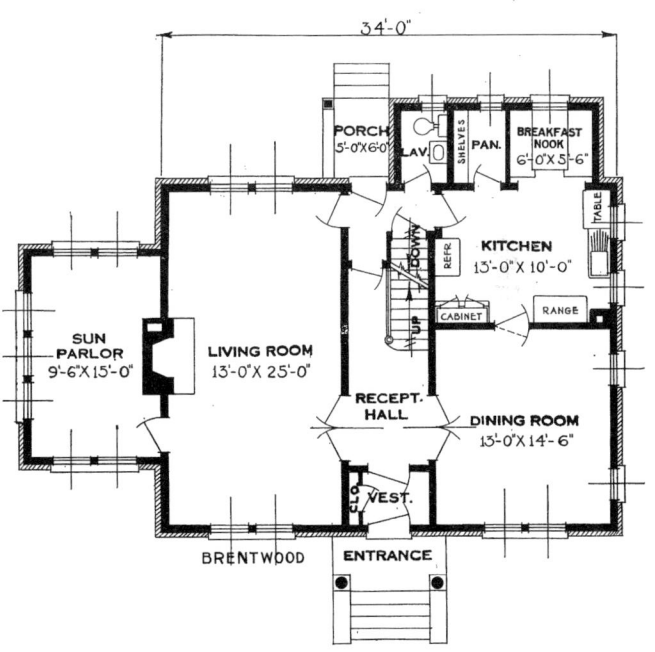

The BRENTWOOD (Size 34x26')

The Brentwood is a masterpiece in architecture. Its stately individuality causes it to stand alone in any community as a home of rare grace and permanent beauty; and yet so carefully have its designers considered economy in construction, that it is well within the means of those contemplating the erection of a home of its dimensions.

11

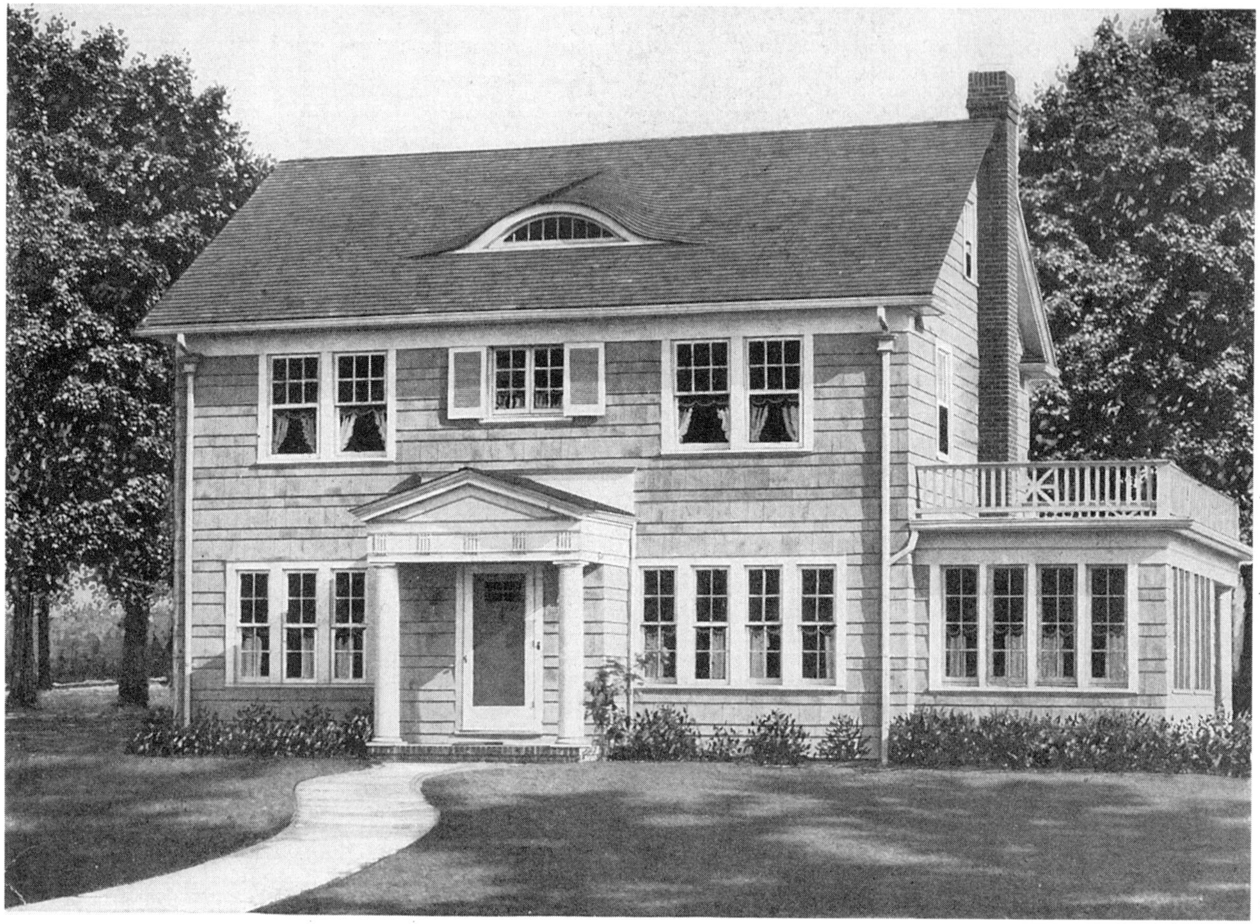

The HAVERHILL (Size 36x28')

The hearth that glows with good fellowship warms chilly hearts and drives out the dampness of discord and disappointments. Such hearths are guarded constantly by women who worship sacred home ideals. The Haverhill will make an ideal home for those who yearn for better conditions in which to demonstrate the power of right thought.

All plans are so prepared as to permit frame, stucco, brick or tile construction.

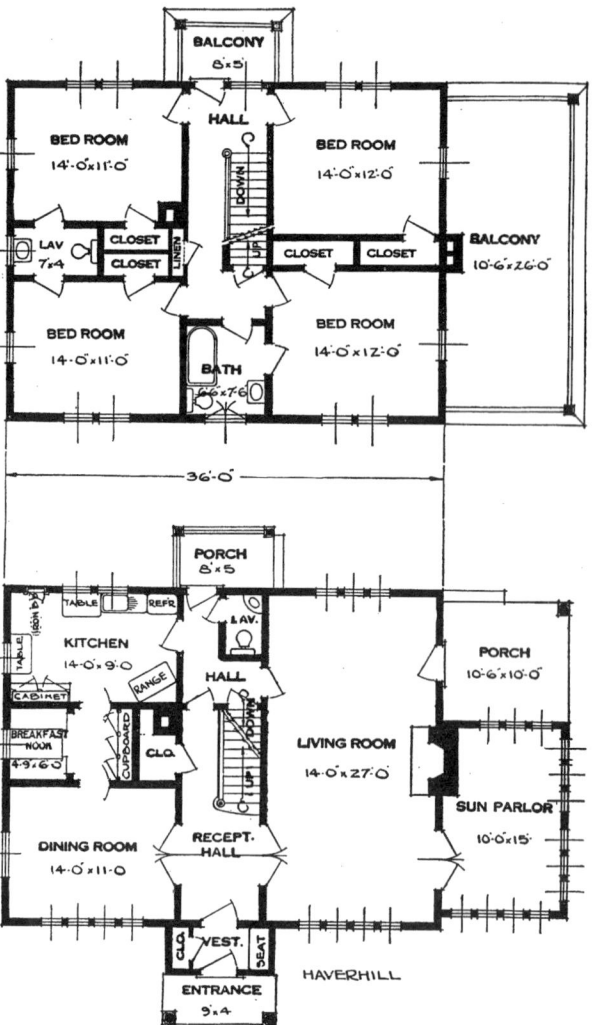

Character of sterling worth is invariably developed in the home.

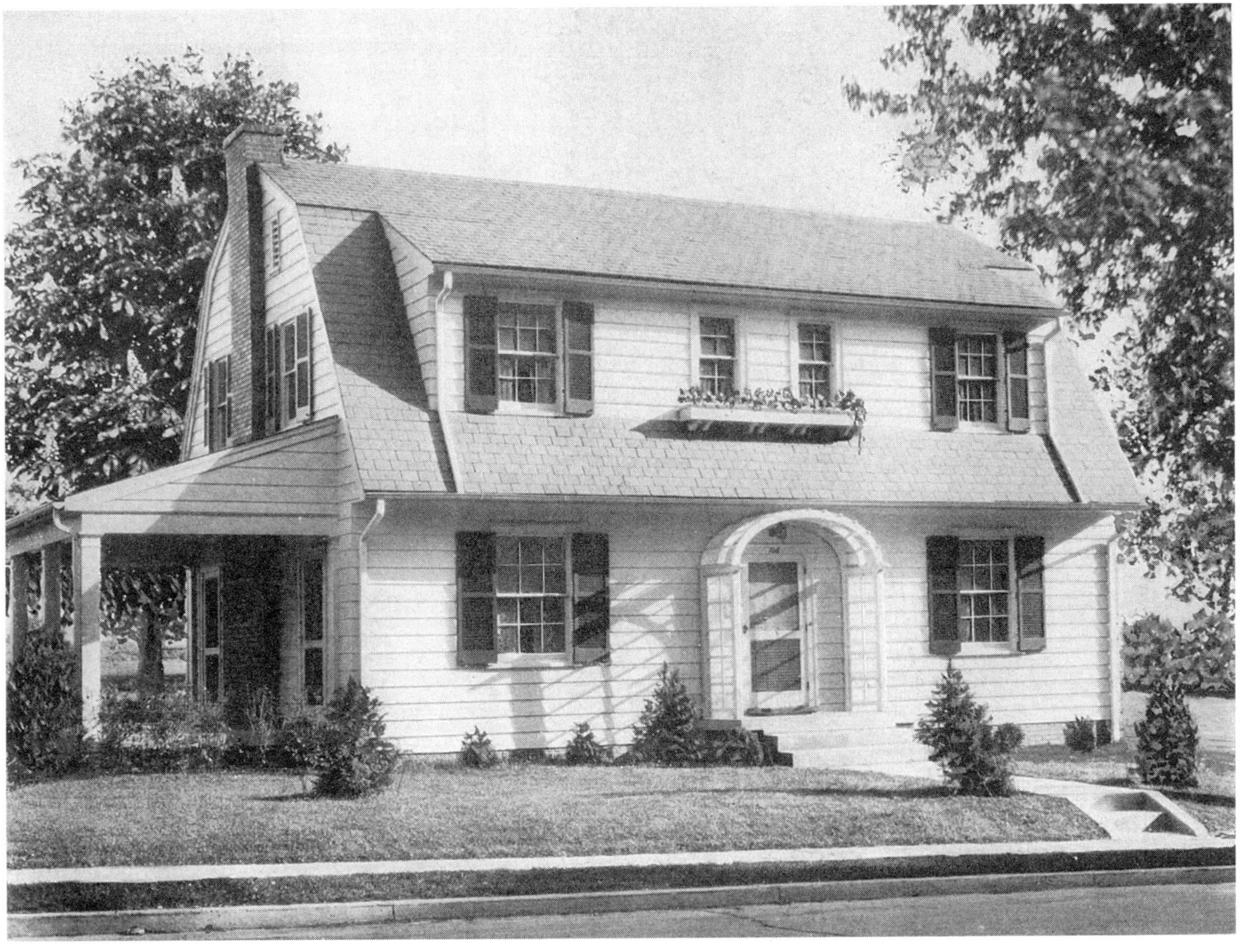

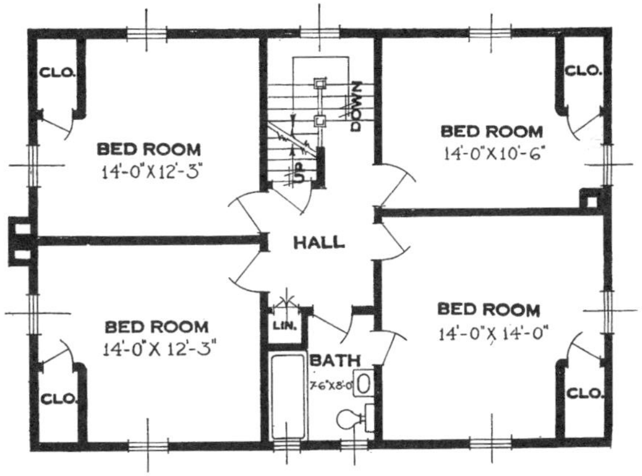

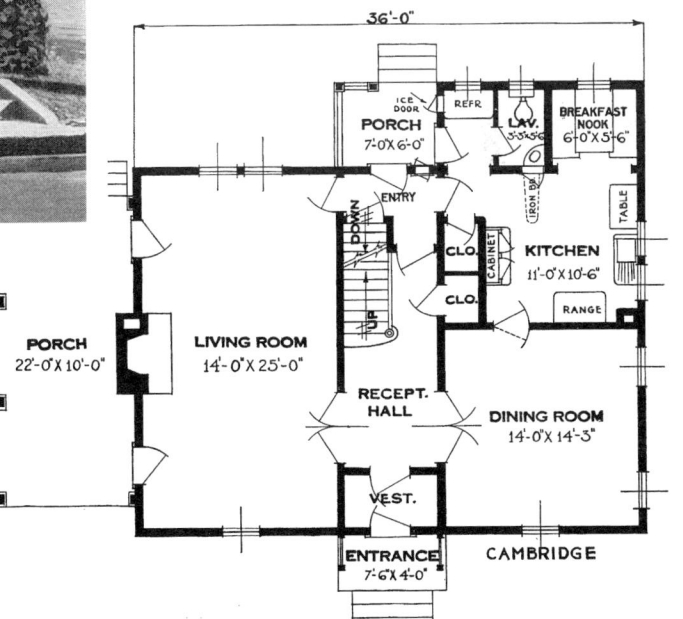

The CAMBRIDGE (Size 36x26')

When one looks thoughtfully at the colonial style of architecture as shown in The Cambridge, his thoughts go back to the days when the love of home and family were the most sacred emotions in the hearts of men. There are yet many with steadfastness of purpose who long for the sentiment of colonial days, and to such The Cambridge will be an inspiration.

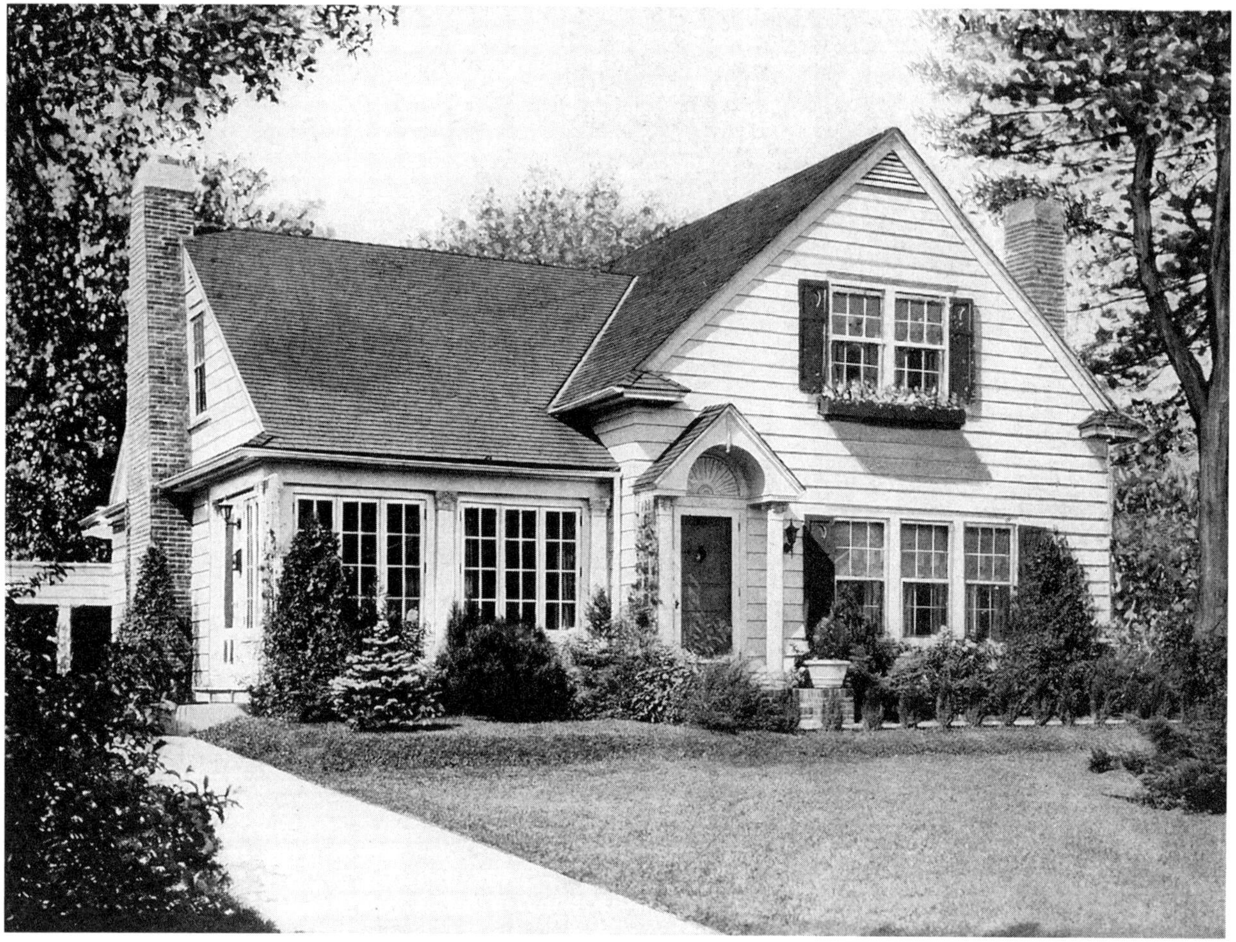

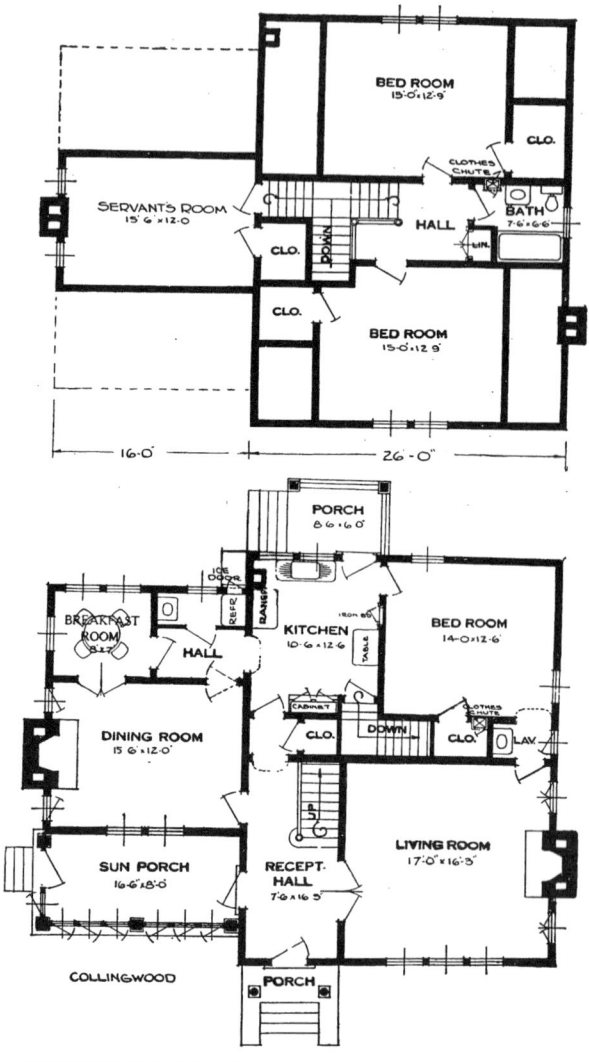

The COLLINGWOOD (Size 42x34')

It is appreciation that humanity really is seeking and not gold. Gold, gained honestly or dishonestly, is in turn paid for appreciation and applause. He is most appreciated by friend and neighbor who contributes to his community a substantial home and unselfishly shares his comforts and pleasures with those of his kind.

In the happiness of the home lies the health and strength of the whole family.

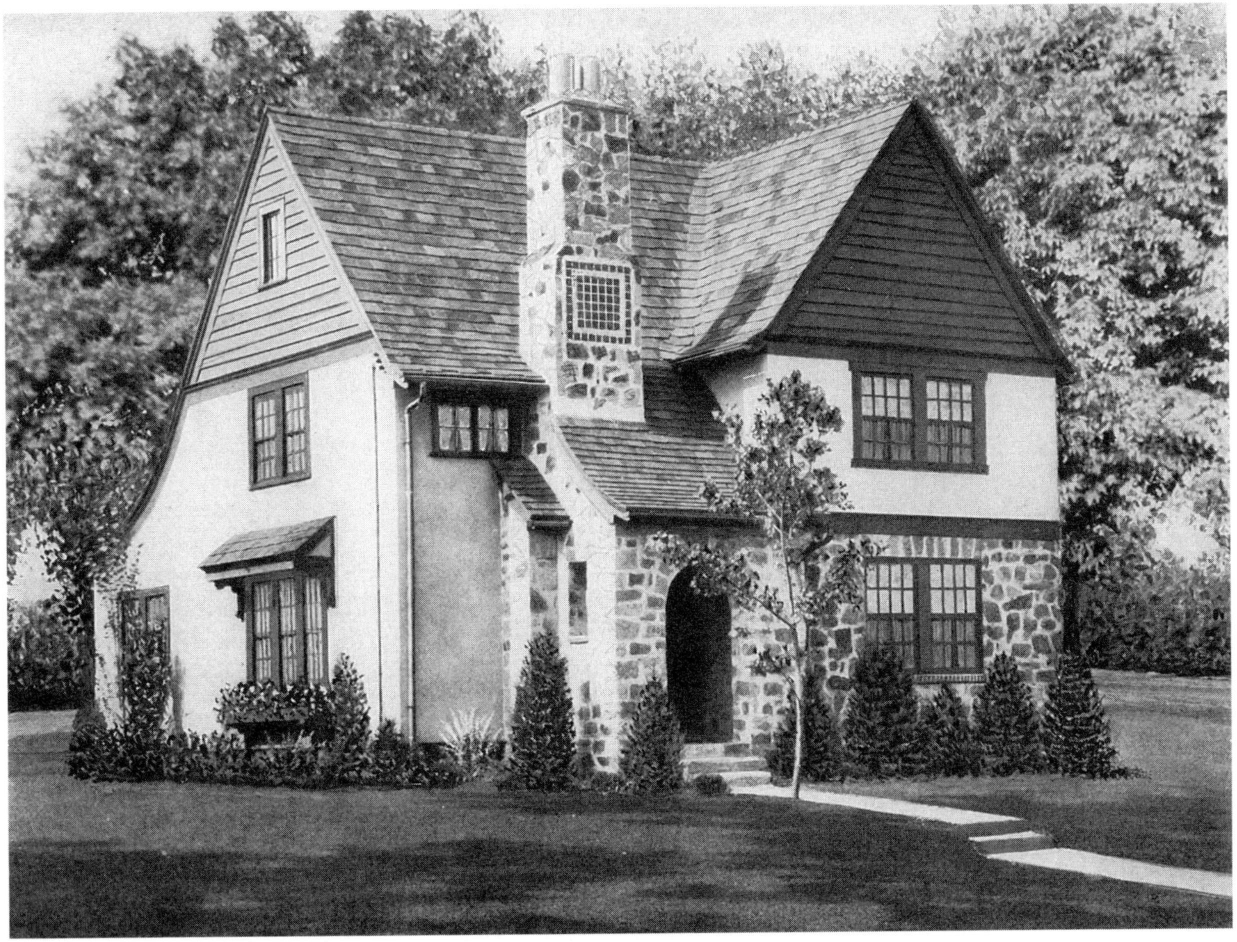

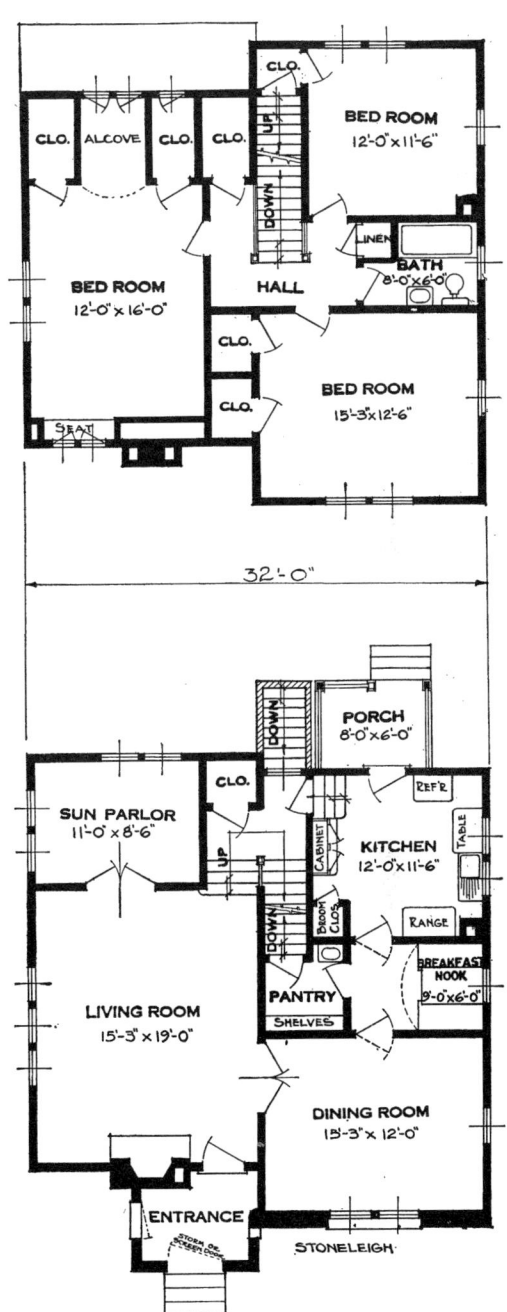

The STONELEIGH (Size 32x32')

The Stoneleigh was designed for those who wish a home of distinction, decidedly different from the many well-known types. There is carefully combined in this home, grace, character, and comfort, and so cleverly have these three features been blended, it will stand as a thing of beauty in any community, regardless of neighboring mansions.

All plans are so prepared as to permit frame, stucco, brick or tile construction.

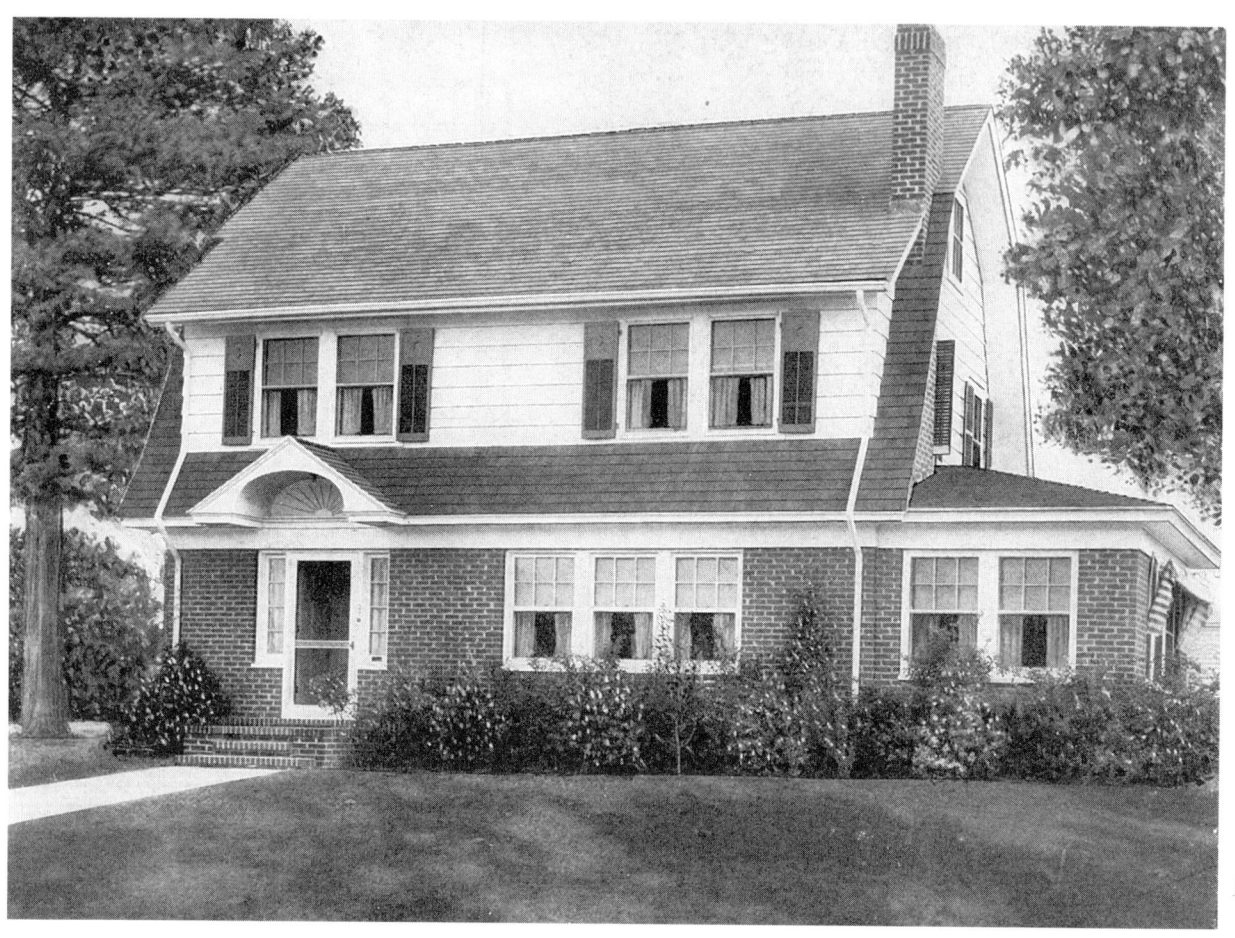
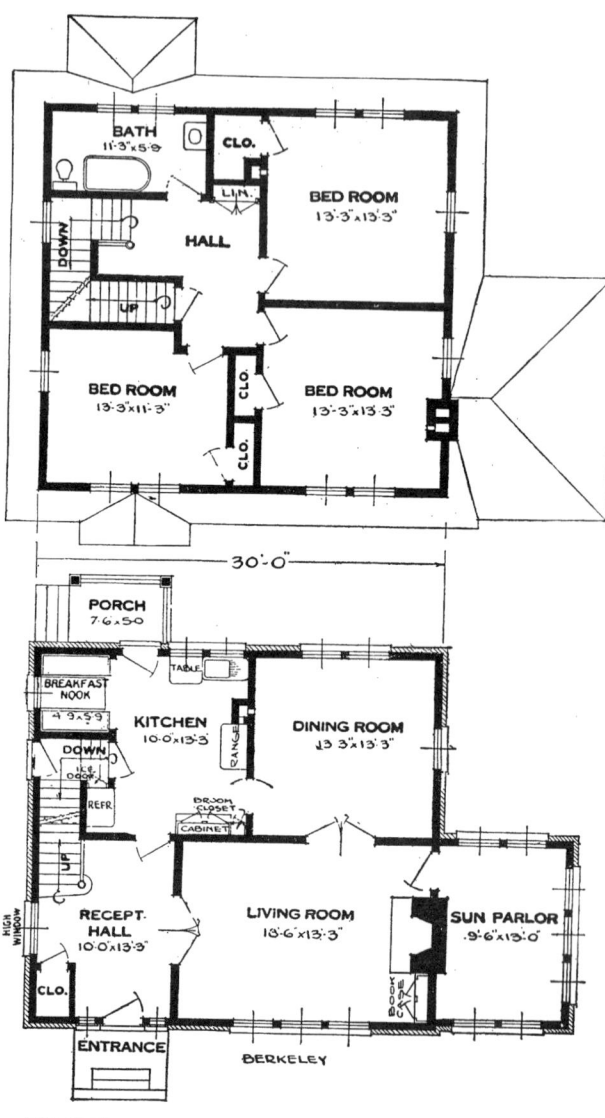

The BERKELEY (Size 30x28')

It is around the firesides of happy homes where children chatter with glee and loving mothers watch over them with divine care that the best and noblest thoughts of men are generated. The germs of selfishness, envy and greed have little chance to multiply in homes of the substantial character of The Berkeley.

All plans are so prepared as to permit frame, stucco, brick or tile construction.

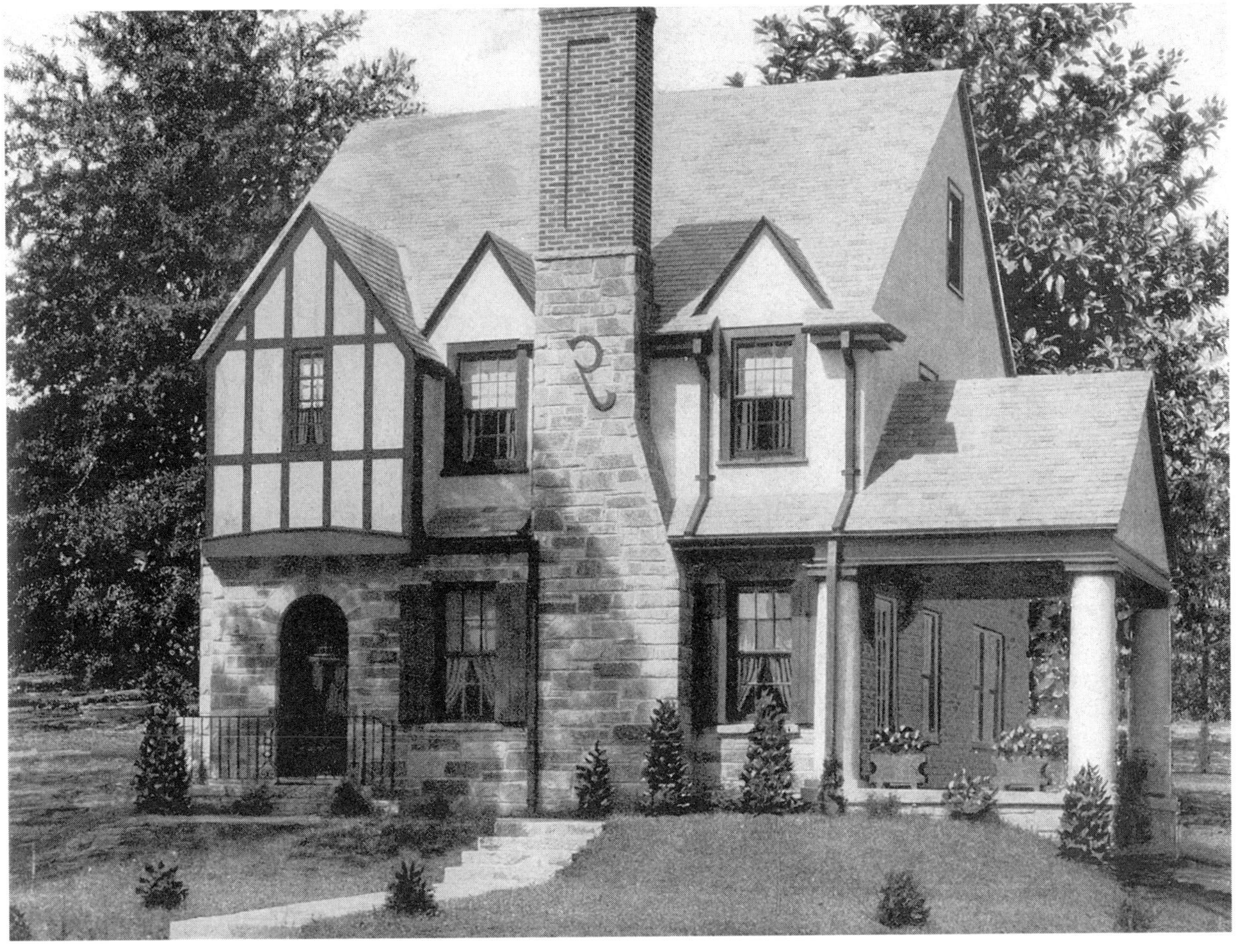

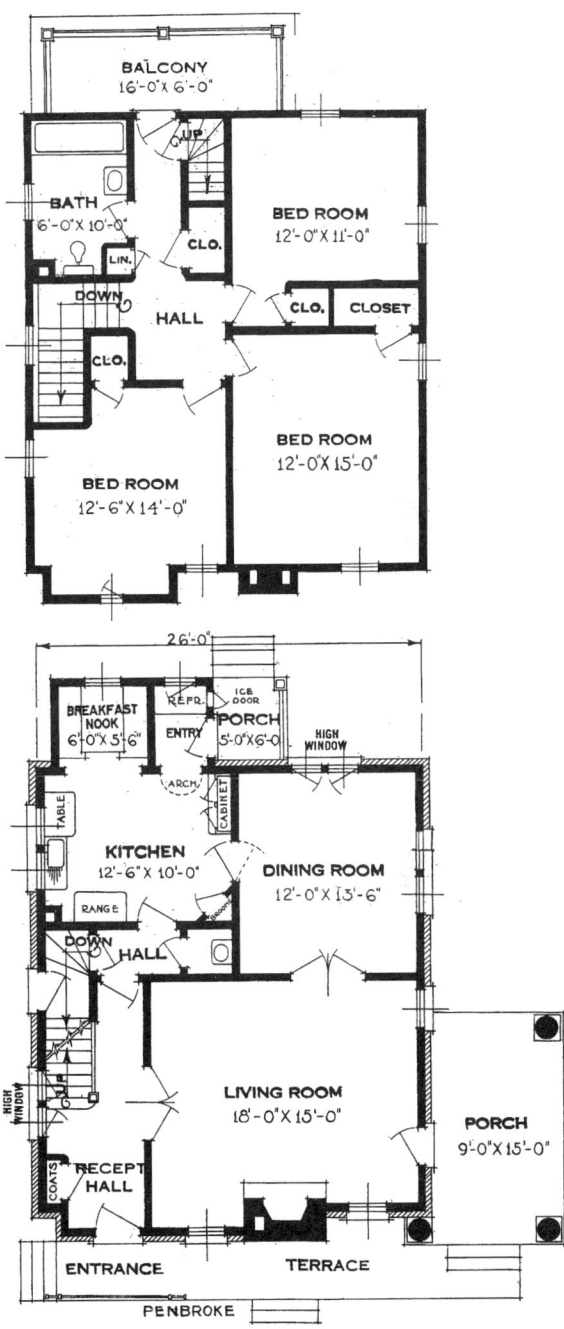

The PEMBROKE (Size 26x30')

Once in a great while a new idea is born, a thing of beauty developed by a dreamer, or something entirely original is expressed by the hand of an artist. For example, The Pembroke is a new idea in the field of architecture, a creation of rare beauty, with originality expressed in every line.

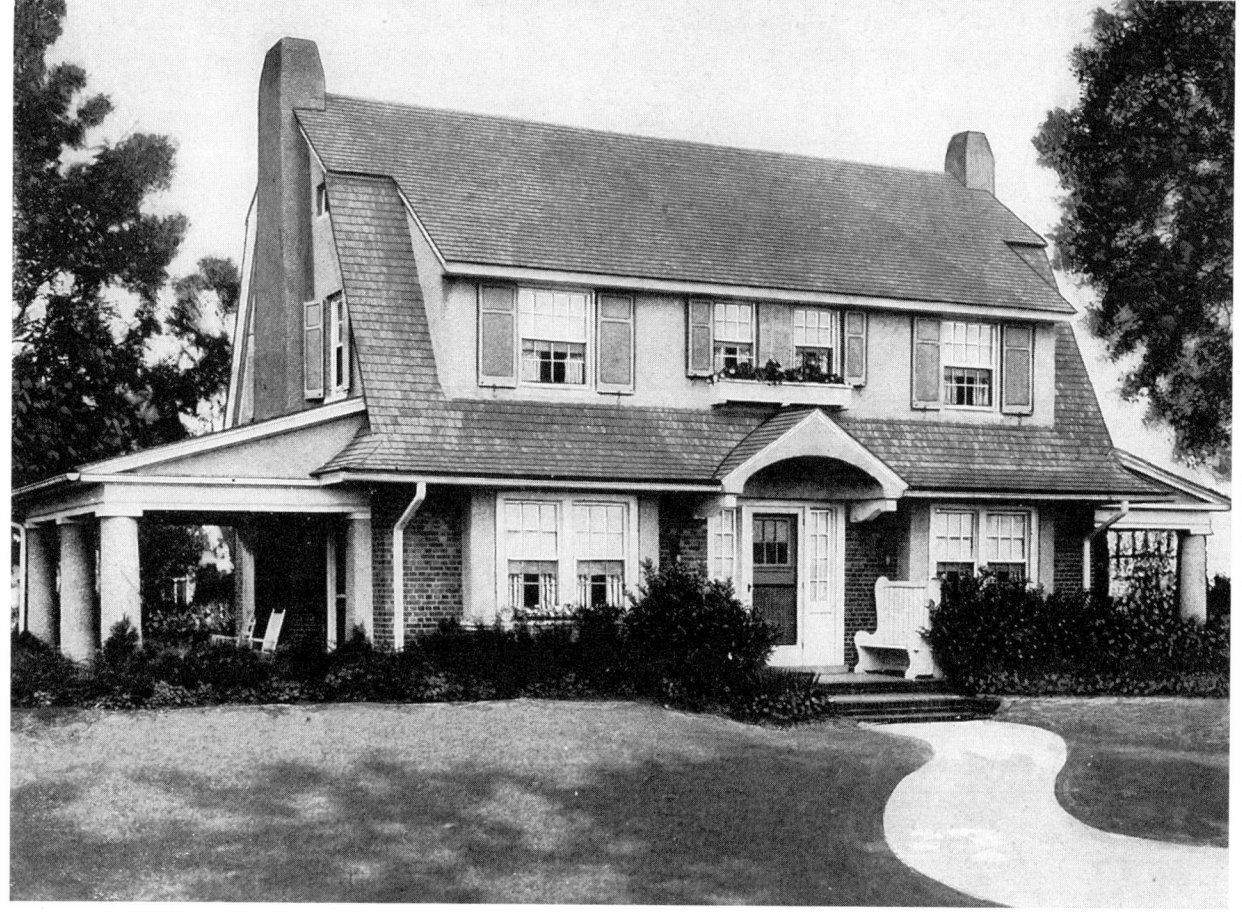

> Only through home liberty and companionship can men and women grow strong.

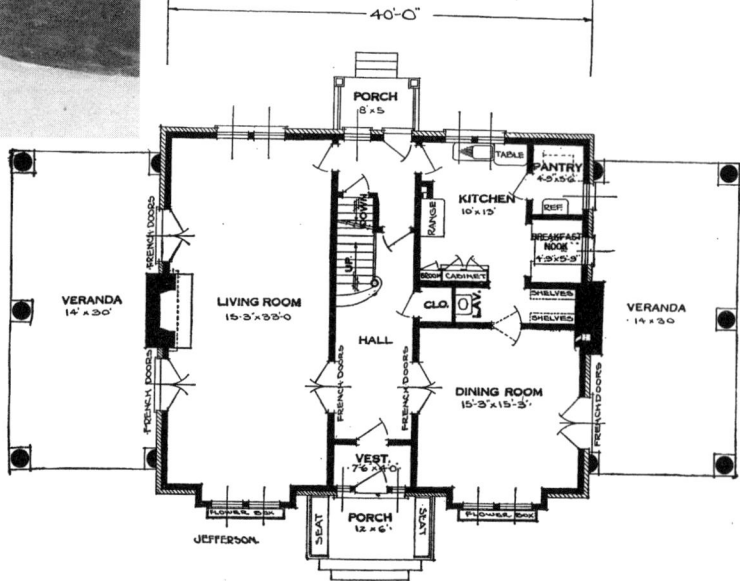

The JEFFERSON (Size 40x34′)

The faculty of inhabitiveness (the love of one's place of birth) is developed far more in the young man or woman whose home has been one of sunshine and freedom than in those whose place of habitation has been sordid and cramped. One would naturally expect the youth from The Jefferson to reflect all of the joy and purity of a wholesome environment.

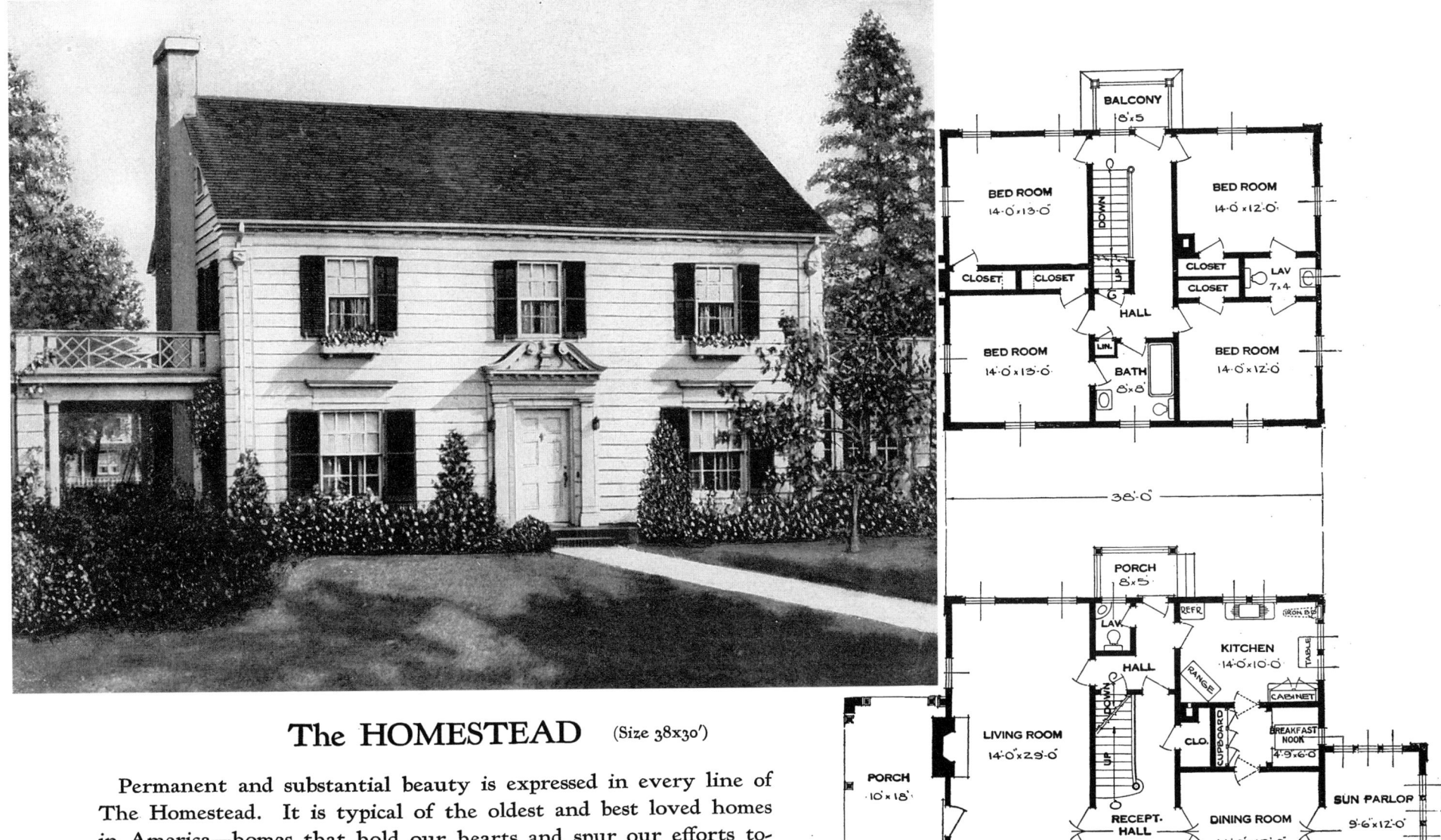

The HOMESTEAD (Size 38x30')

Permanent and substantial beauty is expressed in every line of The Homestead. It is typical of the oldest and best loved homes in America—homes that hold our hearts and spur our efforts toward greater achievements. Surely the comforts of such homes as The Homestead cannot pass with a single generation.

All plans are so prepared as to permit frame, stucco, brick or tile construction.

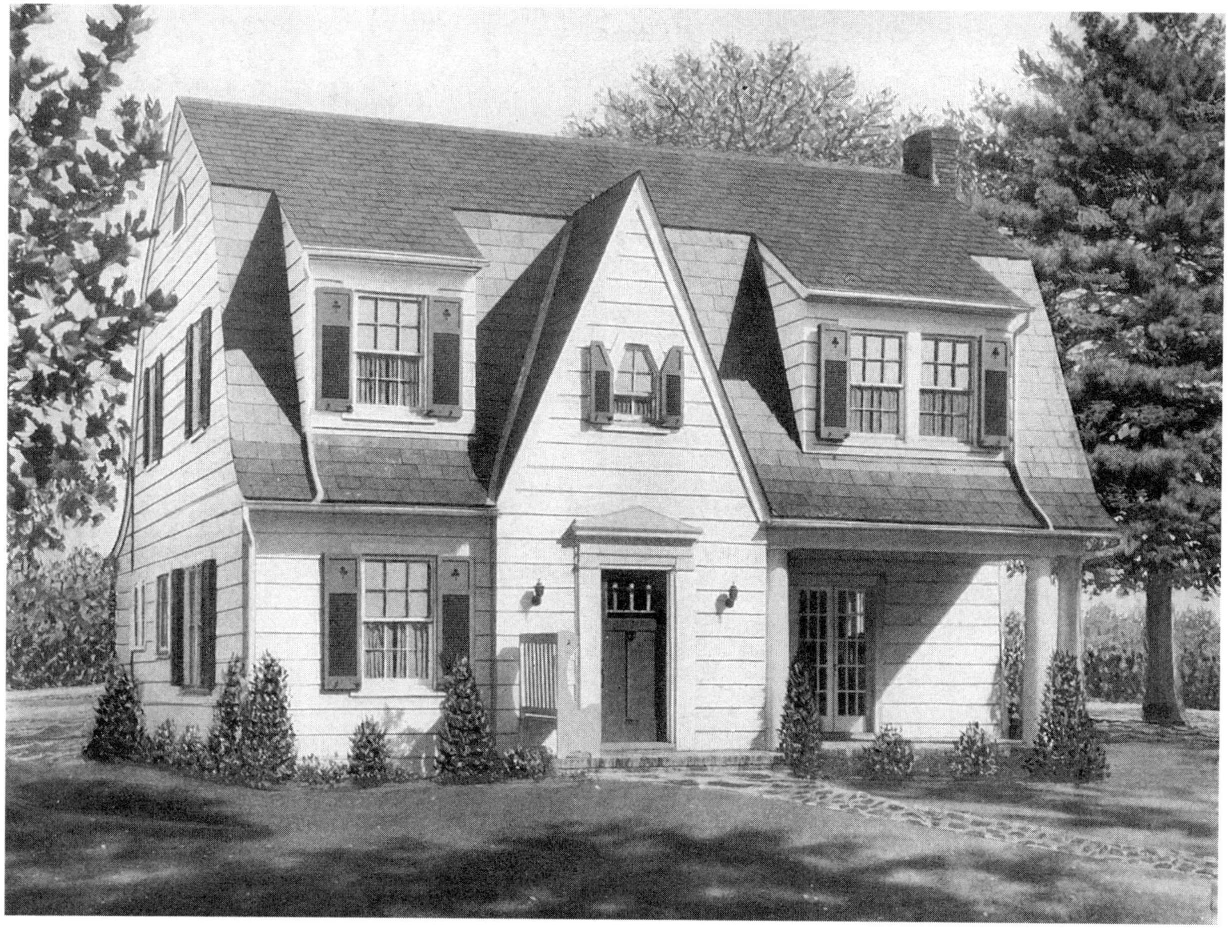

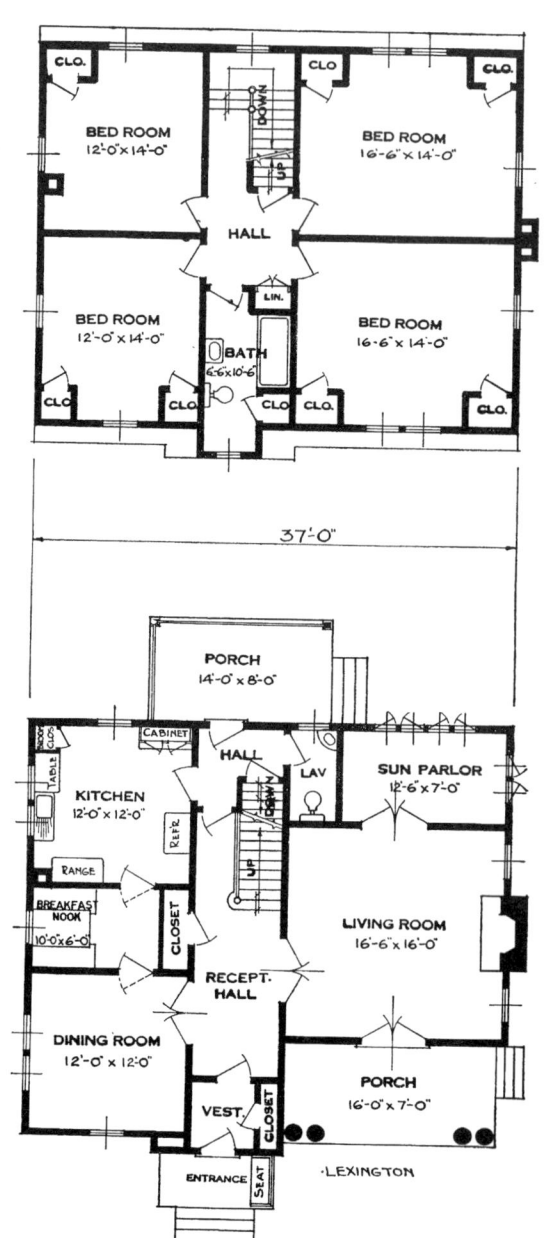

The LEXINGTON (Size 37x32')

Spacious homes like The Lexington are usually constructed in the suburbs by those whose generous natures lead them away from the cramped and crowded districts where limited space and unlimited noises tend to choke their creative thoughts. Furthermore, The Lexington is strictly practical as well as peaceful and restful, and its dignity is undeniable in any community.

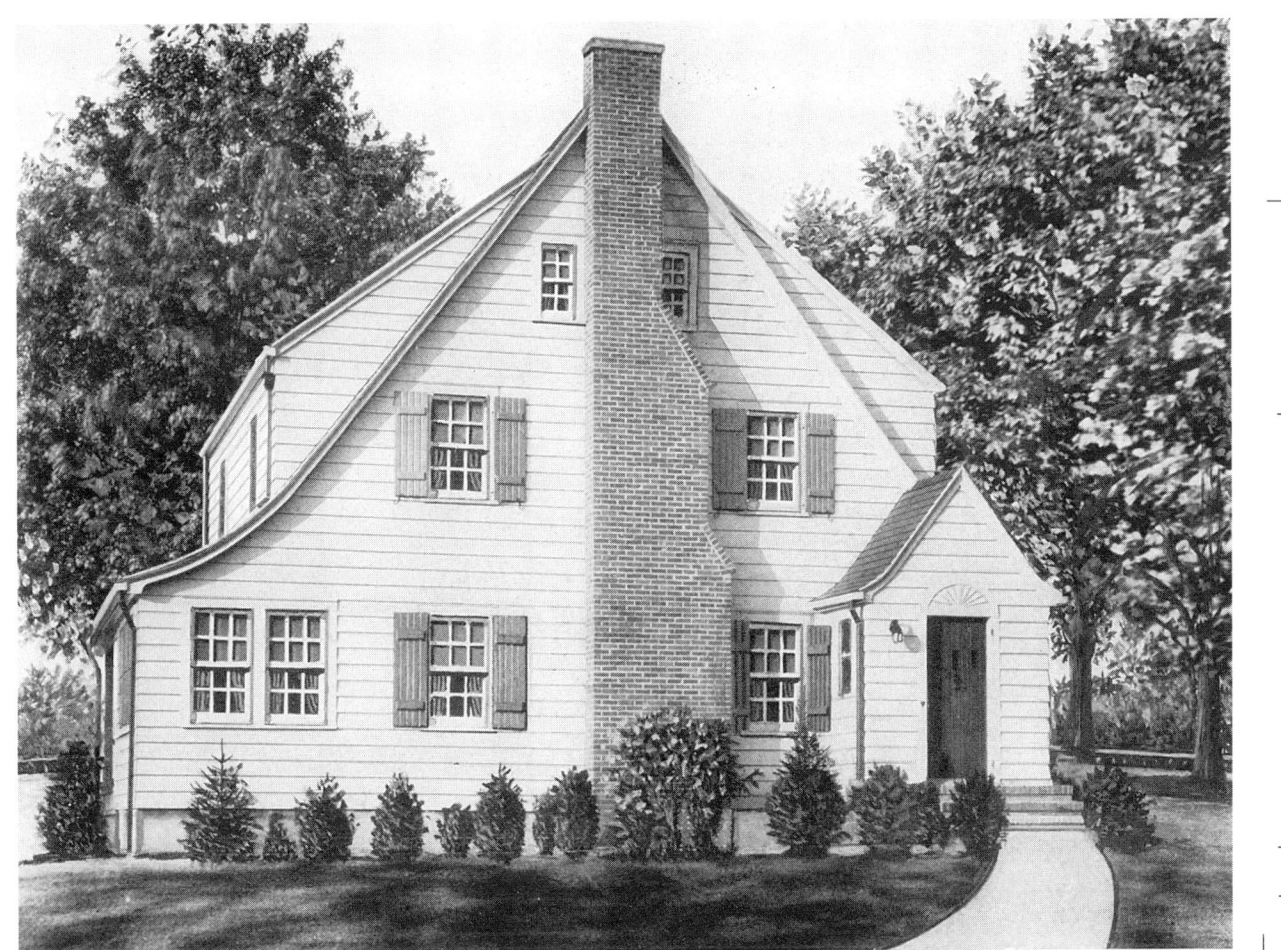

The CHADWICK (Size 28x28′)

Men change only as their environment and associates change. A good home and a good wife will enable any man to become stronger and more efficient. Any man is worthy of the highest trust who saves from his earnings sufficient to build The Chadwick, and whose life companion is in sympathy with him and his work.

All plans are so prepared as to permit frame, stucco, brick or tile construction.

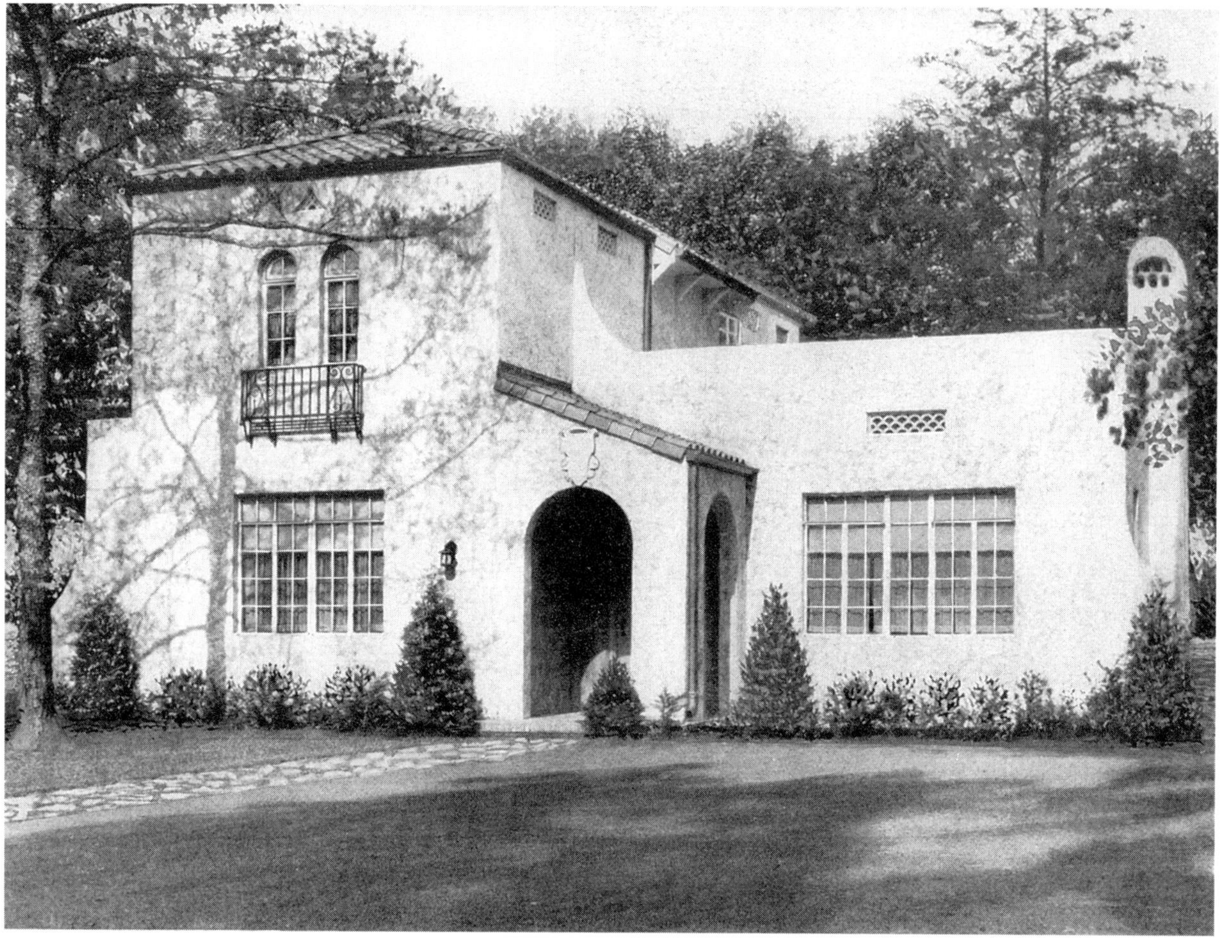

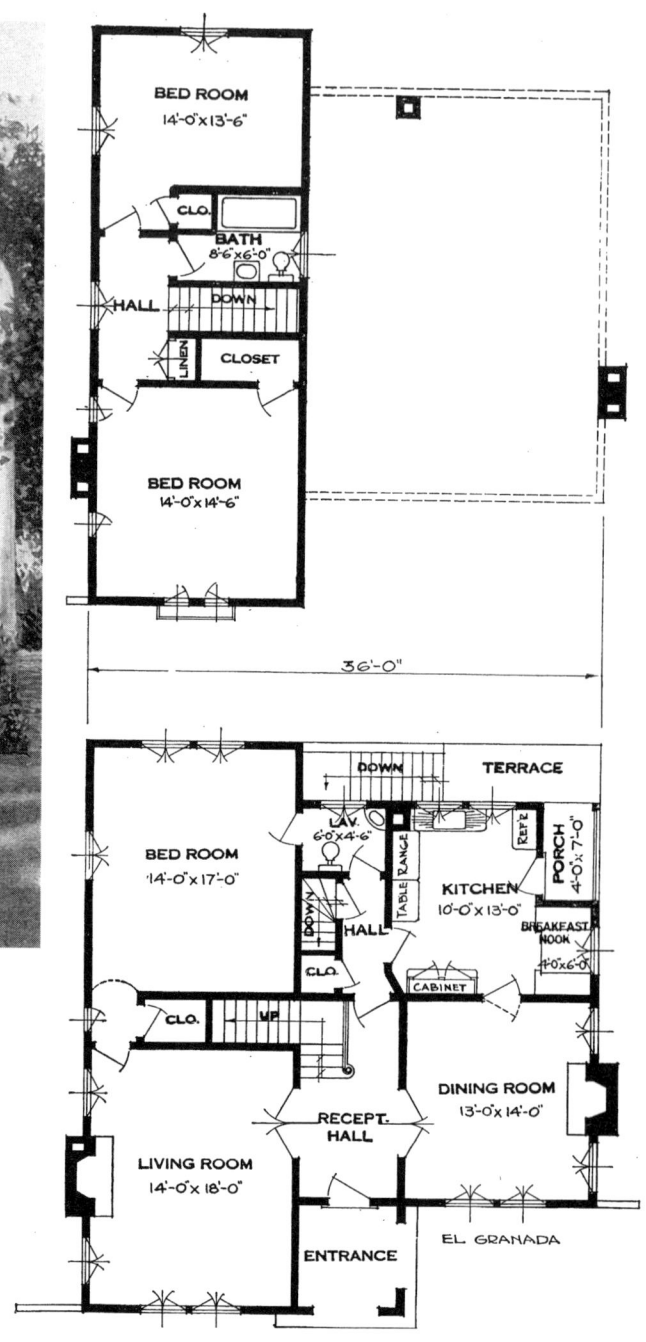

The EL GRANADA (Size 36x40′)

Selfishness seldom strangles the man whose pride and ambition lead him to build a home of The El Granada design. Pride in one's home is the fire that kindles power for success, and ambition is the invisible voice that ever calls man successward. It is home and its accompanying sentiments that develop character of sterling quality.

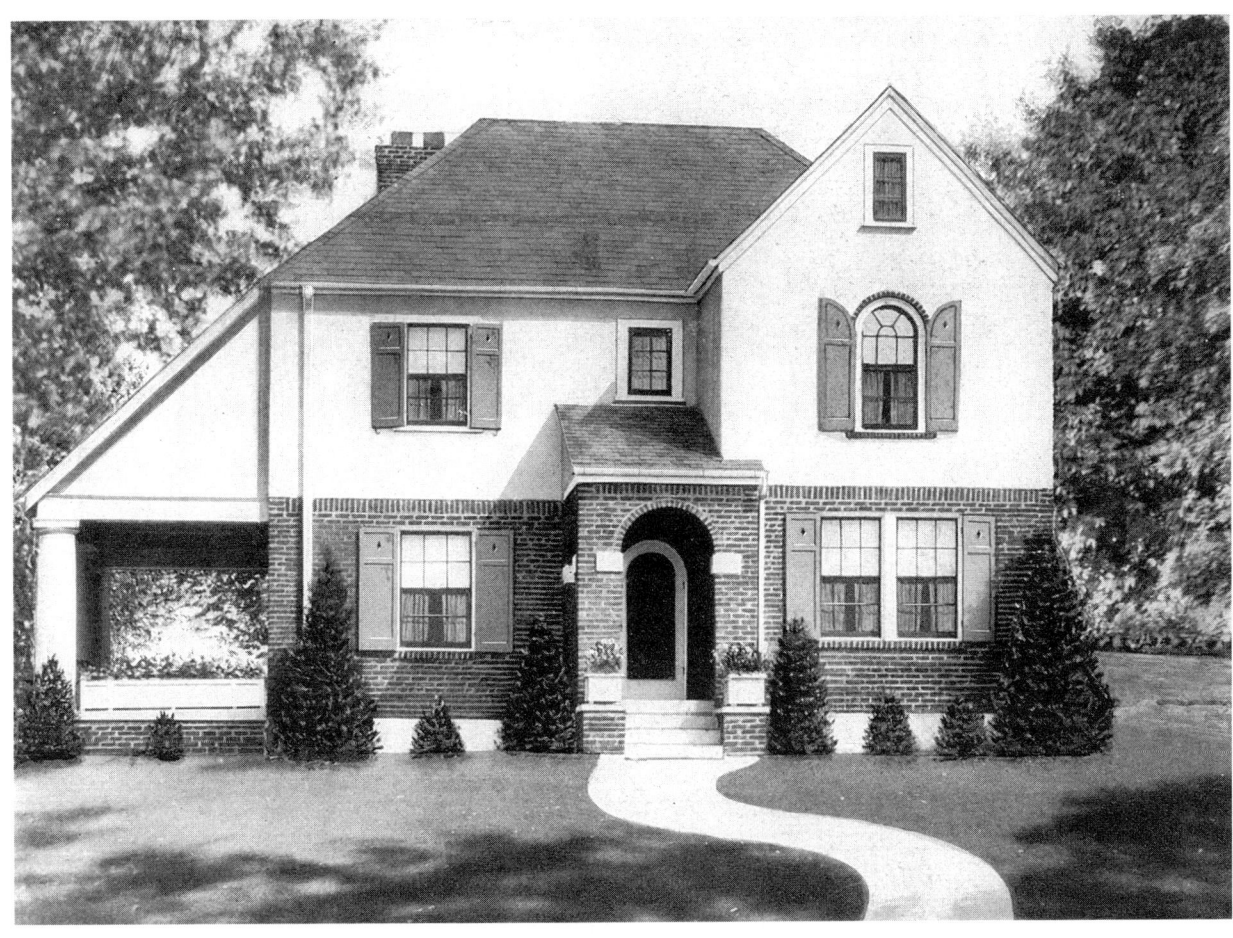
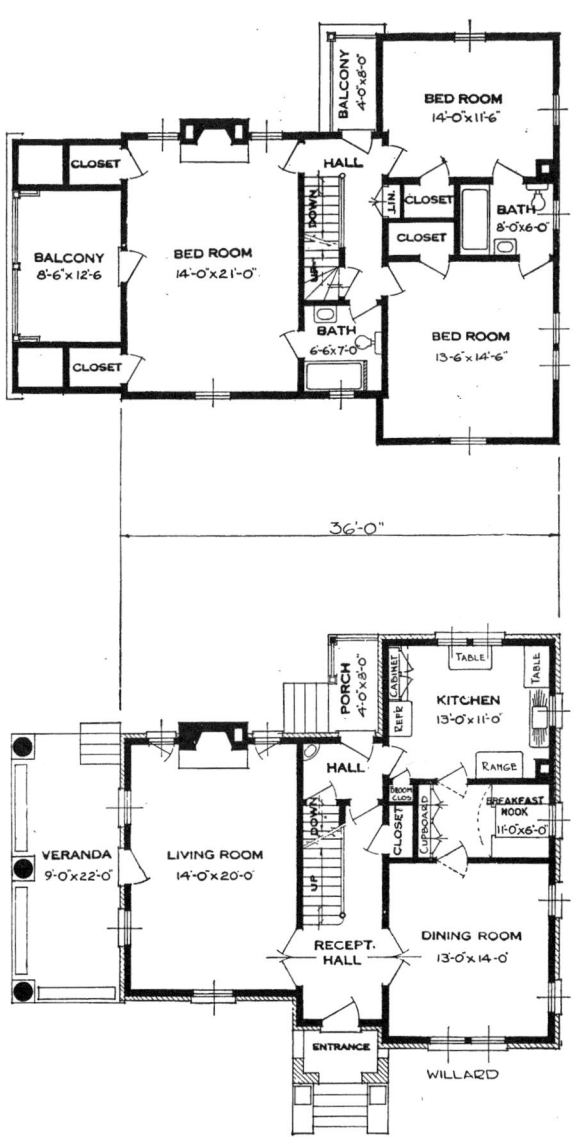

The WILLARD (Size 36x34')

All obstacles stand aside for him who firmly fixes his gaze on a coveted goal, and goes forward with a steady step and a strong heart. Homes in The Willard class are within reach of those whose ideals demand beauty in abundance, and whose wills calmly and fearlessly affirm that substitutes are unacceptable.

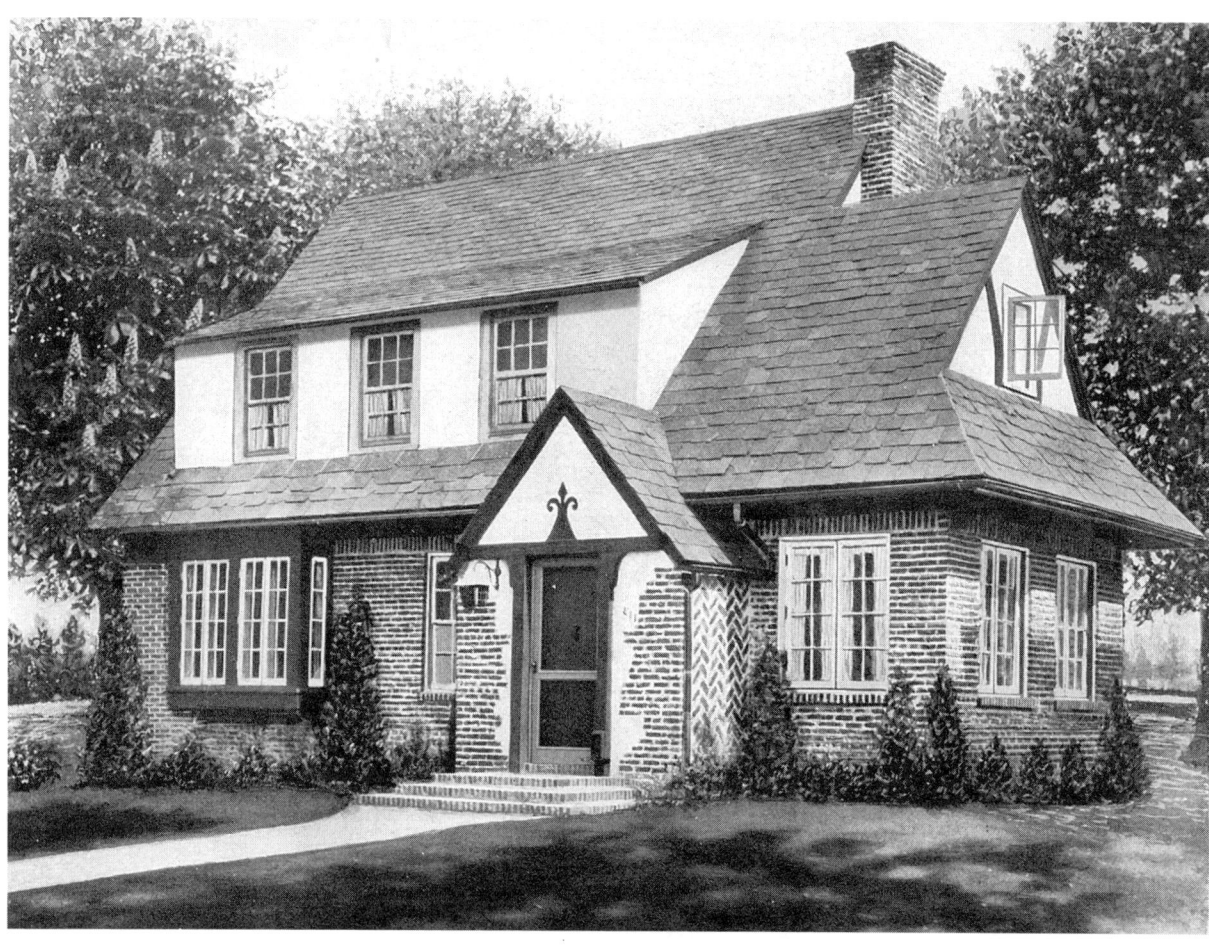
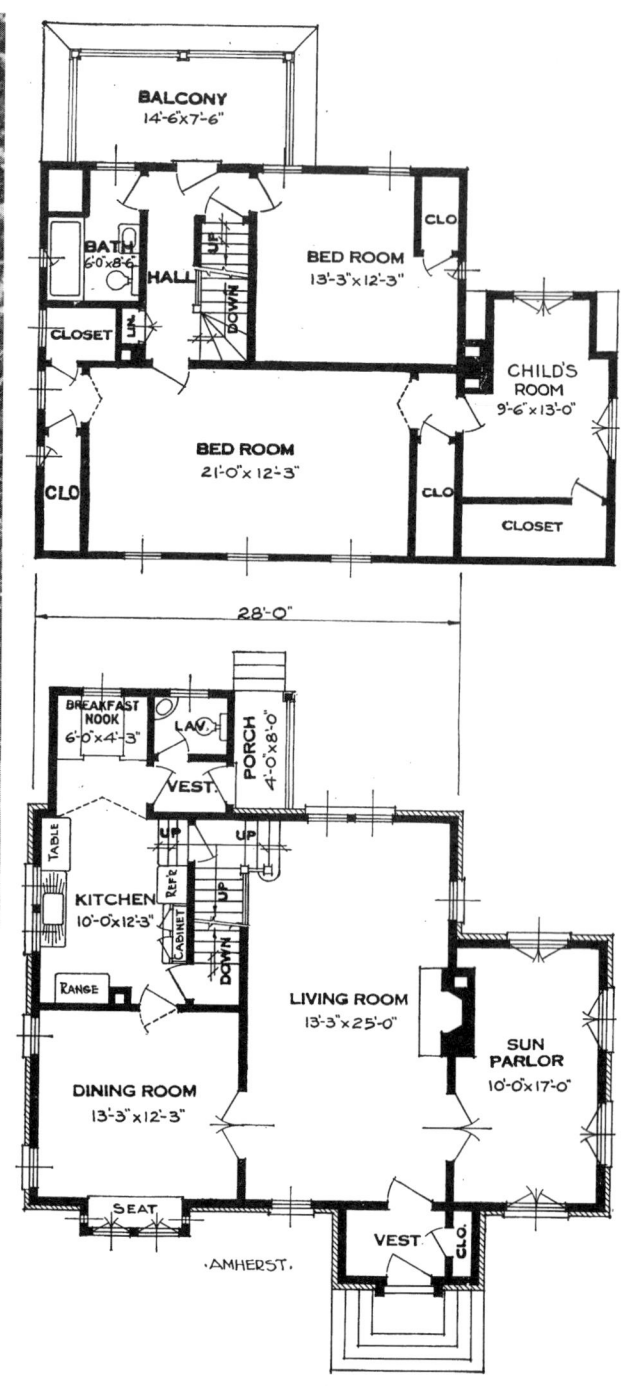

The AMHERST (Size 28x26')

A child seldom becomes a burden on society whose home life has been one of happiness and contentment. The home is the localized center from which initial impulses for good or evil go out. Those who select The Amherst as a home in which to purify the environment for their children may well pay the debt to humanity which all of us owe.

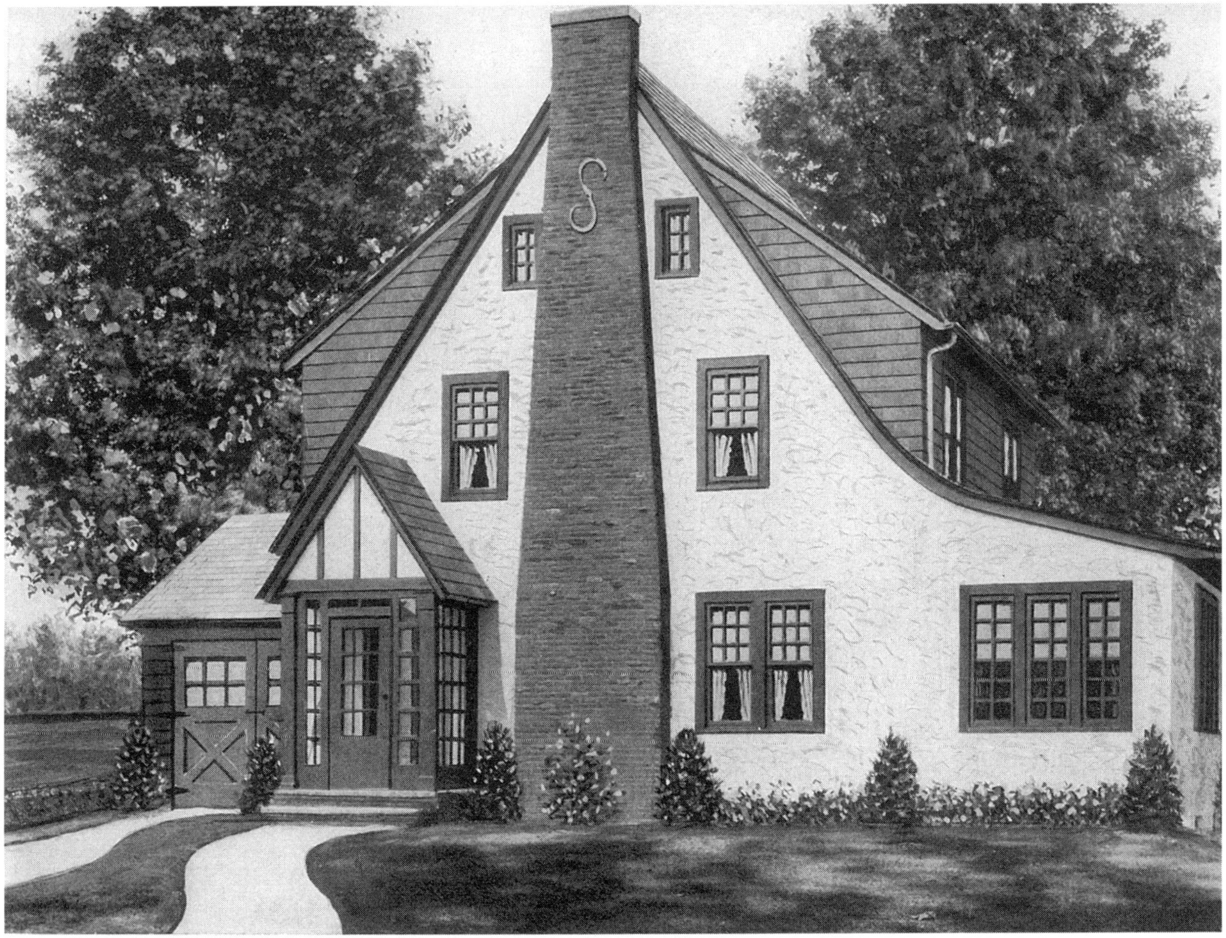

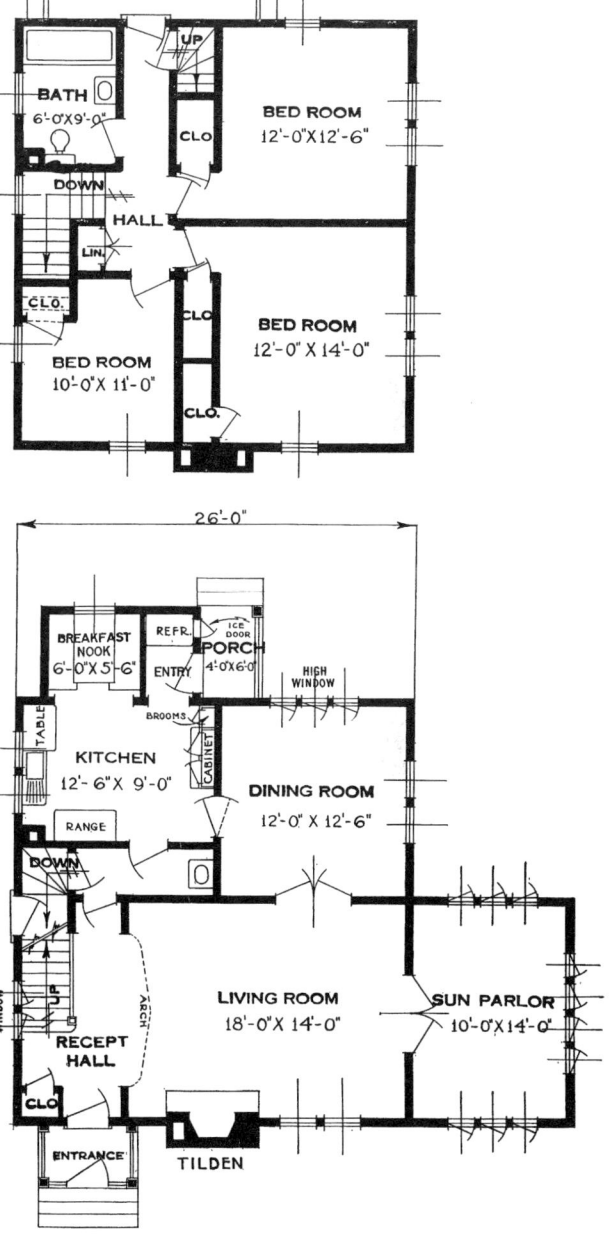

The TILDEN (Size 26x28′)

Sunshine is to the physical body what joy is to the heart. Those frail of body should seek the sun porches of homes of The Tilden plan, and those frail of heart can find inimitable balm in the building and making complete a new home and a new environment. Health and home joy come to those who prepare expectantly for their reception.

All plans are so prepared as to permit frame, stucco, brick or tile construction.

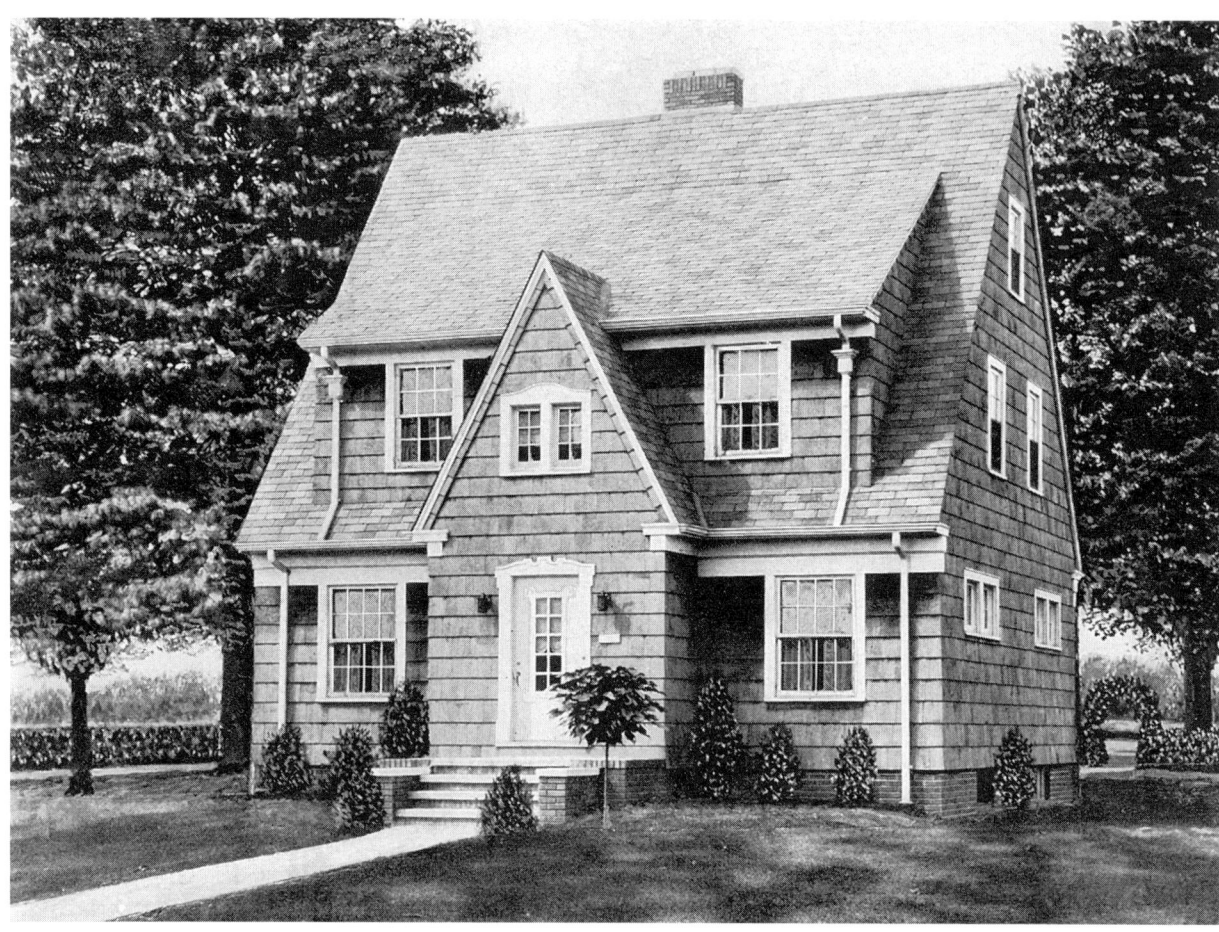
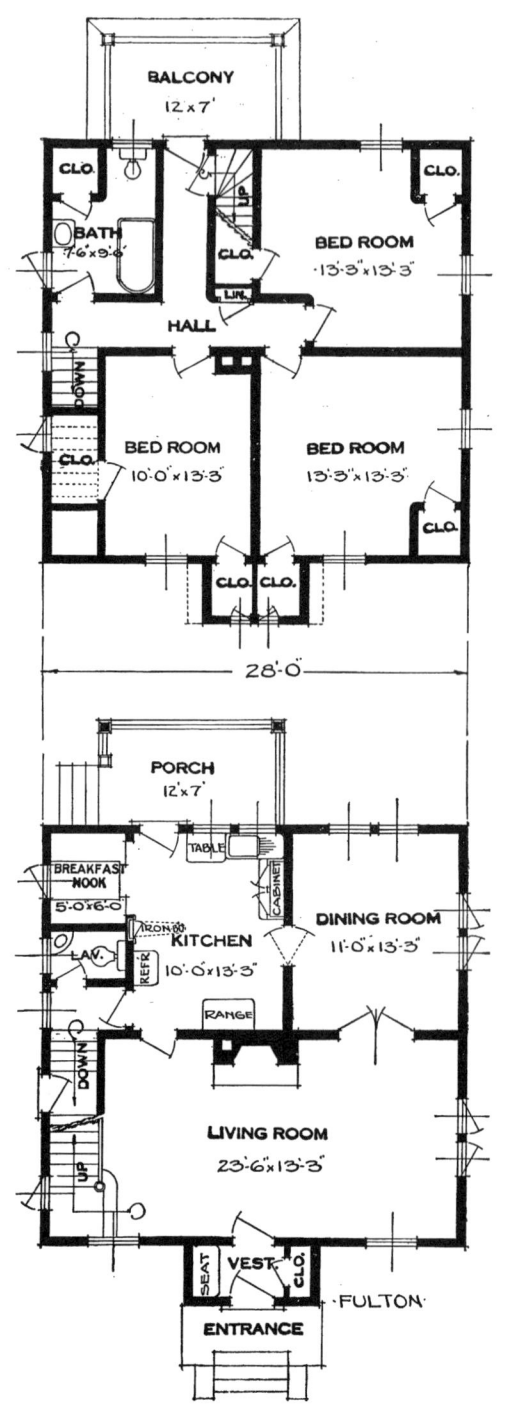

The FULTON (Size 28x28')

The woman who knows that the surest way to a man's heart is through his sense of taste, and that sympathy and appreciation will lead him over mountains while criticism causes him to balk stubbornly on a level, can make any home an influence for permanent good whether it is of The Fulton style of architecture or a more humble cottage.

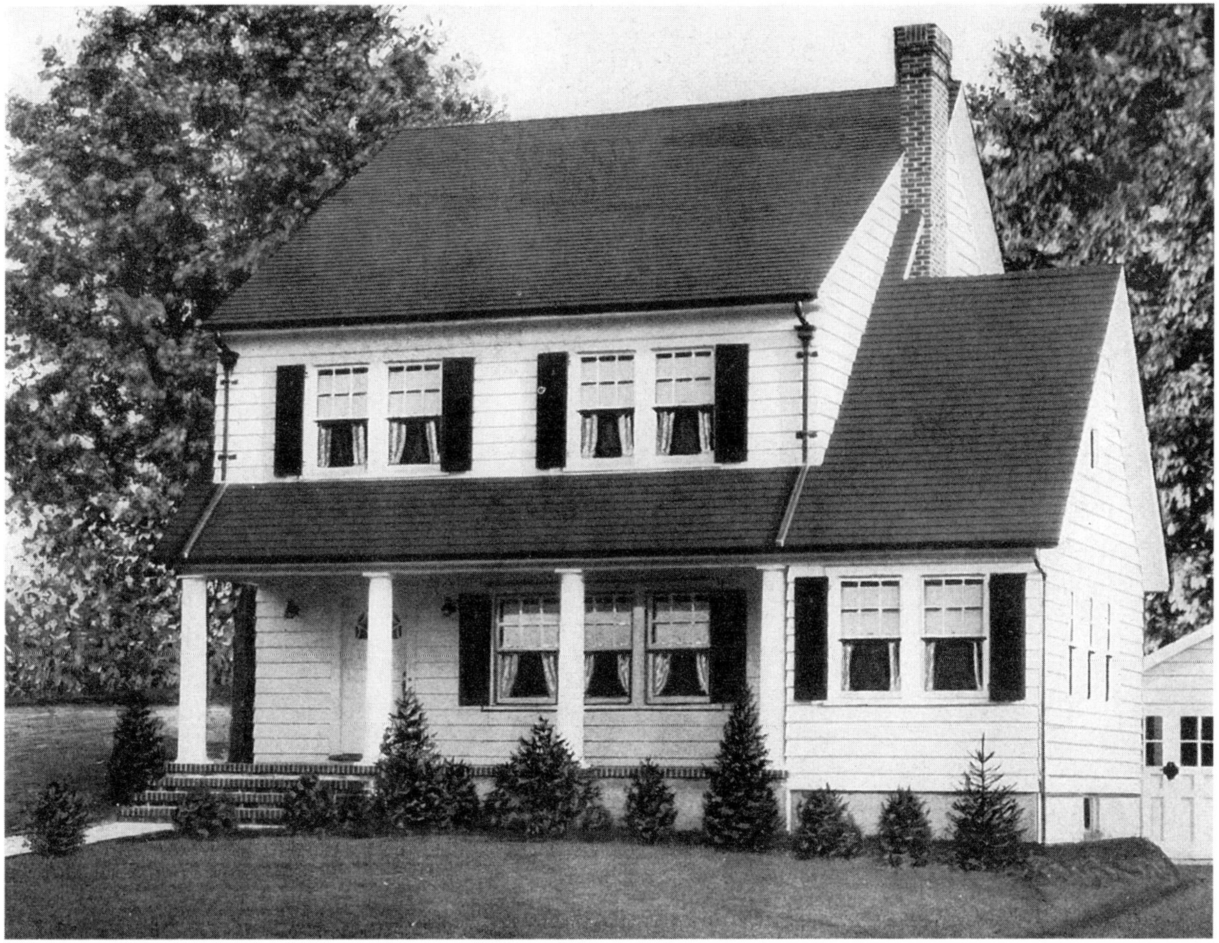

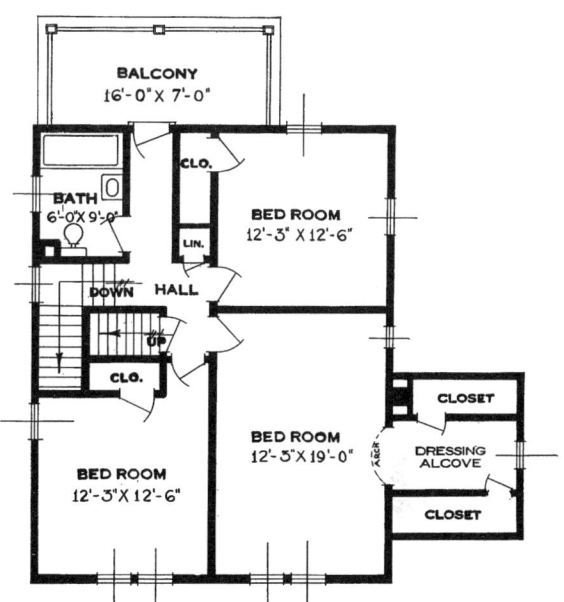

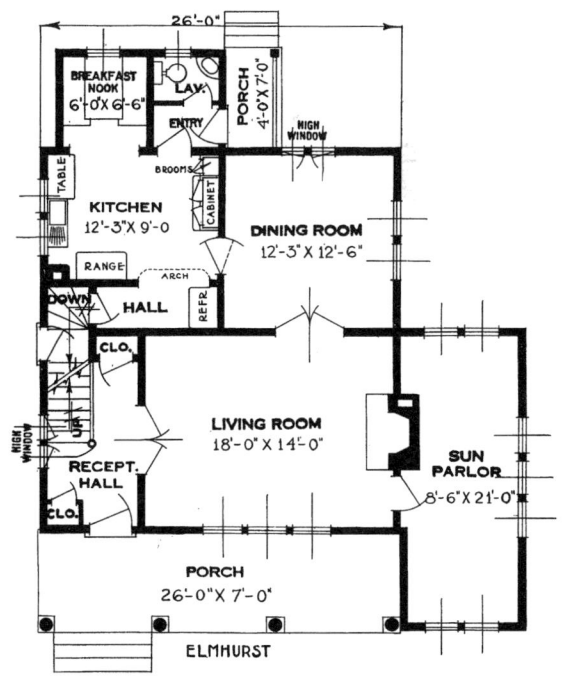

The ELMHURST (Size 26x28')

When a normal woman comes to herself at the age of twenty, twenty-two or twenty-four, according to her physical and mental growth, she realizes that her highest ambition is for a home of her own, affection and children, but her happiness is never complete until the home in which she lives becomes her very own.

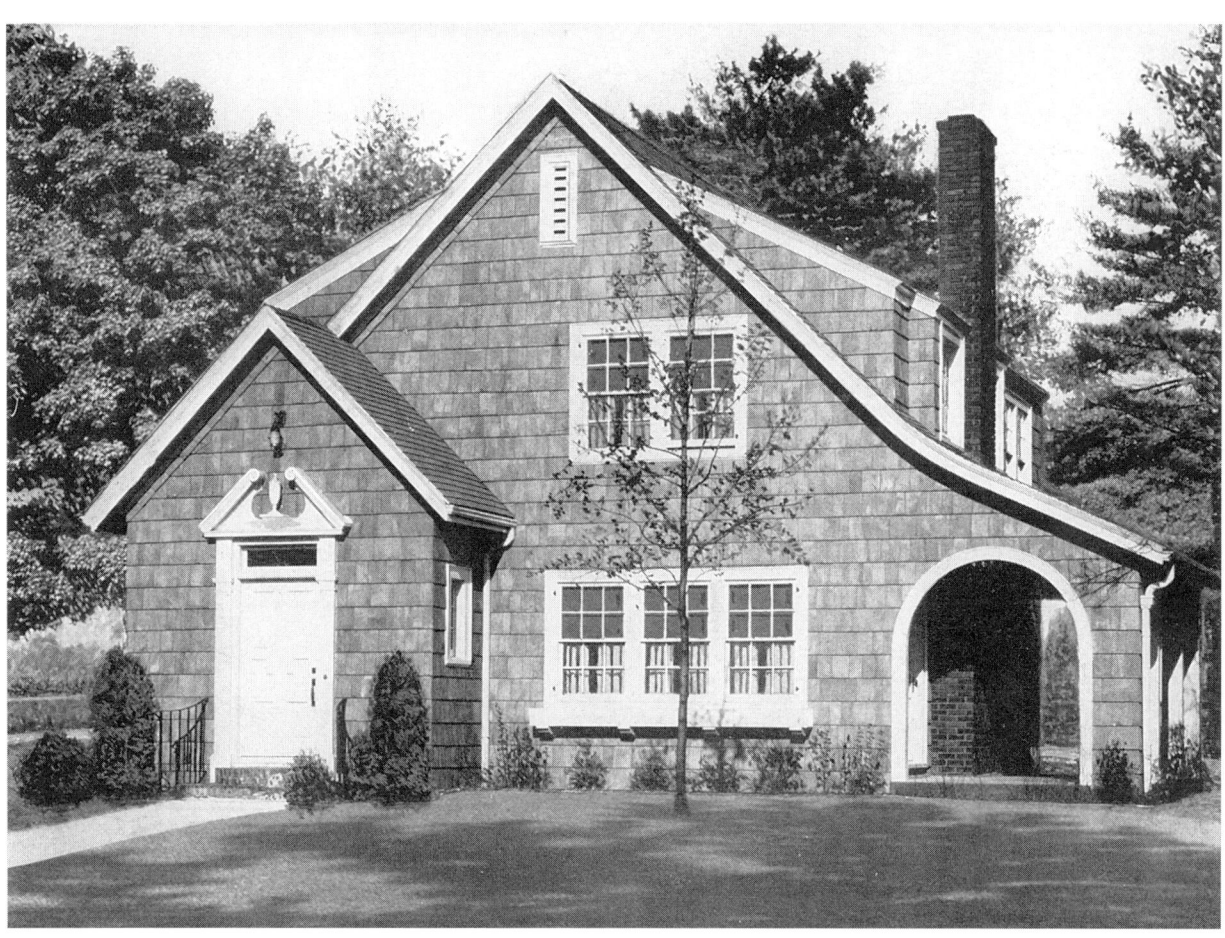

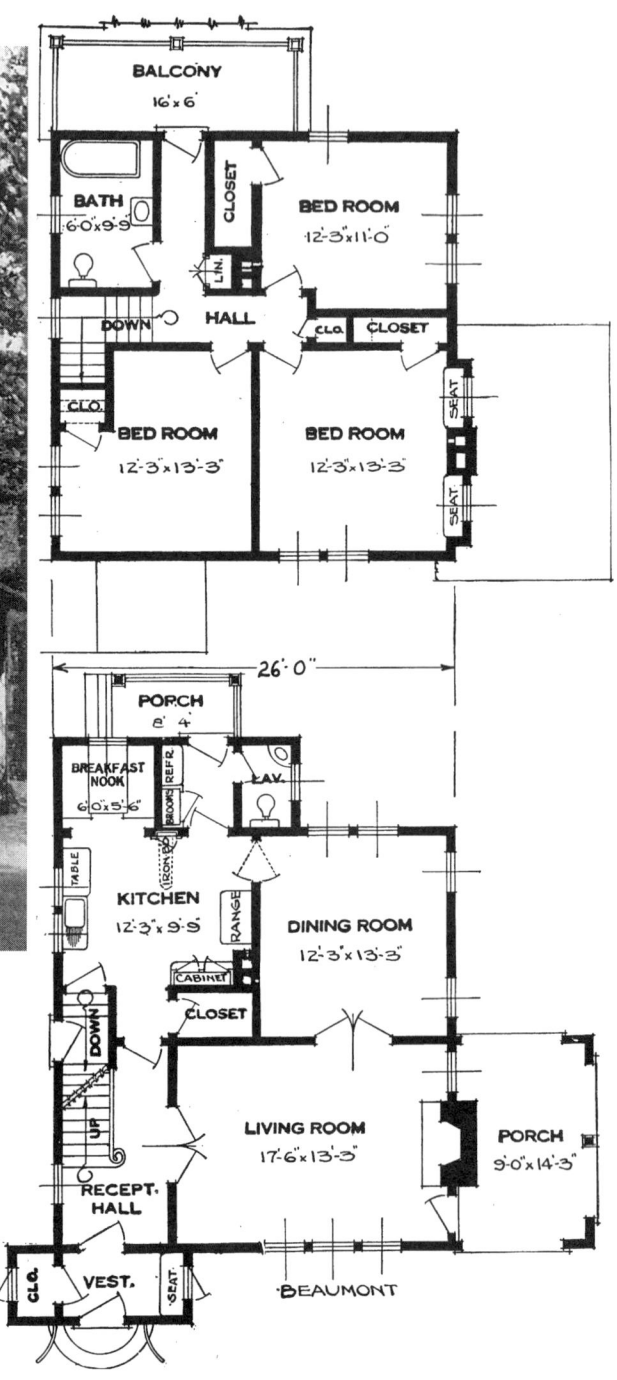

The BEAUMONT (Size 26x28')

Those only are great who love and are kind, and these greatest of human faculties are best developed in the home. Those who strive hardest to attain a home, strive hardest for the development of the best in themselves and in turn bring out the best in others they meet. Striving for a home such as The Beaumont, elevates, educates and ennobles.

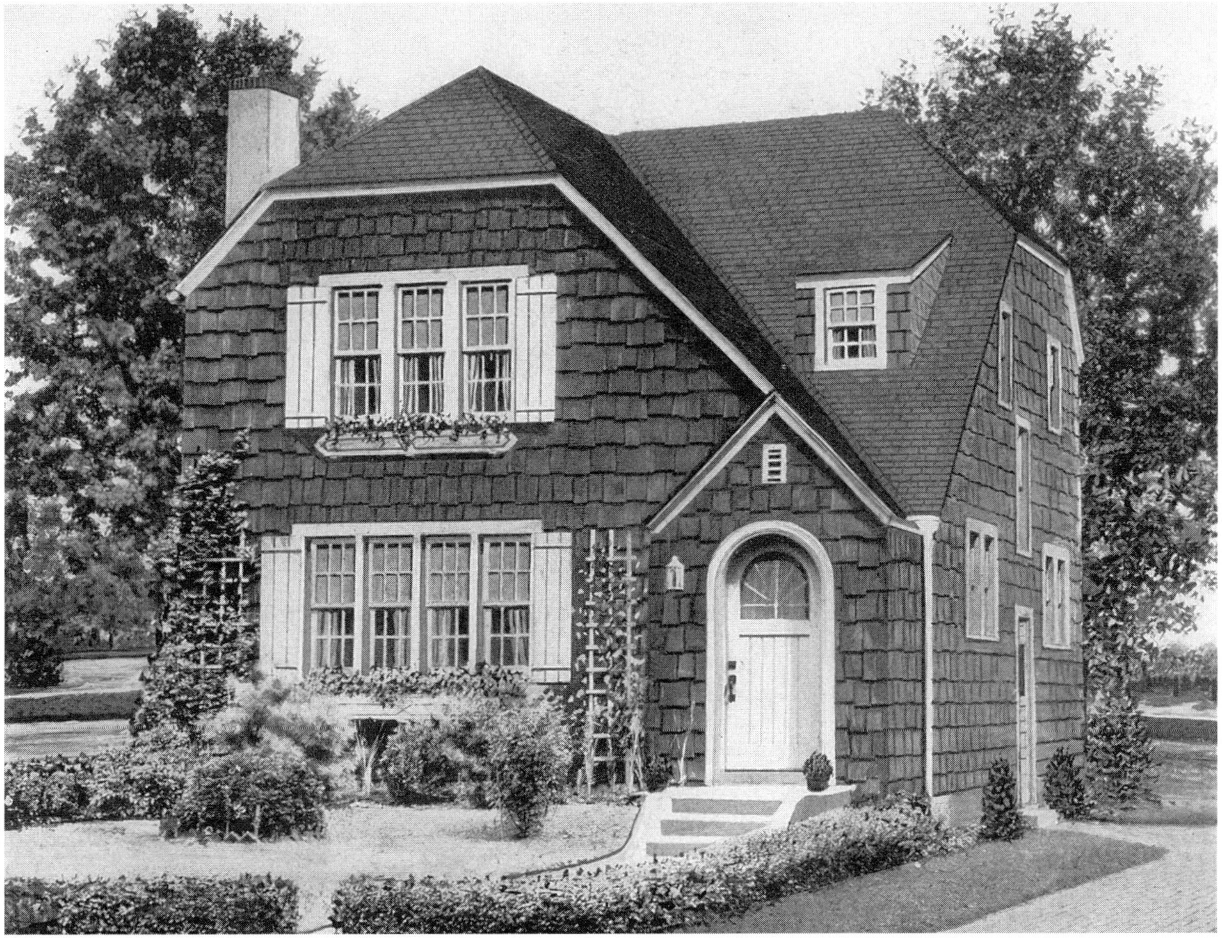

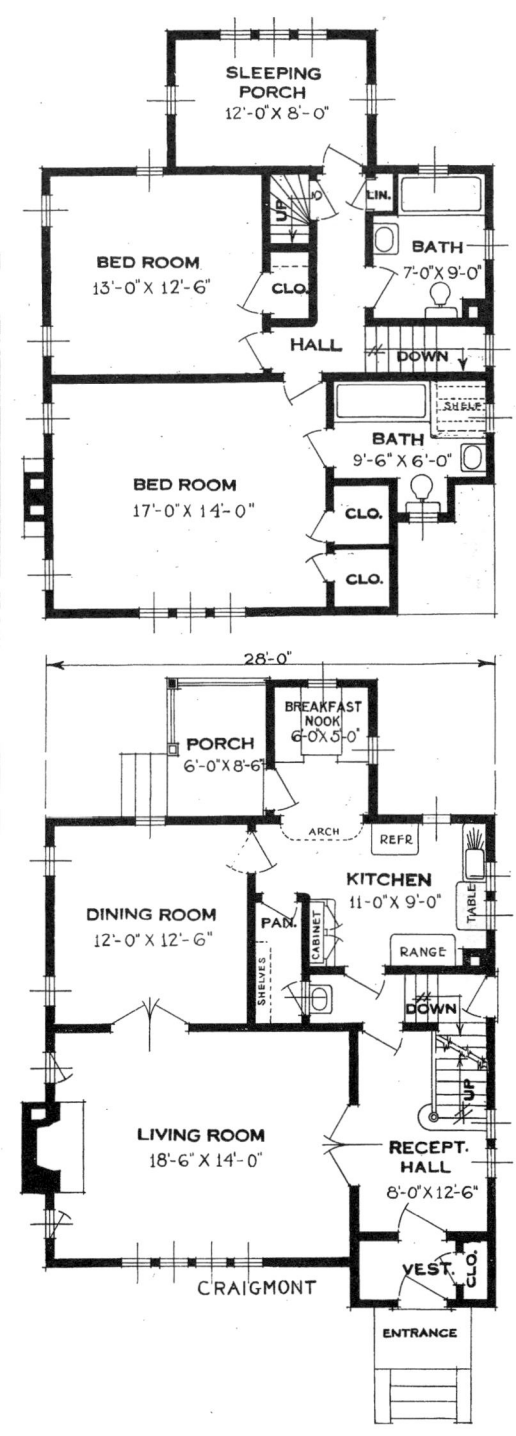

The CRAIGMONT (Size 28x28')

The authority who said, "Give every family a home of their own with garden and flowers and crime will vanish with a single generation"—knew well the inspiration which everyone gains consciously or unconsciously from such surroundings. Truly garden and flowers spell the difference between house and home.

All plans are so prepared as to permit frame, stucco, brick or tile construction.

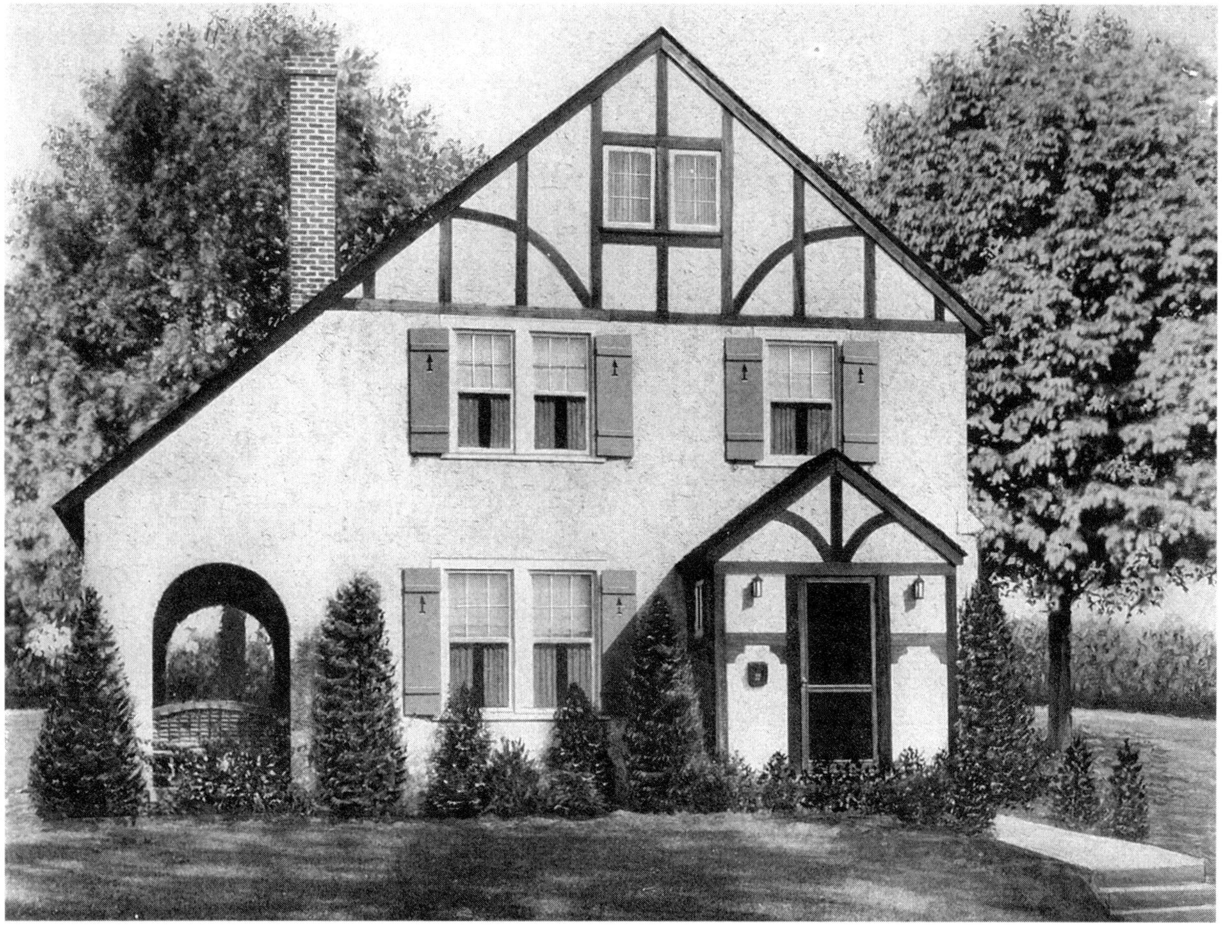

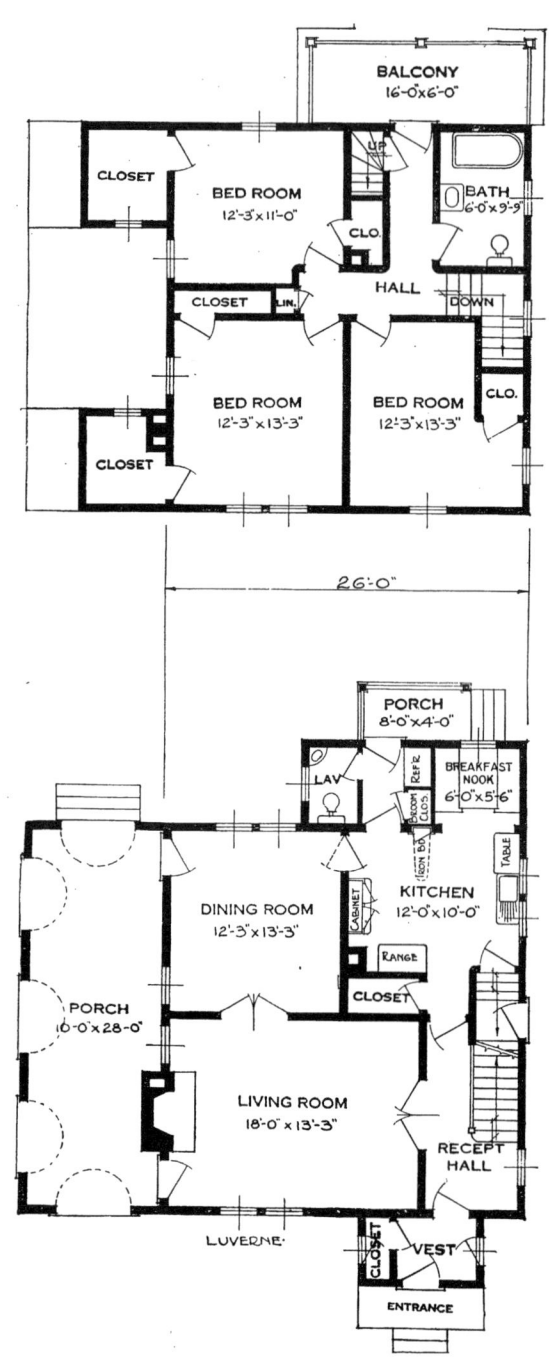

The LUVERNE (Size 26x28′)

Men and women never so fully realize their oneness with life and the natural Law of Perpetual Progress as when their best efforts are directed toward the creation of a home and family. To build The Luverne for a home, and to make that home vibrate with joy and mutual interest, is to join the front ranks for permanent advancement.

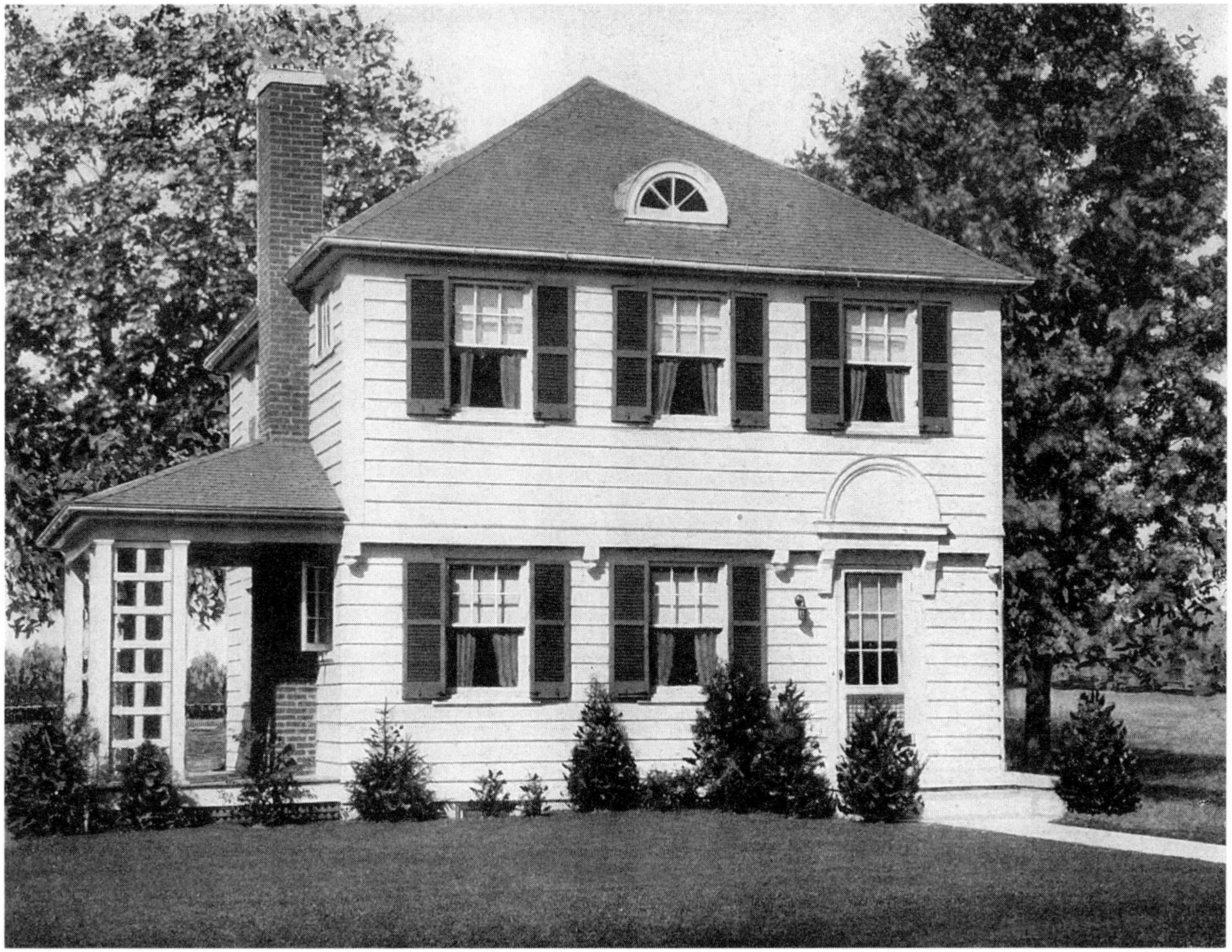

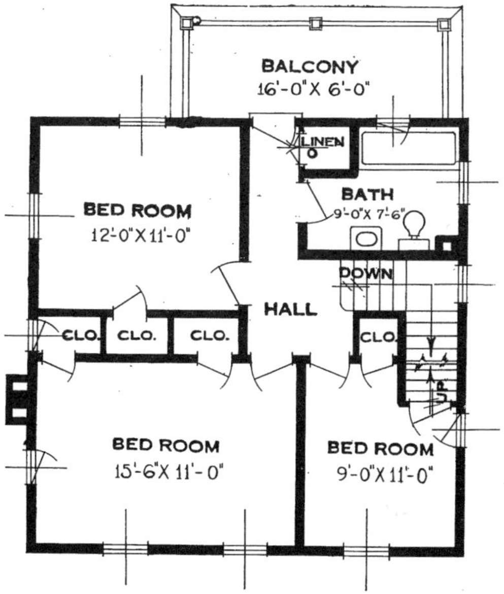

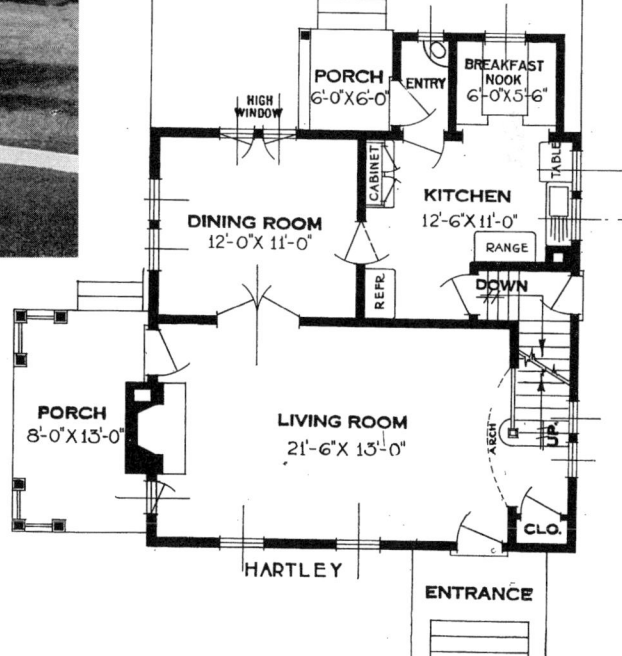

The HARTLEY (Size 26x26′)

As the human mind unfolds, new possibilities are seen and new strength is developed for greater tasks. Those who see in The Hartley a home of exceptional advantages, comforts and conveniences, and firmly fix their hearts on its possession, can surely develop the strength necessary to enable them to materialize the mental pictures which they hold.

31

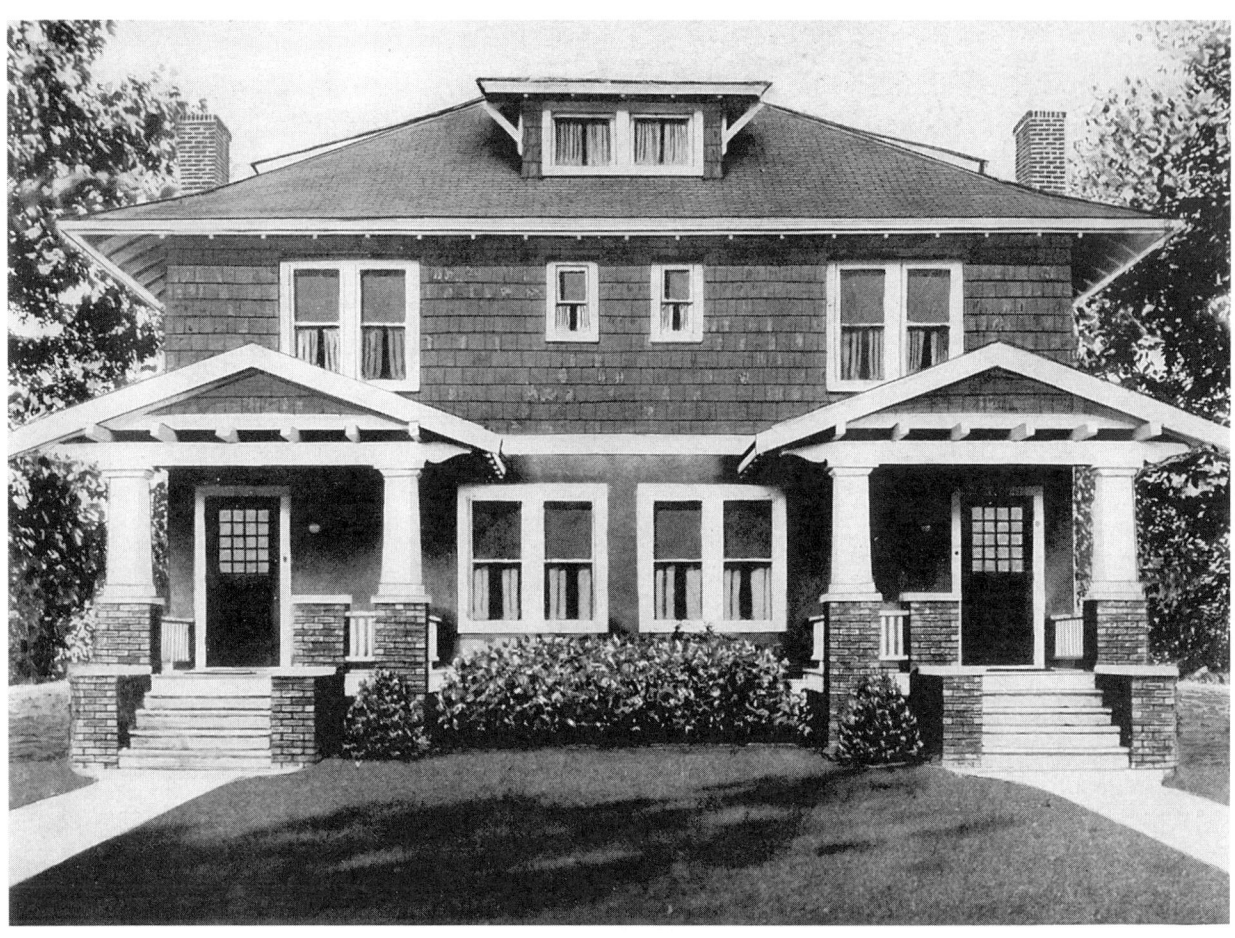
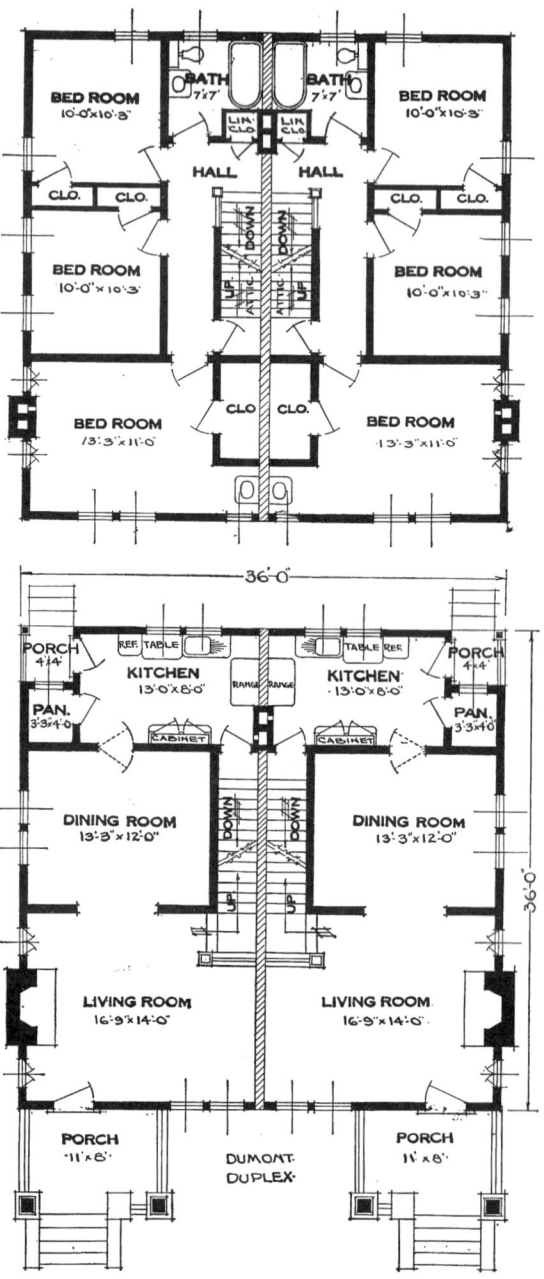

The DUMONT DUPLEX (Size 36x36′)

The Dumont is hard to surpass as a double house, and will make homes of exceptional advantages for those whose experience and education have taught them the value of good fellowship and neighborly kindness. Learning to co-operate with our fellow creatures is the secret of overcoming selfishness and all of its poisoning effects upon our better selves.

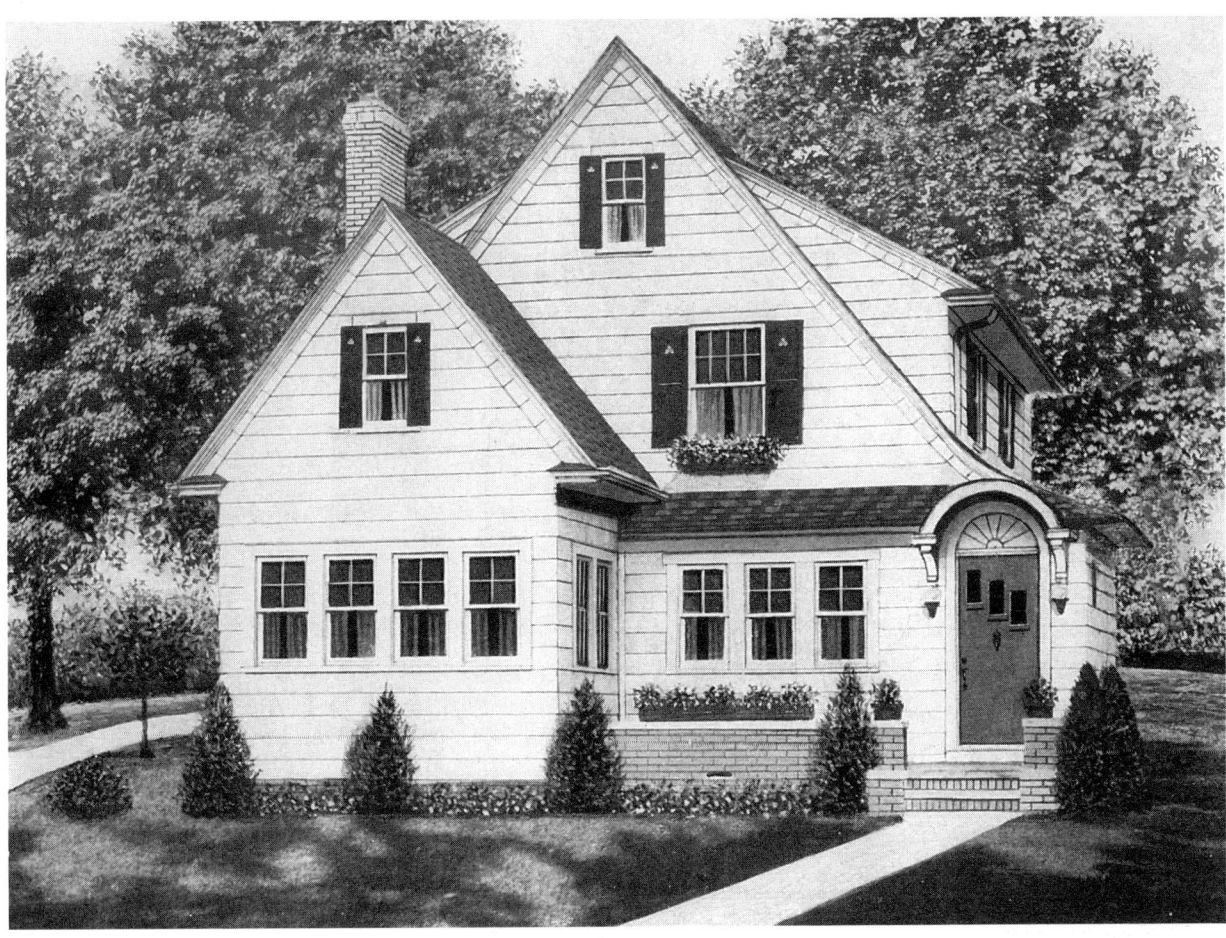
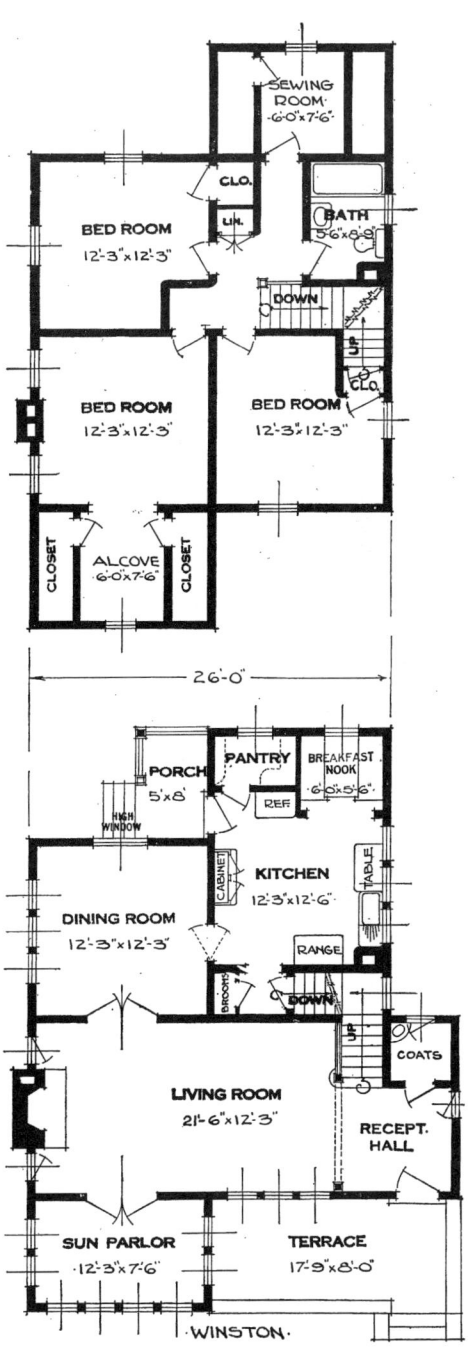

The WINSTON (Size 26x26')

The unprecedented progress of the American people can be attributed more than anything else to the freedom which American women enjoy in the home. When a woman of culture selects a home like The Winston for her kingdom, in which to practice the principles of freedom and co-operation, a new star is manifest in the firmament of civilization.

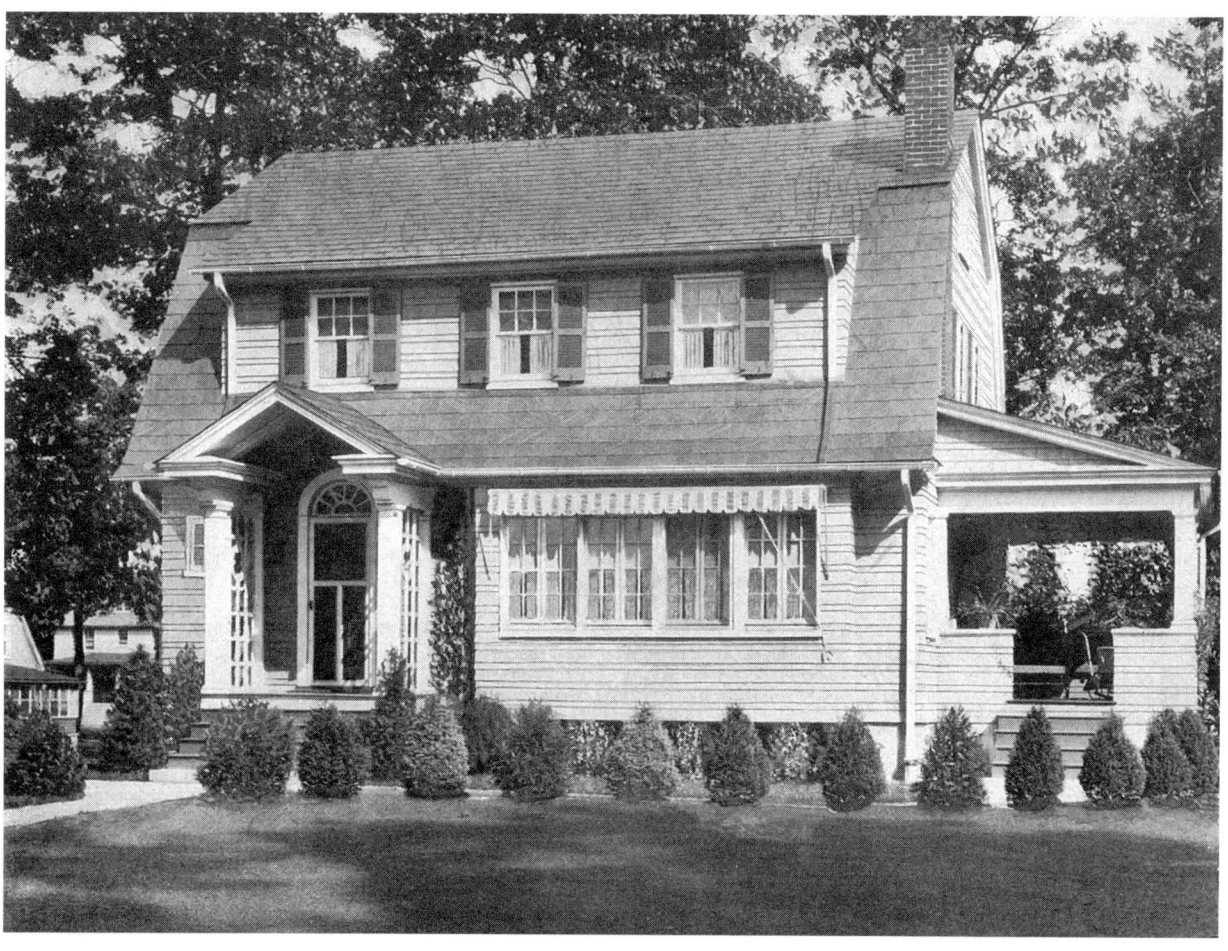

The GLEN AVON (Size 28x26′)

Woman is by nature more economical than man, and her better judgment always offers protest against avoidable avenues of waste. To her, rent receipts are constant reminders of funds foolishly spent, and constantly she sees a vision of a home, perhaps of The Glen Avon style, which the rent money would shortly purchase.

All plans are so prepared as to permit frame, stucco, brick or tile construction.

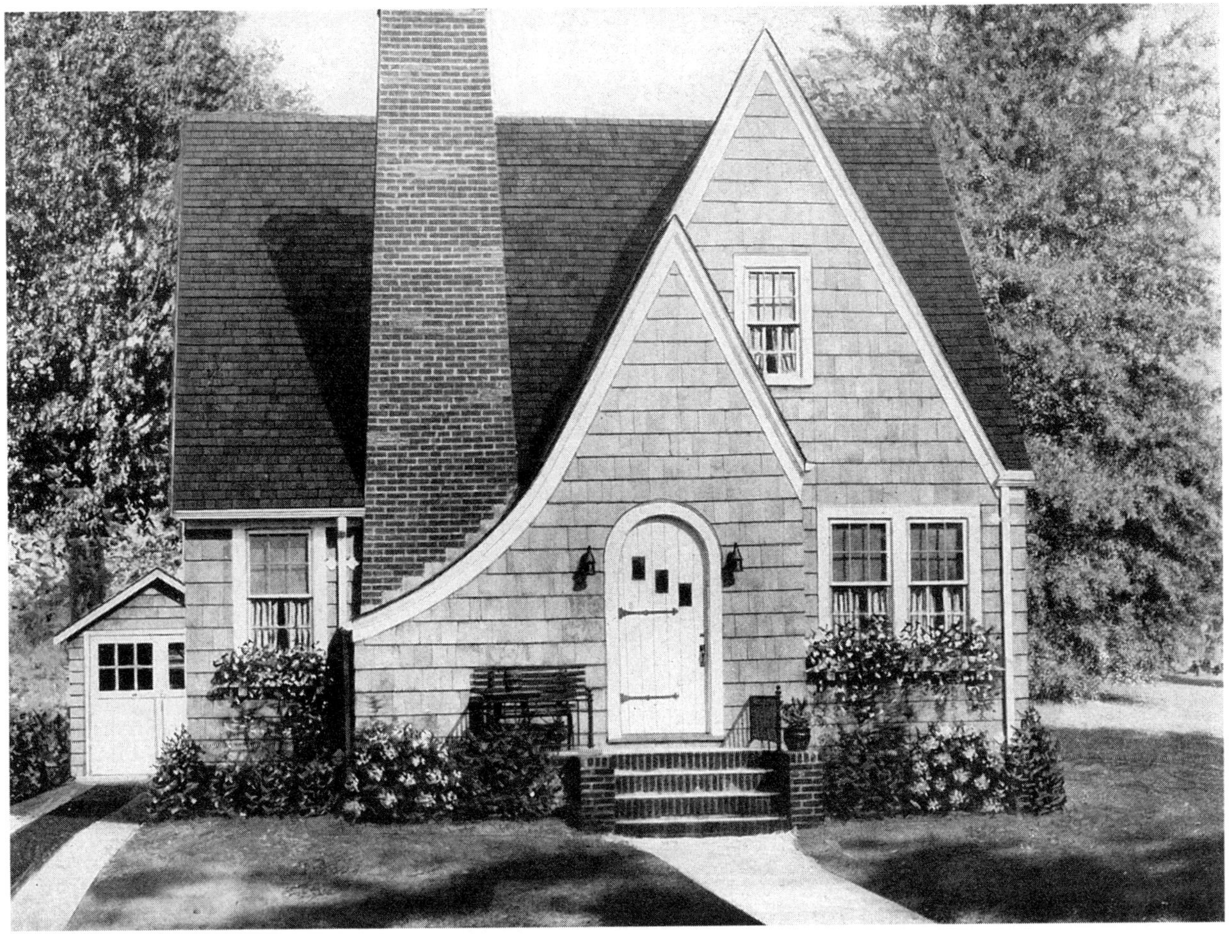

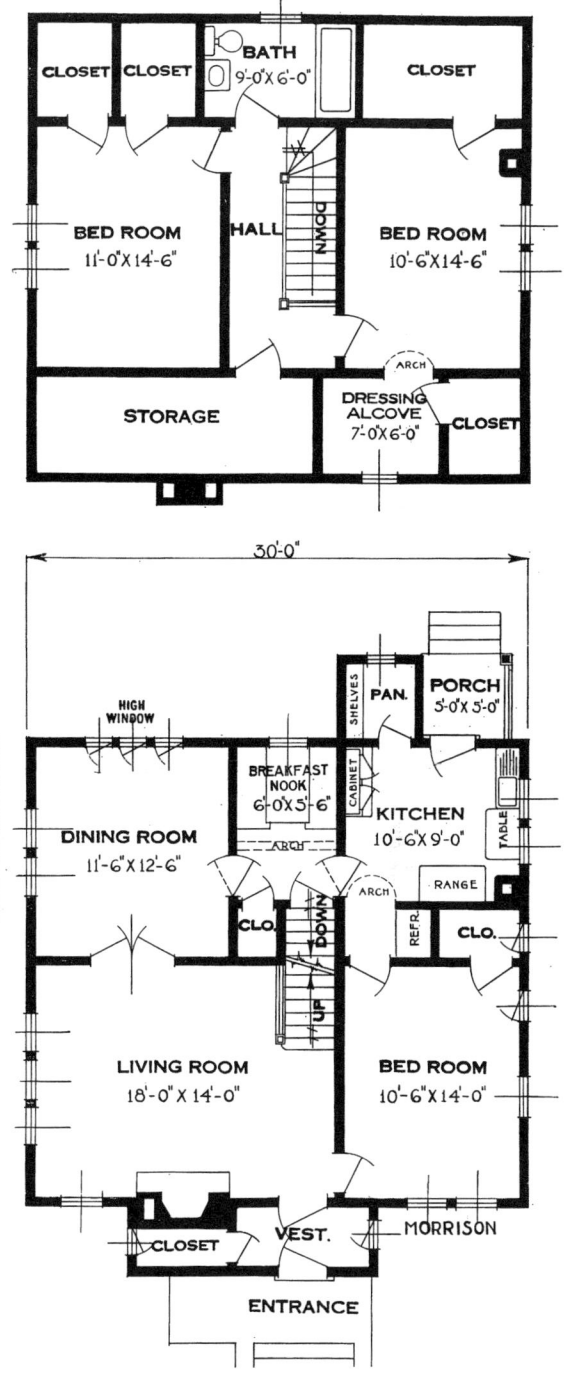

The MORRISON (Size 30x28′)

An English cottage of gray shingles, moss green roof and a massive chimney which suggests glowing warmth within. What home could be more inviting? But go further—look thoughtfully at the floor plan, the ample closets and every possible convenience that helps to make a house a home.

All plans are so prepared as to permit frame, stucco, brick or tile construction.

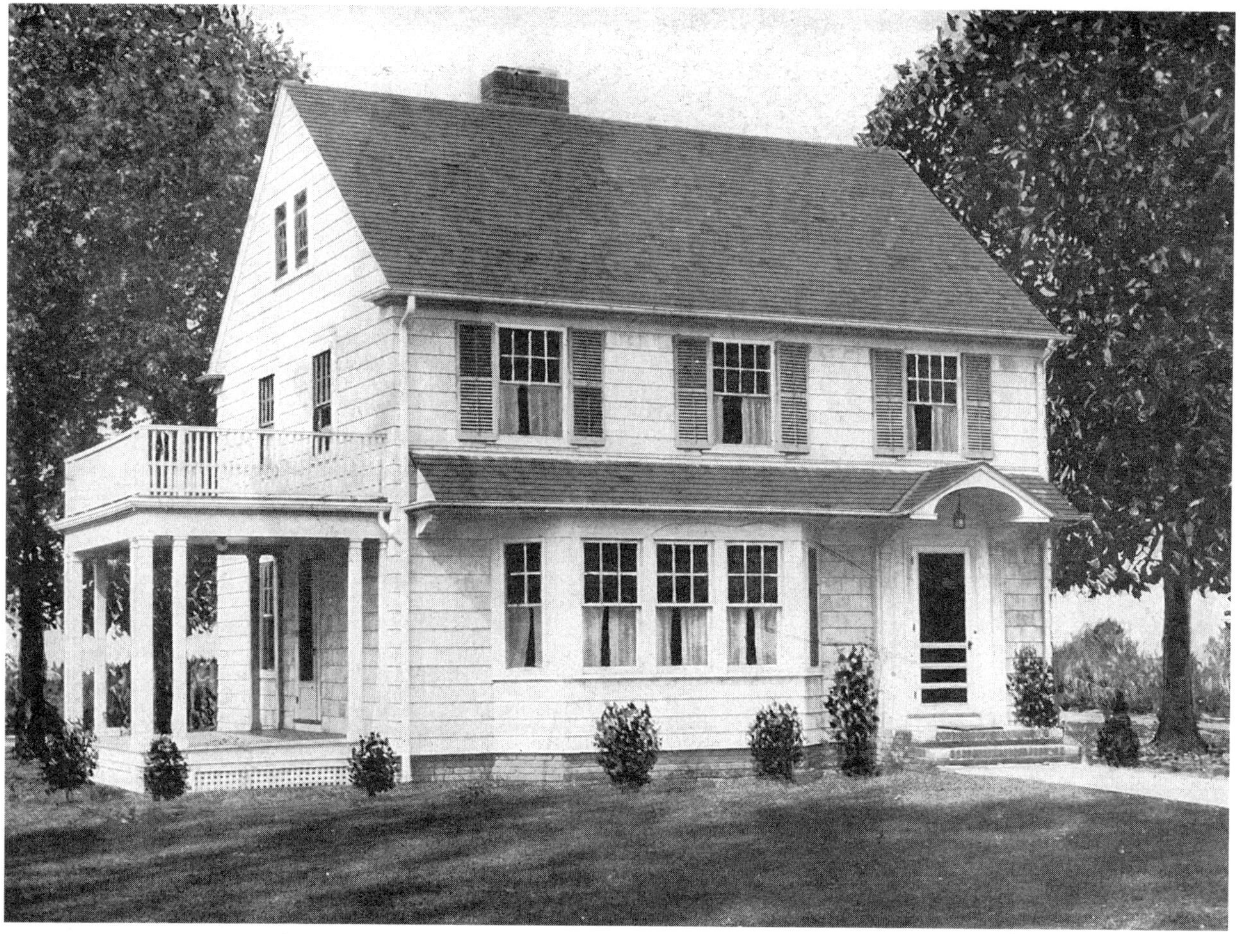

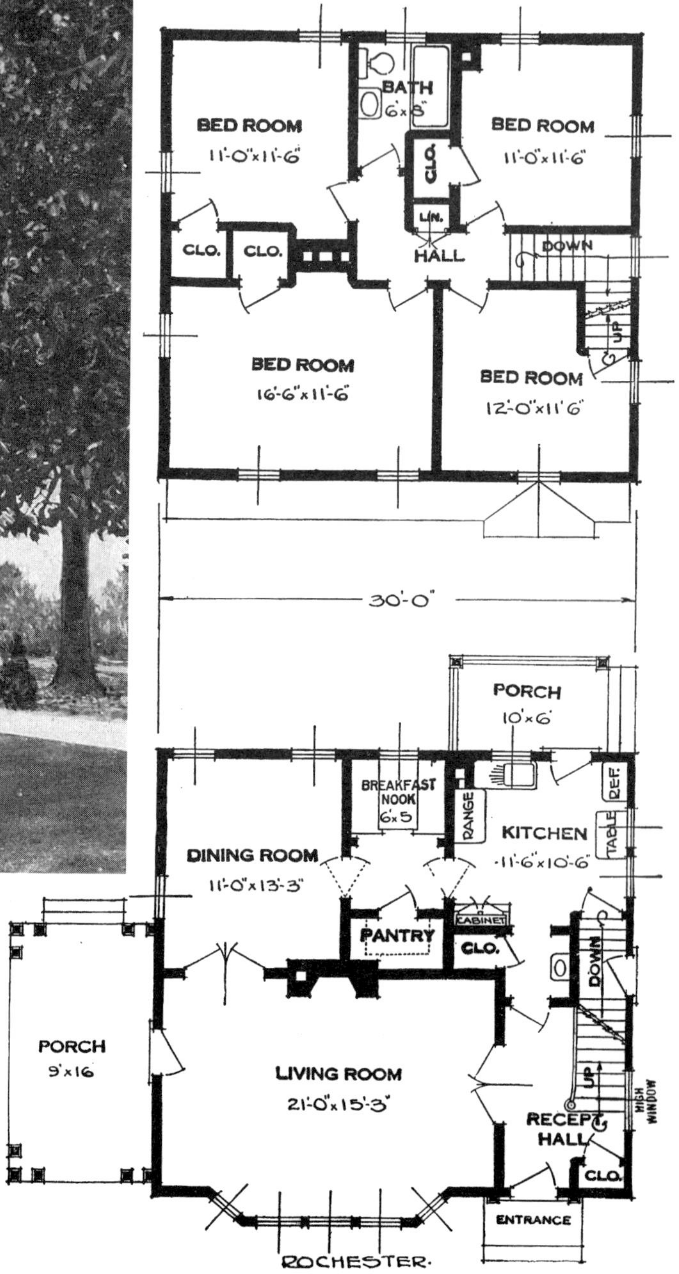

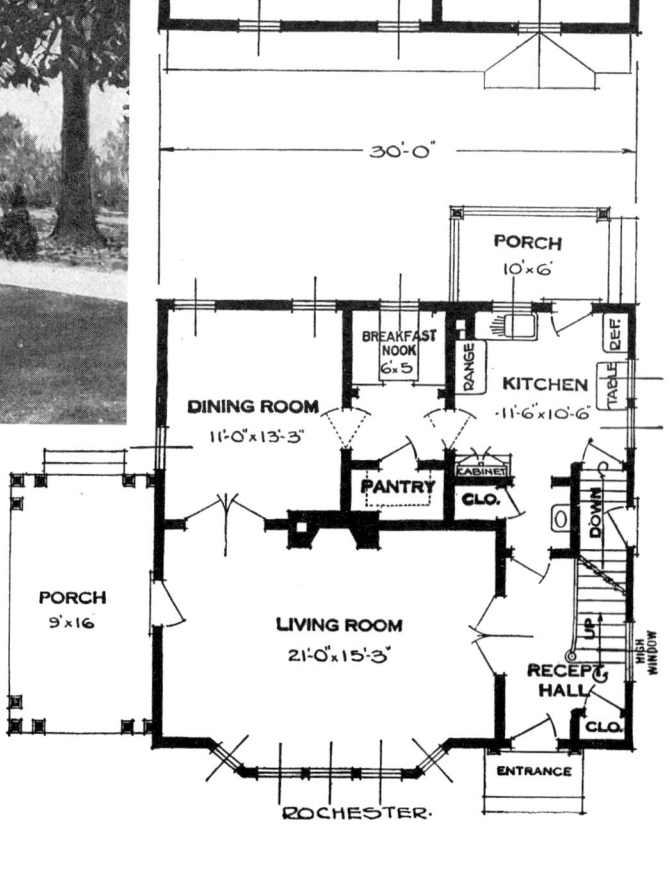

The ROCHESTER (Size 30x28')

Every child has the right to be born and reared in an environment free from discord and paternal unrest. It is far easier for parents to maintain a wholesome atmosphere for their children in a private home like The Rochester than it is in a crowded tenement or apartment house where conditions are neither sanitary nor homelike.

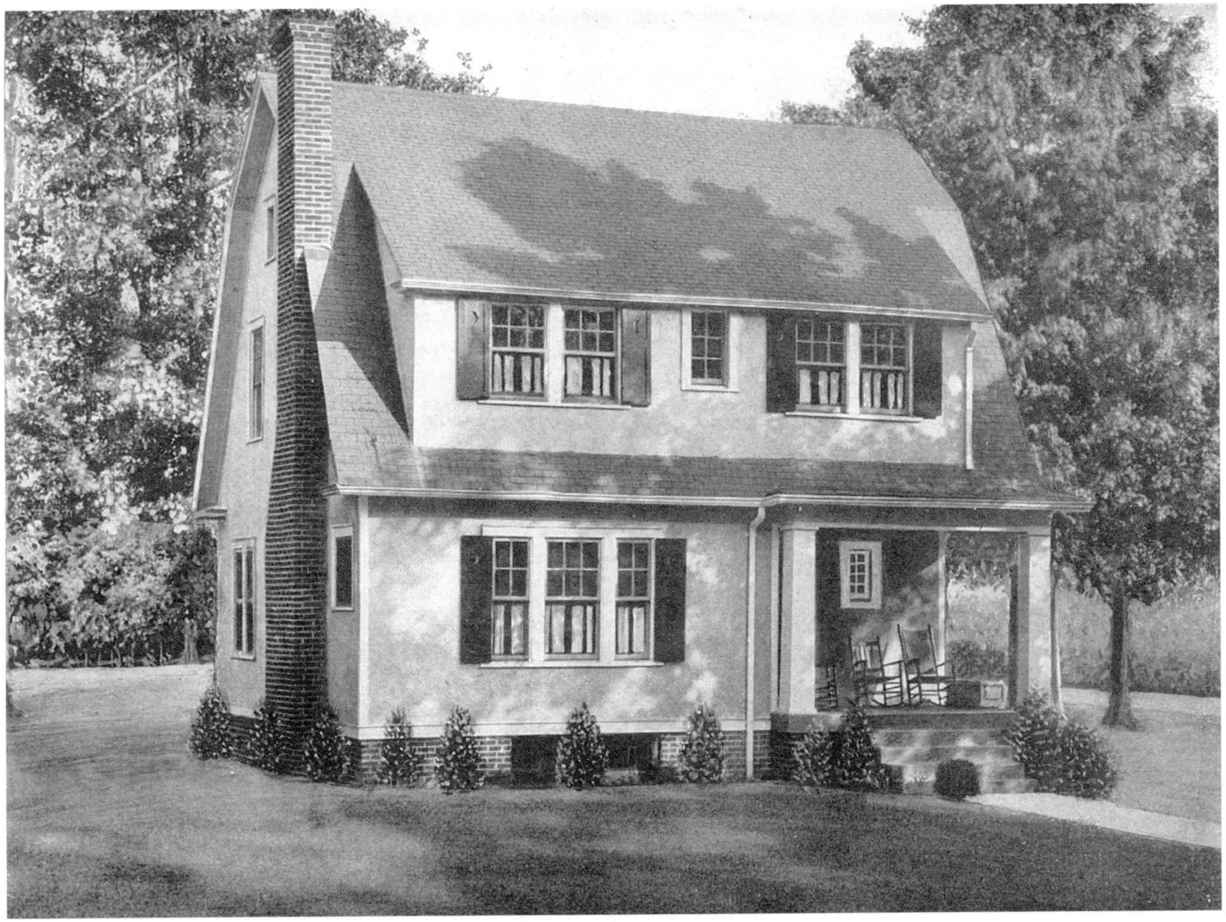

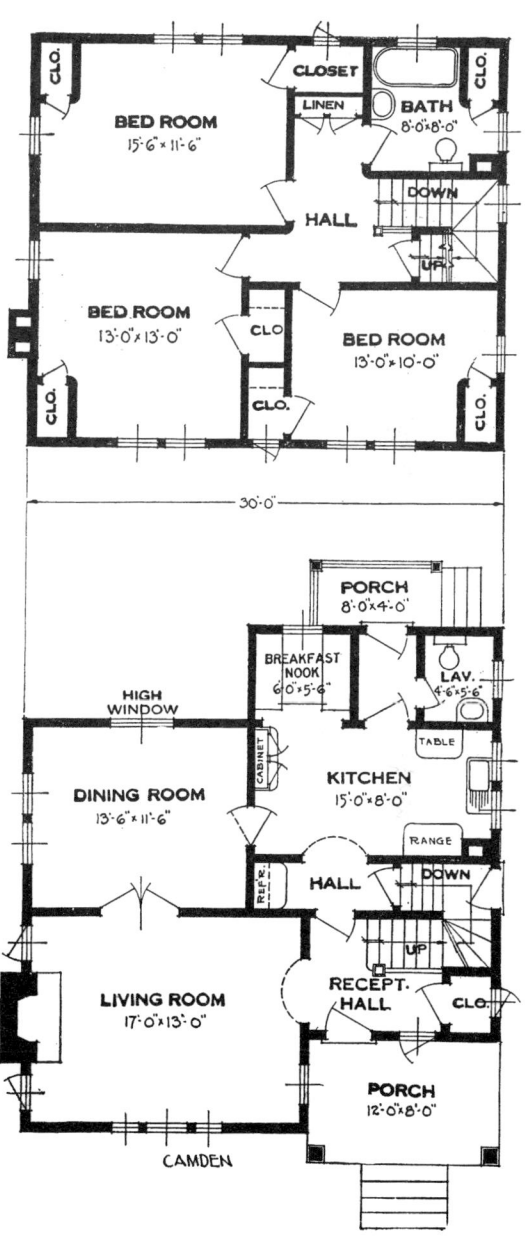

The CAMDEN (Size 30x26′)

Those who put their savings into get-rich-quick schemes instead of homes of their own are, as a rule, the most dependable support for landlords. The suburban streets of all cities could be lined with artistic homes similar to The Camden with the money which is yearly fooled away with fakers who play upon the imagination of the inexperienced.

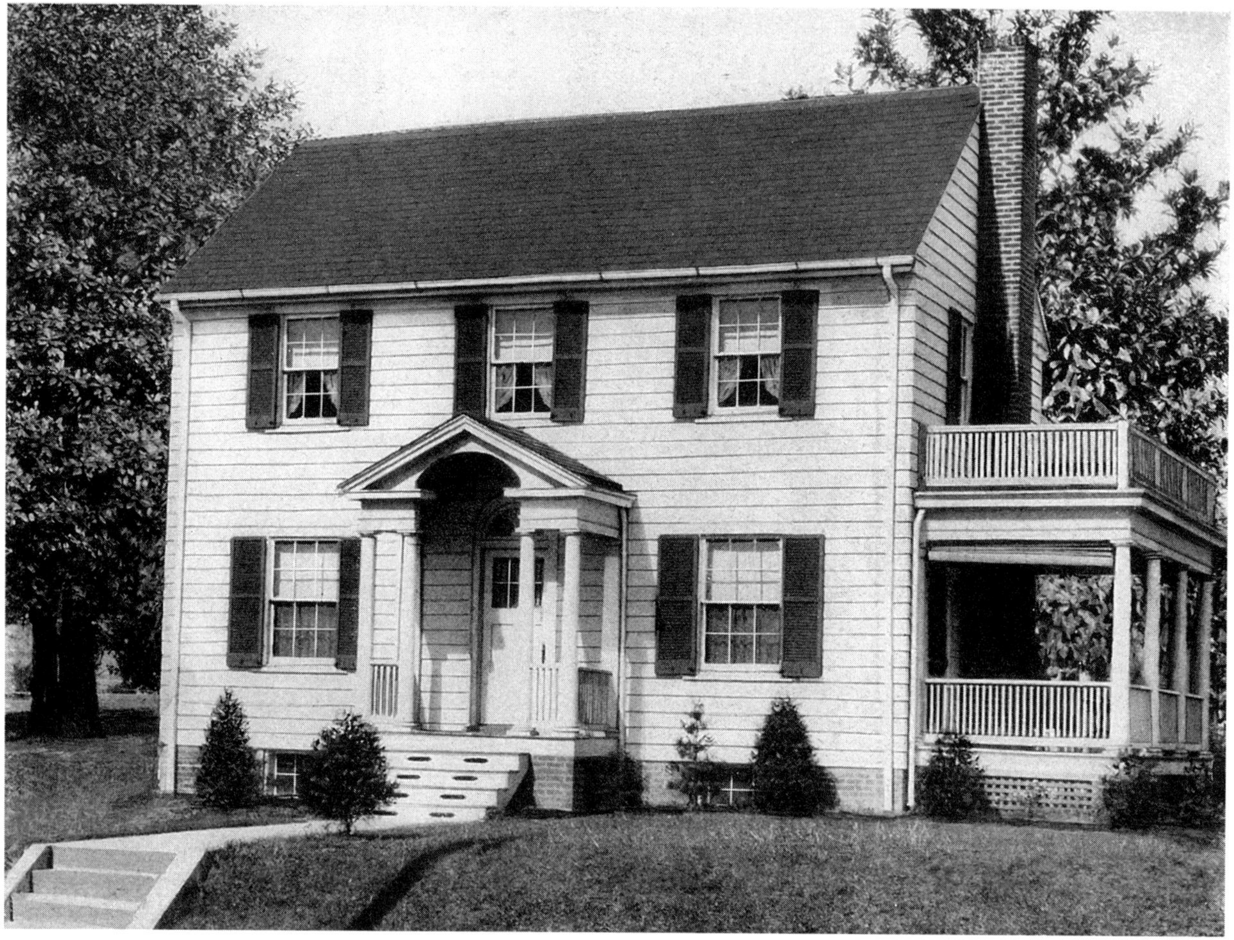

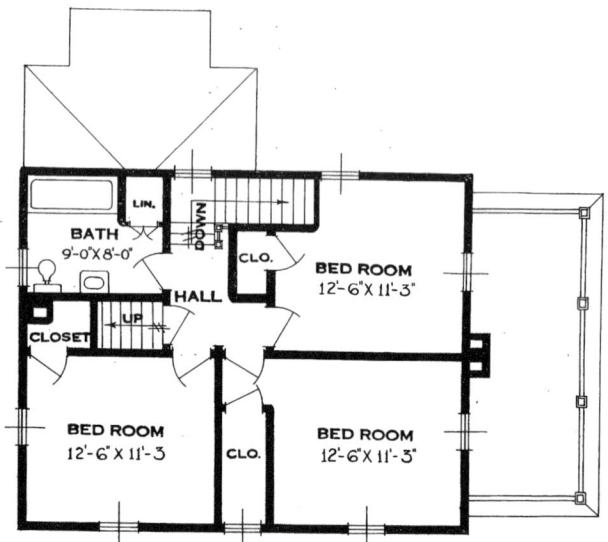

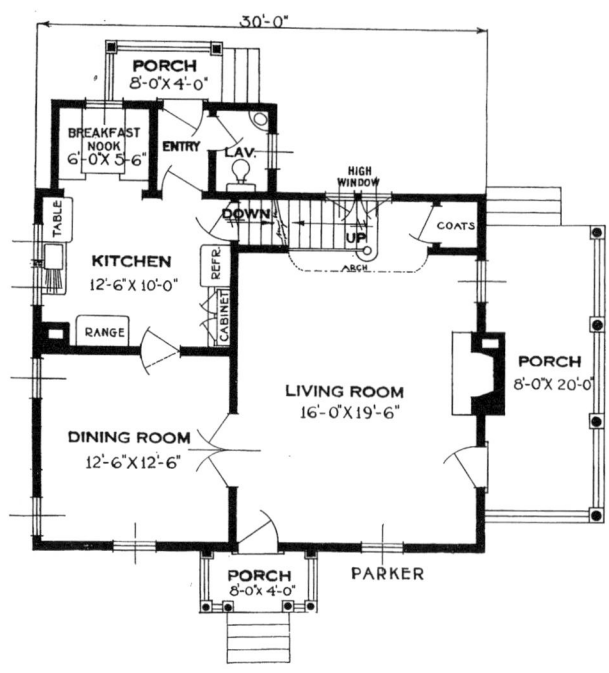

The PARKER (Size 30x24')

If all women knew how much easier it is for a man to be contented in a home he has helped to build and learned to love, countless numbers would lose no time in learning the cost and easy terms of payment on artistic homes like The Parker. Such homes are inexpensive to build, yet they hold a world of joy for earnest homeseekers.

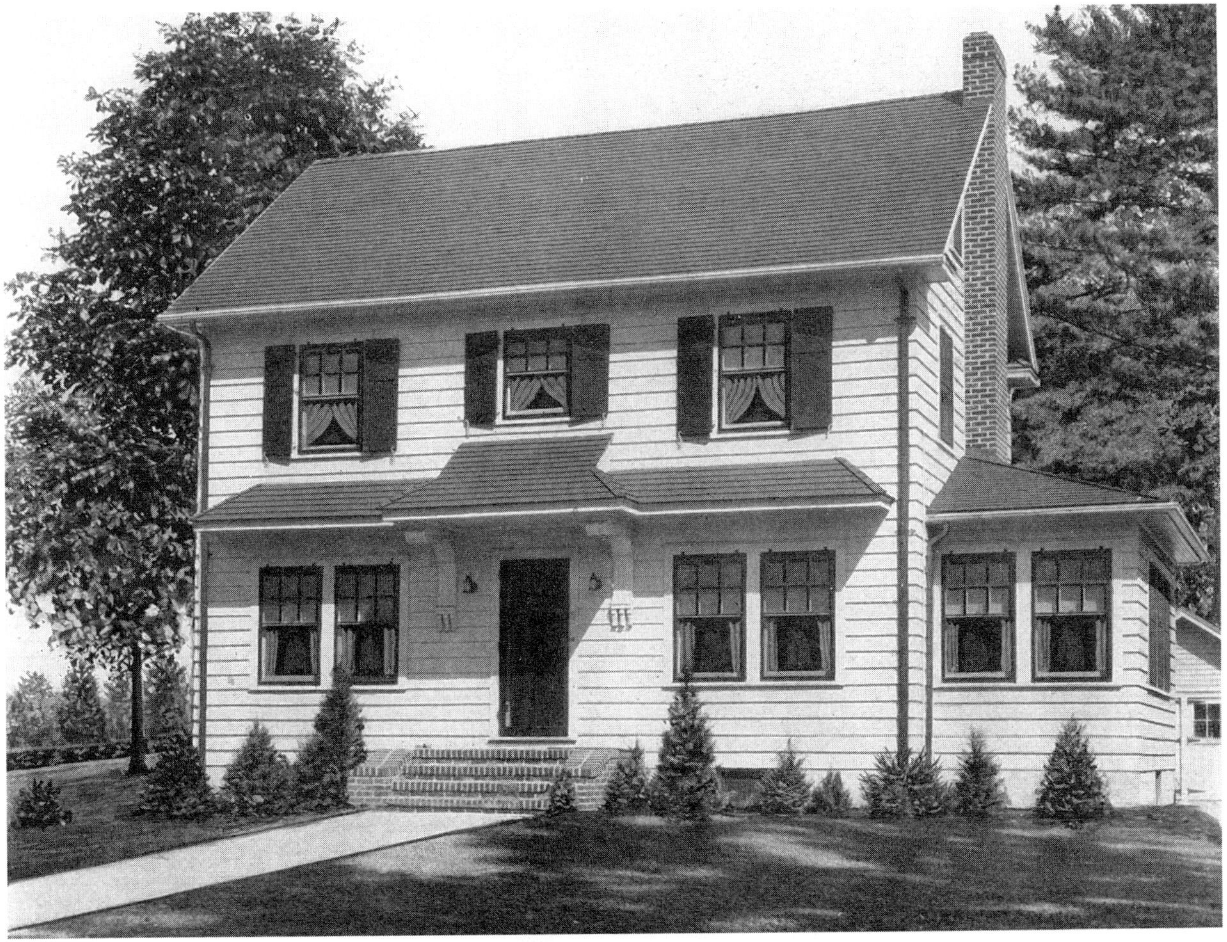

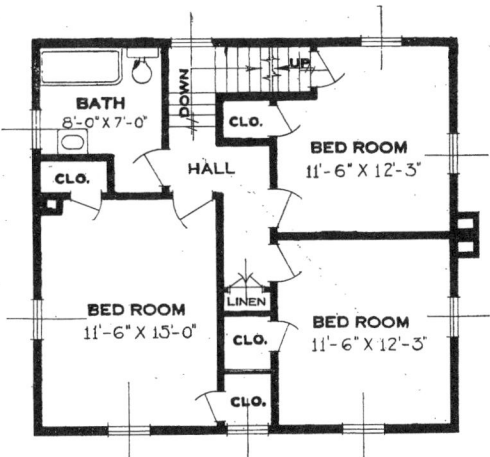

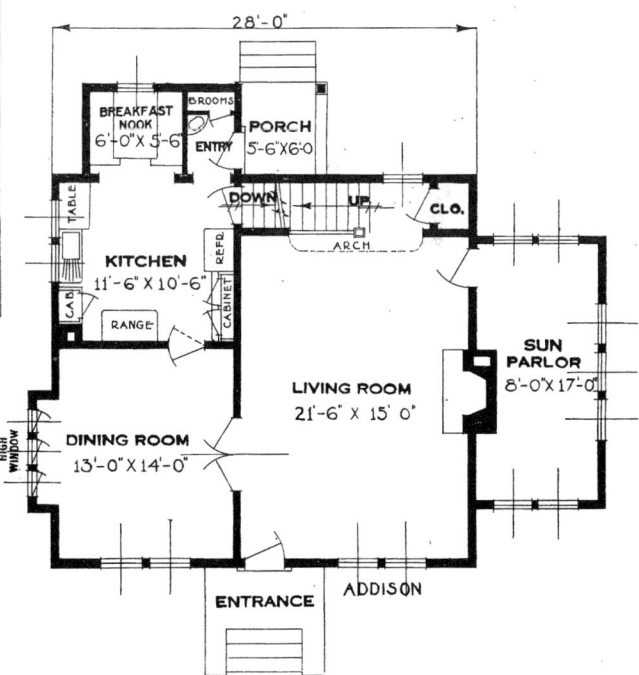

The ADDISON (Size 28x26')

Homes are not constructed alone of brick and stone and wood. These are merely the materials out of which the walls are fashioned. Artistic structures like the Addison are simply inviting, comfortable places where ambitious hearts can quietly and undisturbed build homes of culture, refinement and love which neither climate nor man can mar.

All plans are so prepared as to permit frame, stucco, brick or tile construction.

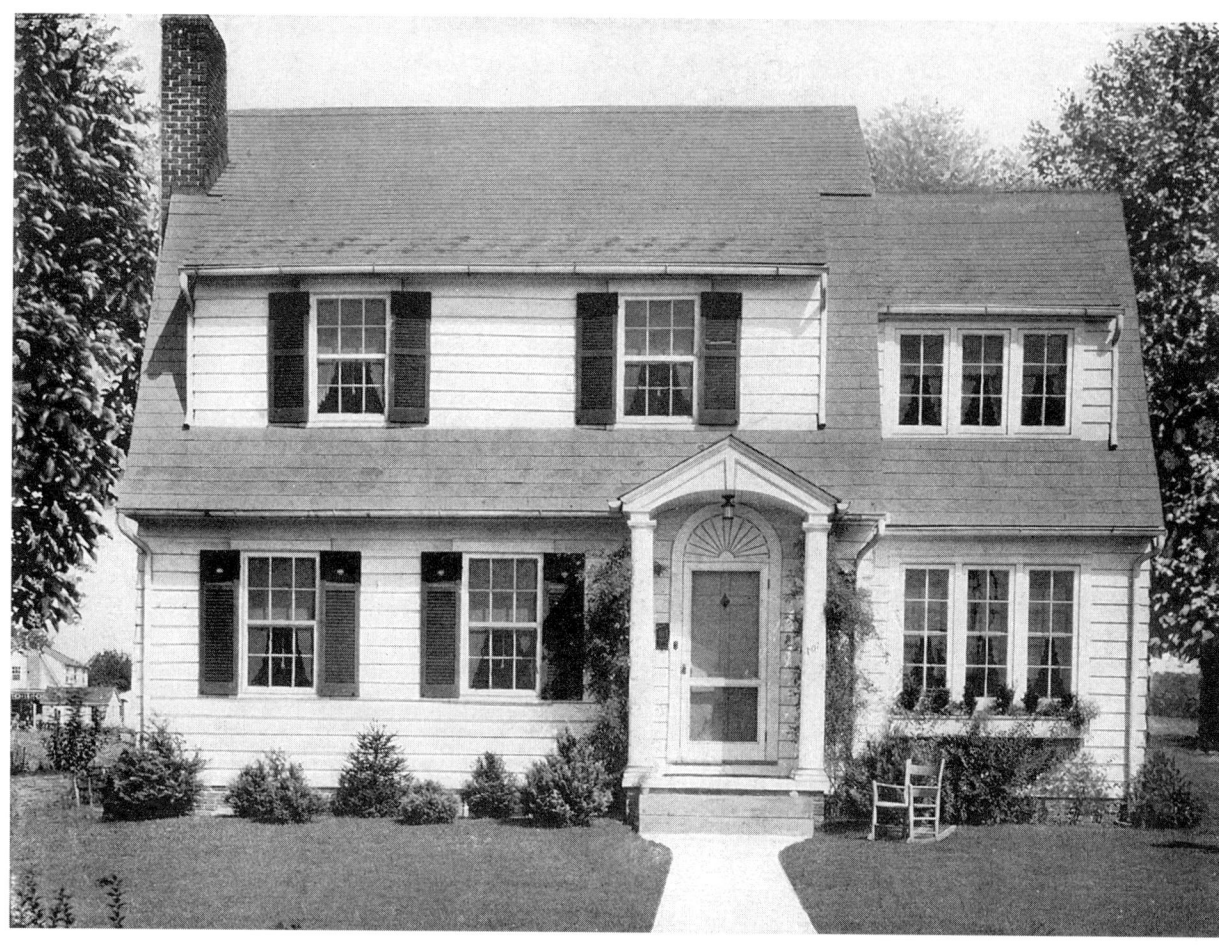
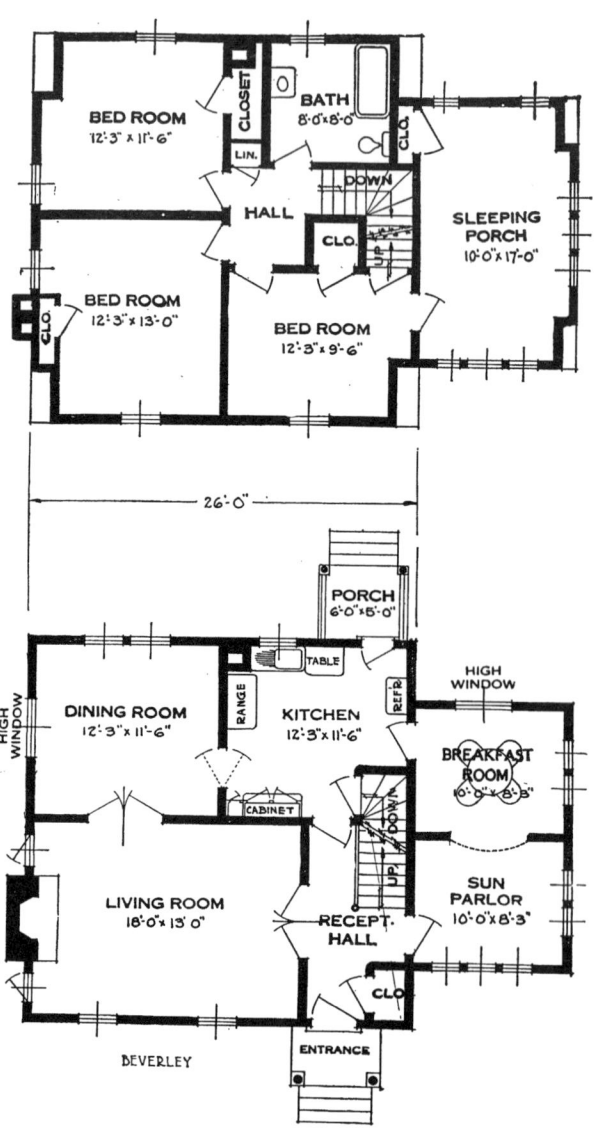

The BEVERLEY (Size 26x26')

The first step in the path of progress is to fix in the mind a clear vision of better conditions, better surroundings and a better place for normal and unhampered growth. Growth comes from freedom of thought and an inner feeling of independence. In no other place can a family so well realize this desired freedom as in a home of their own—such, perhaps, as The Beverley.

All plans are so prepared as to permit frame, stucco, brick or tile construction.

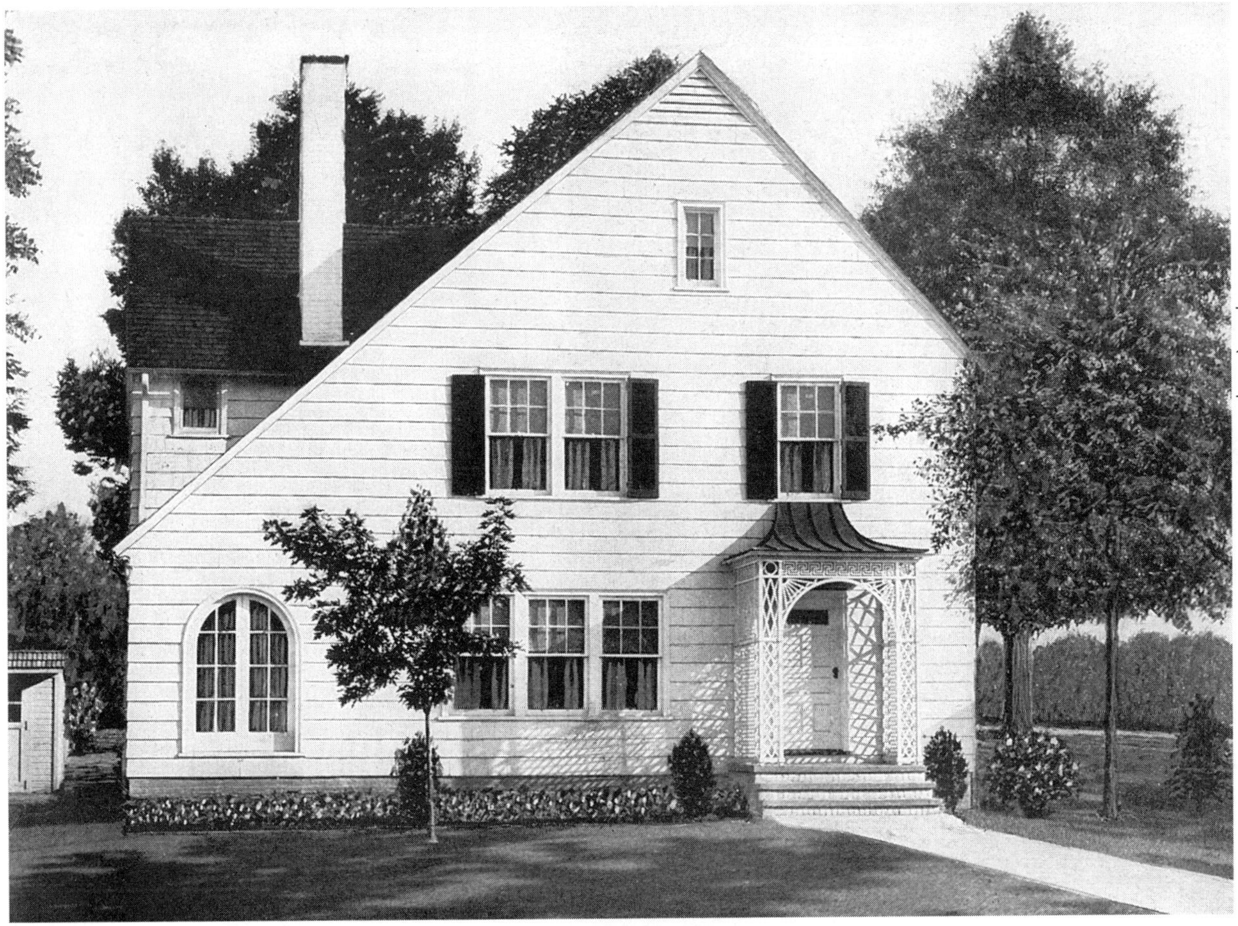

The LAWRENCE (Size 28x28')

A man is often judged as much by the home he builds as by the company he keeps or the clothes he wears. One would expect to find the owner of The Lawrence a man of good judgment and thoughtful purpose, of influence and solid character. Men who select and build homes of this style are, as a rule, sentinels of progress in their communities.

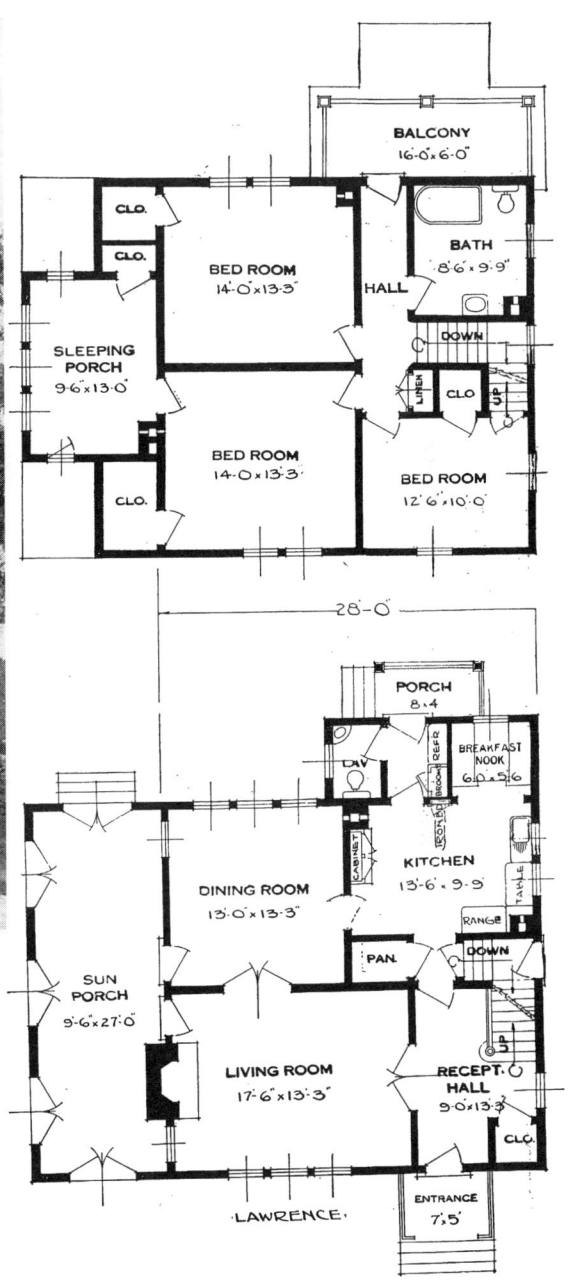

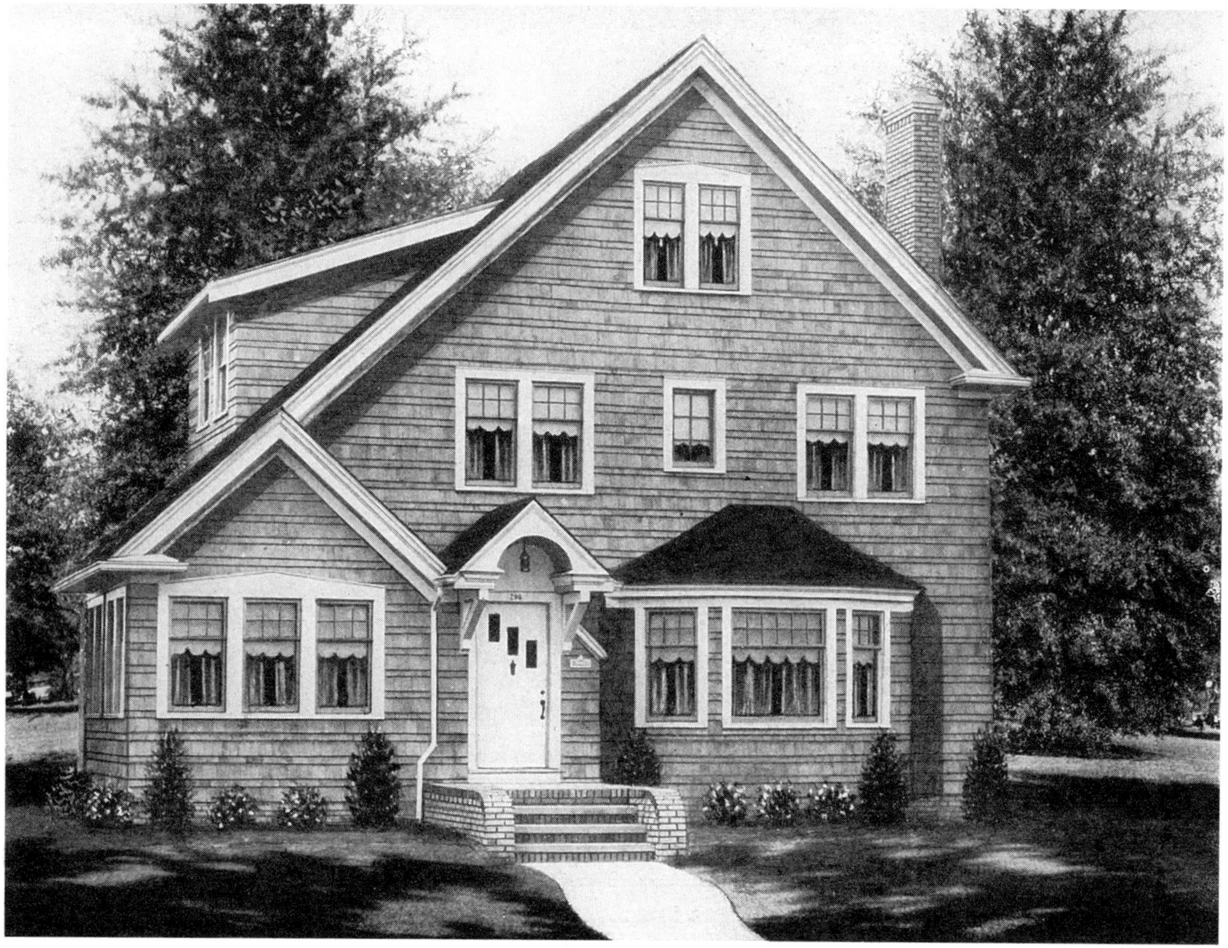

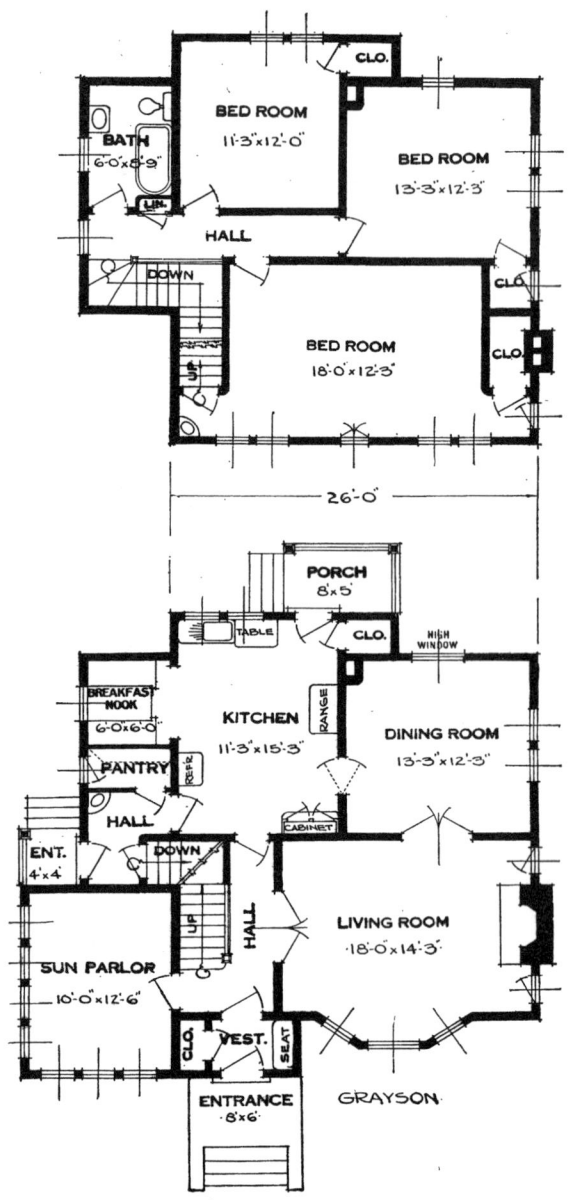

The GRAYSON (Size 26x26')

If all bachelors could purchase insurance against mishaps and discords in marriage and be assured that their life companions would be real helpmates in the building and keeping of their homes, contracts for new houses would be let by the thousands, and the loss of help from the workshops and offices would paralyze business for the time.

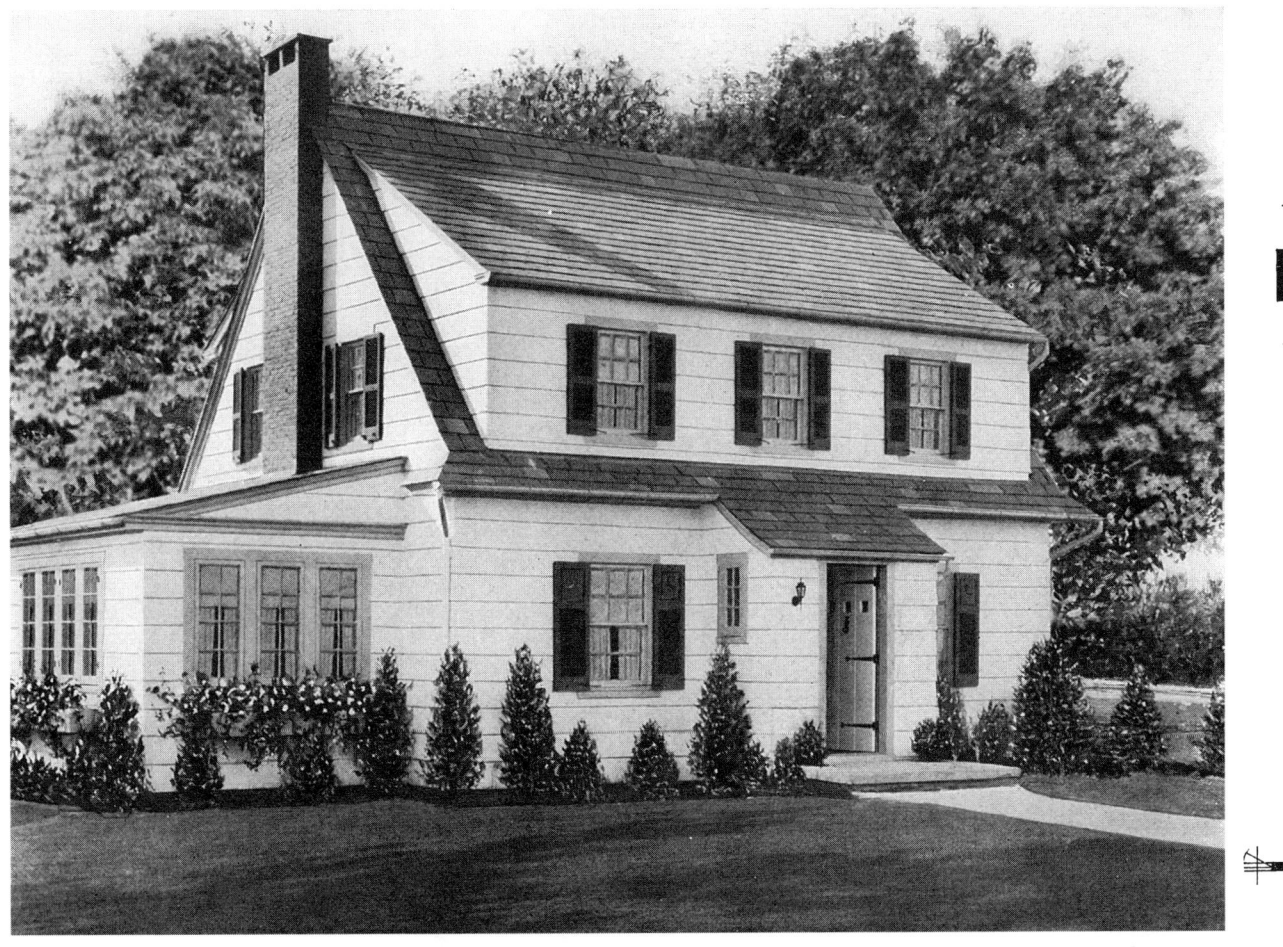

The AVONDALE (Size 28x26′)

To know the value of right environment is one of the first steps in the mastery of self. It is impossible for anyone to think his best thoughts or do his best work when his home life is not in keeping with his ideals. Those who firmly fix their hearts on The Avondale for a home may be assured of the refining influence which its possession will bring.

All plans are so prepared as to permit frame, stucco, brick or tile construction.

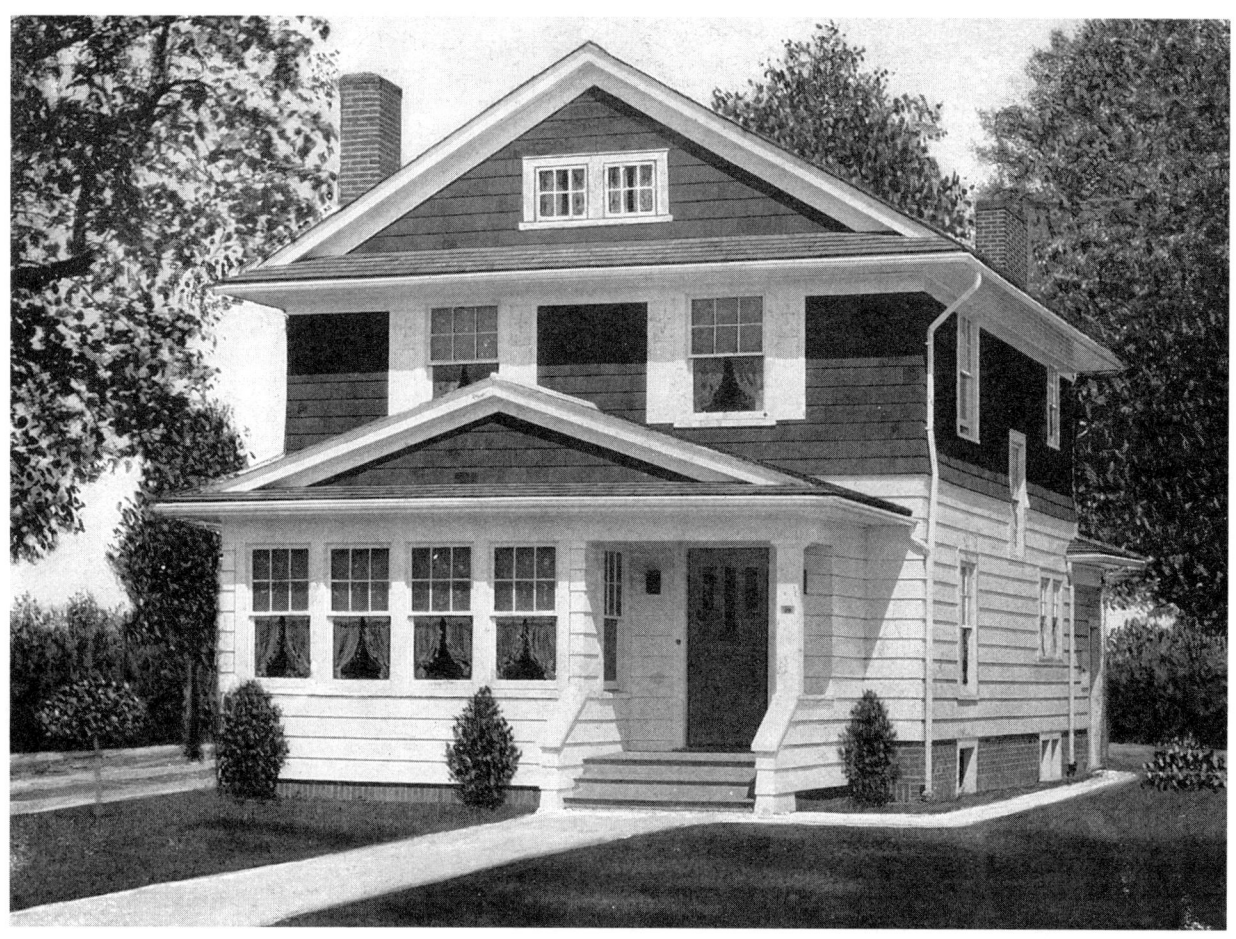
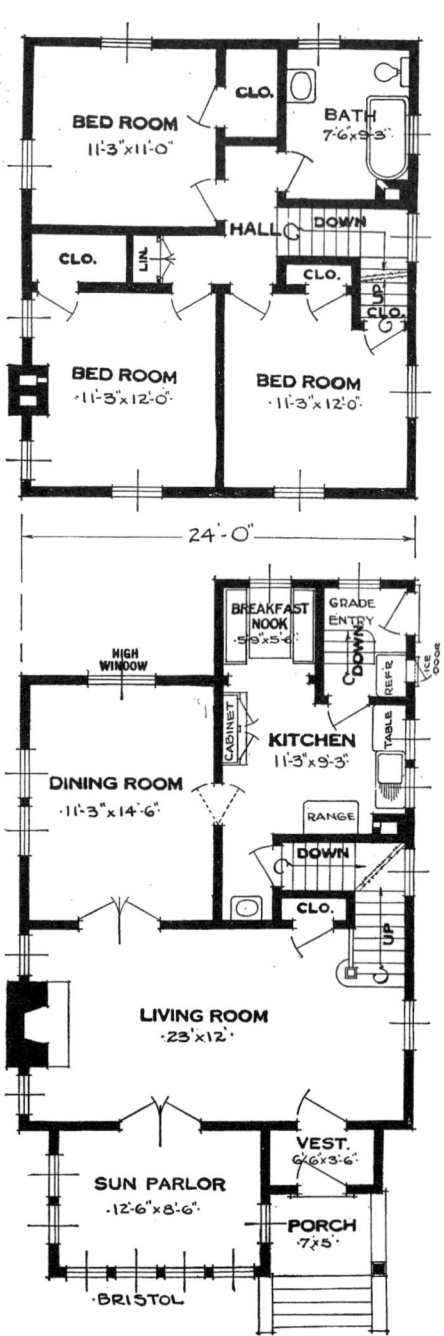

The BRISTOL (Size 24x28')

To the wife and children home means infinitely more than to the husband whose duties are elsewhere. To him it is a place for recreation and rest, but to them it is their kingdom. The hearts of many wives will go out to The Bristol, not with selfish designs, but with earnest maternal longings for better conditions for the culture and refinement of their children.

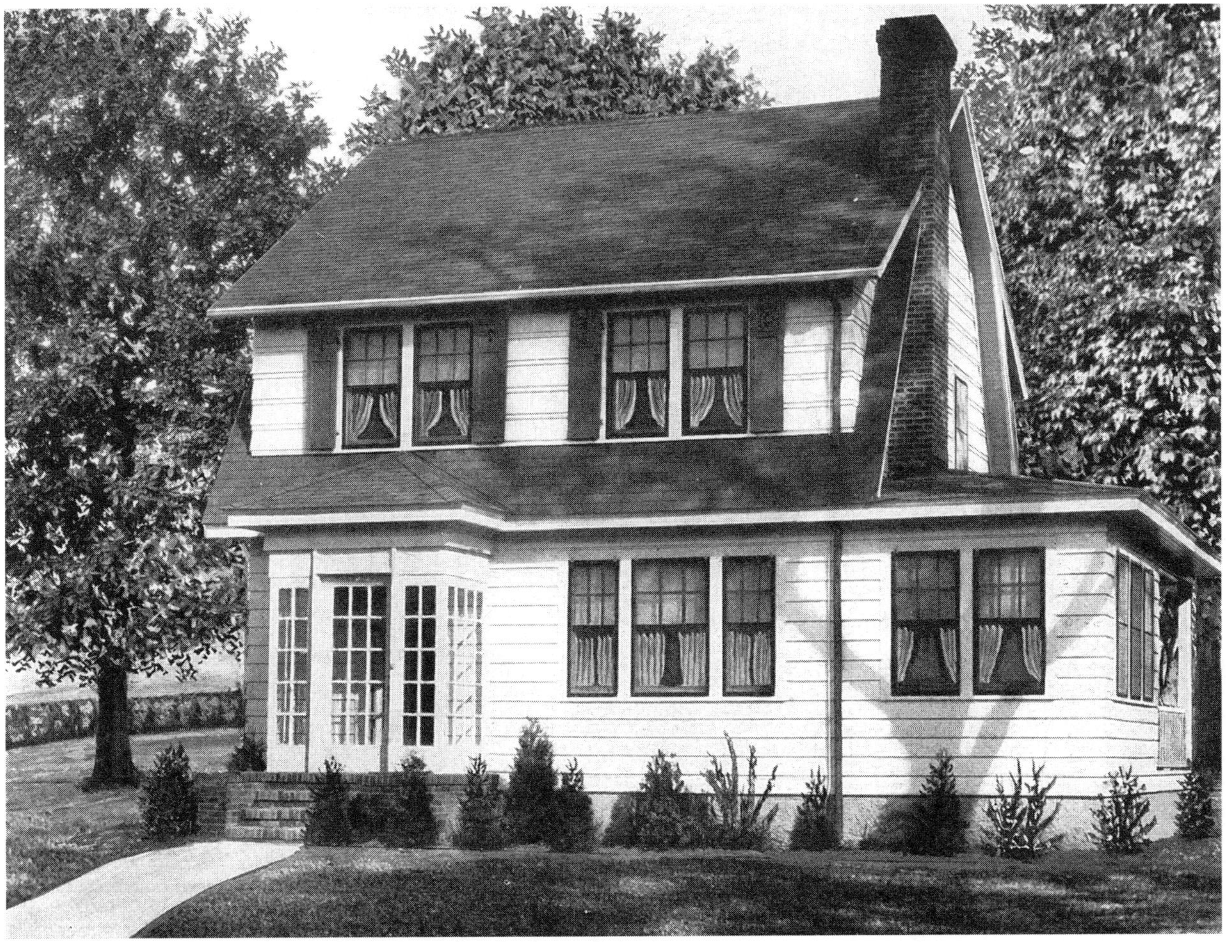

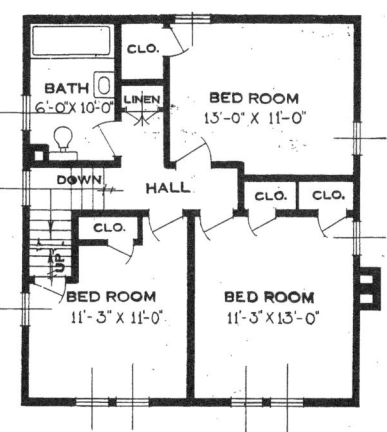

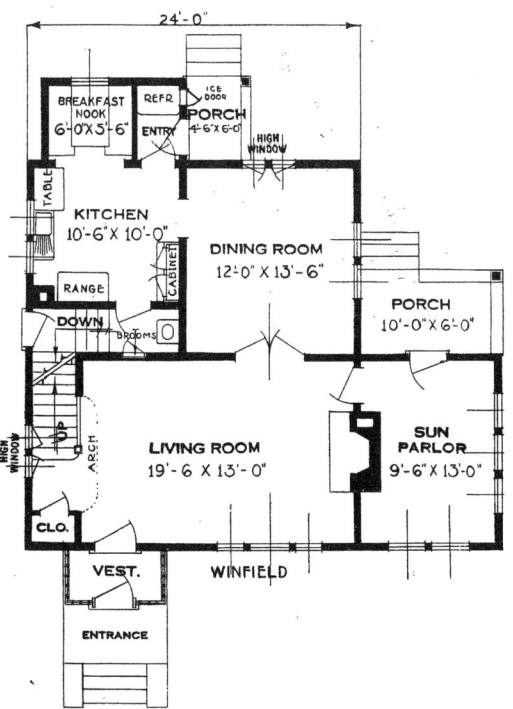

The WINFIELD (Size 24x28')

Nothing beautiful or sweet grows in the darkness. Light and sunshine are the superior forces that develop the finest and purest qualities in all nature. No work of the Creator is so sensitive to environment as woman, nor so susceptible to culture in the light and sunshine of appreciation and kindness such as may be expressed in homes like The Winfield.

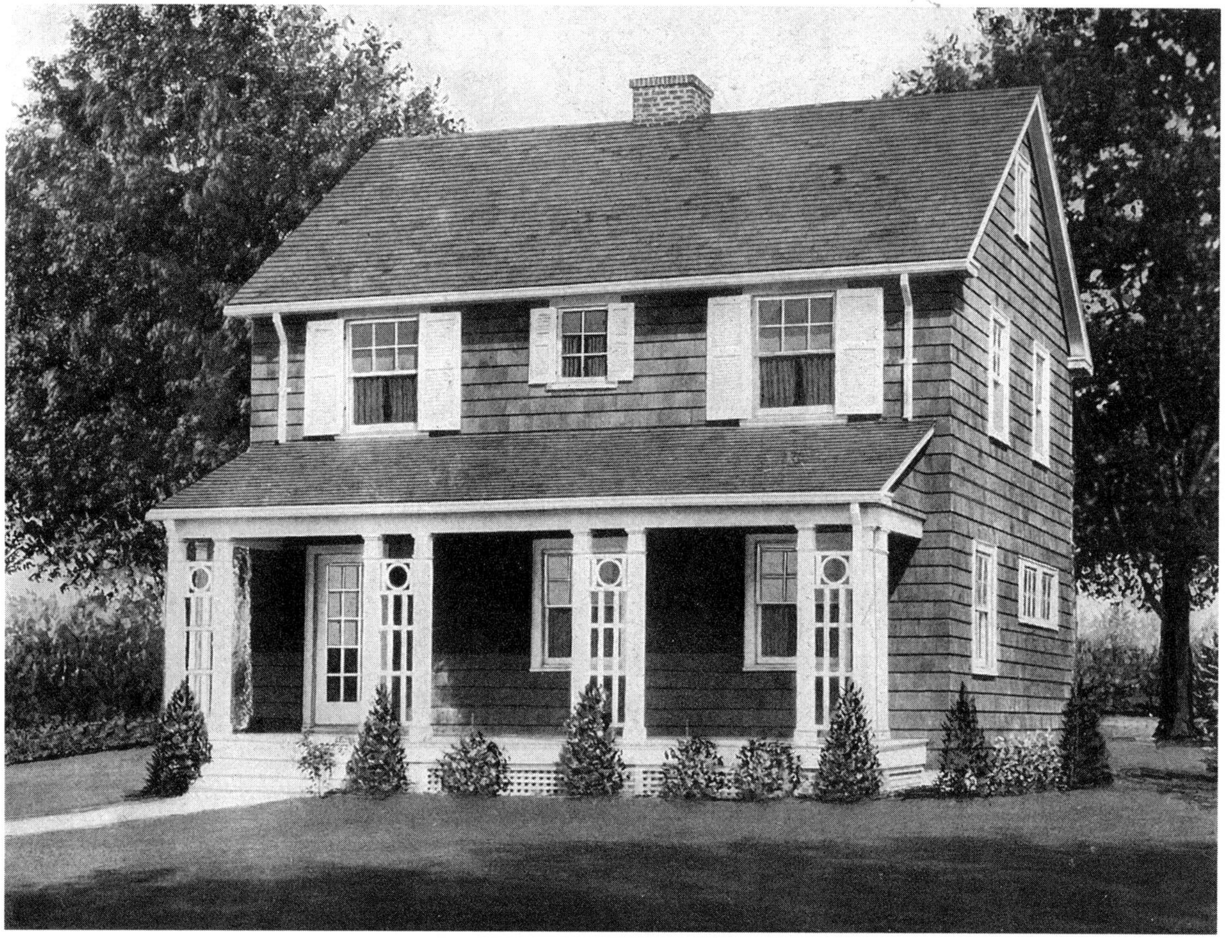

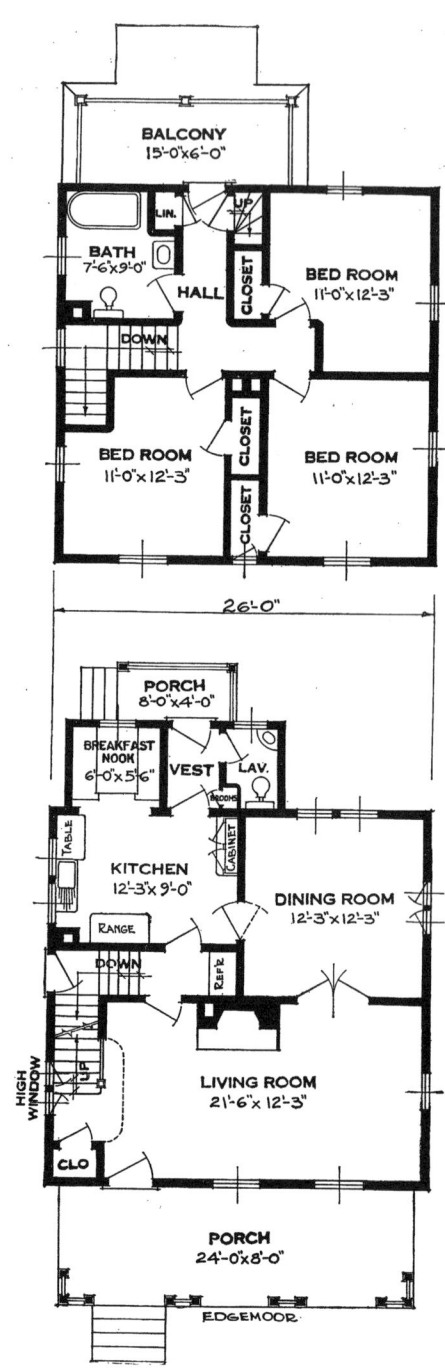

The EDGEMOOR (Size 26x26')

When one wishes to build a home, there are three points to be considered: first, the size of his pocketbook; second, his family and their requirements; and third, the type of house out of which he can realize the greatest profits if it becomes necessary to dispose of it. The Edgemoor is not only a practical house for a home, but is always a salable type.

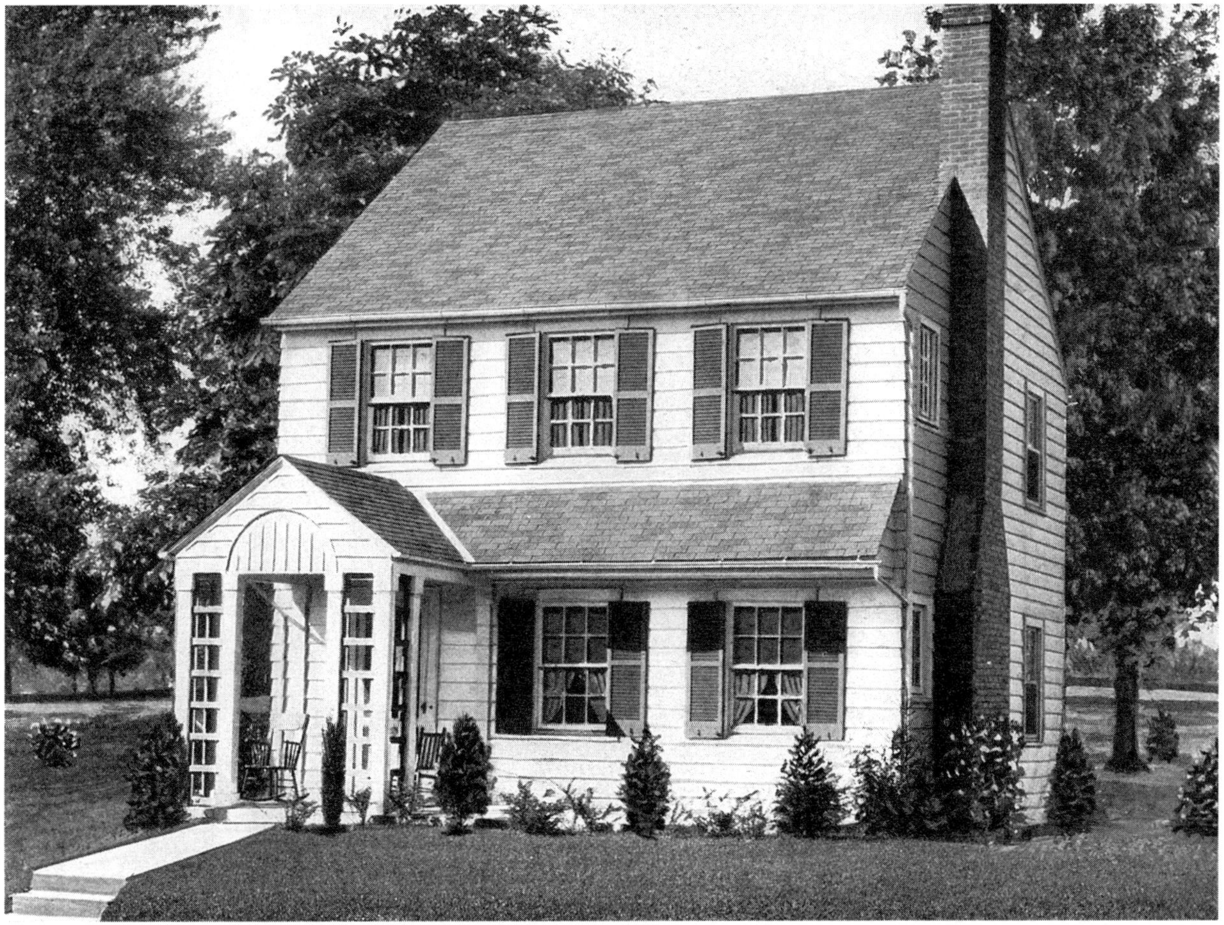

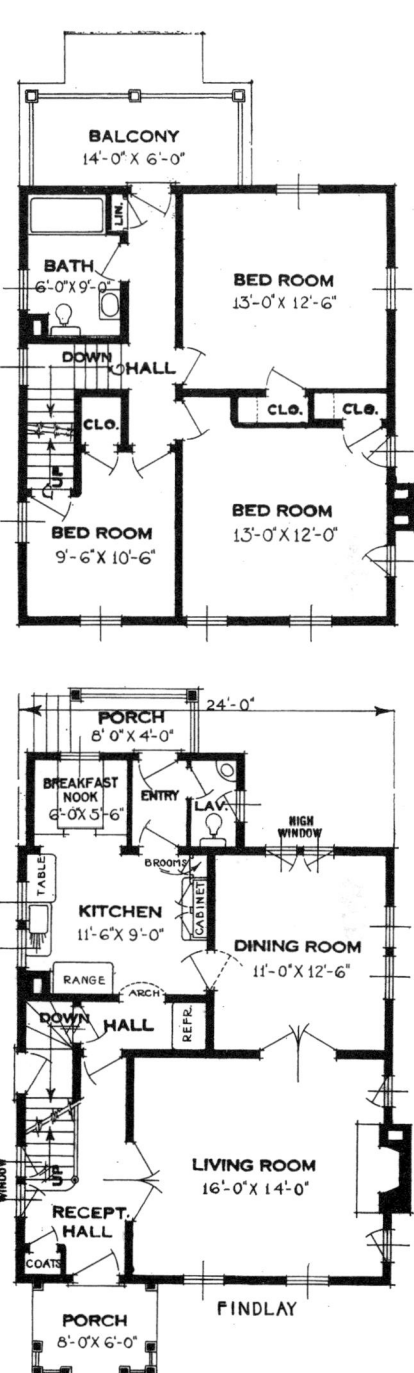

The FINDLAY (Size 24x28')

The happiest homes, like the happiest marriages, are those in which the woman takes the most sacred part, and uses her secret power to guide for permanent good. Any woman who is mated to the man of her choice, and is permitted to enjoy her freedom in a home like The Findlay can surely make it a paradise for worldly peace.

All plans are so prepared as to permit frame, stucco, brick or tile construction.

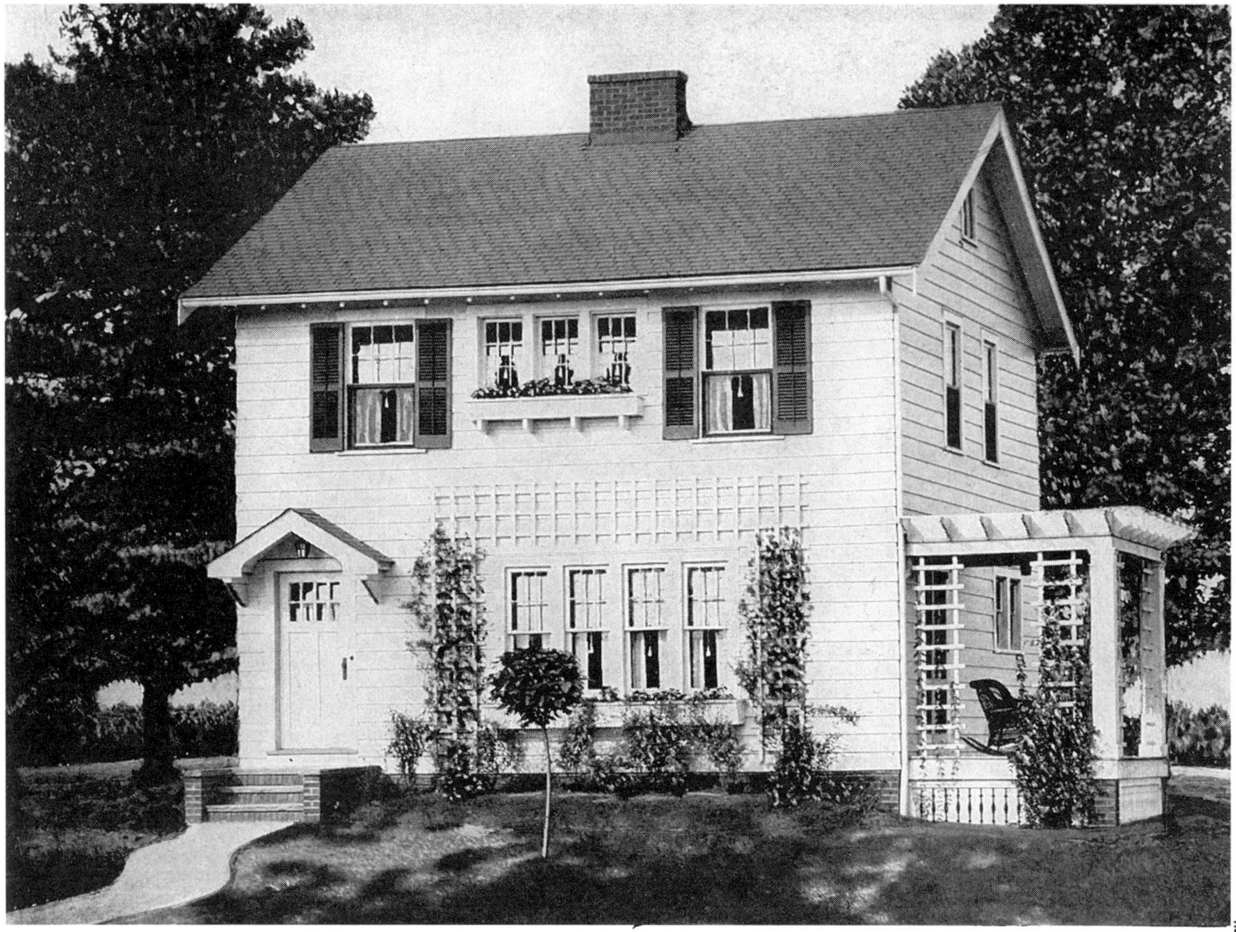

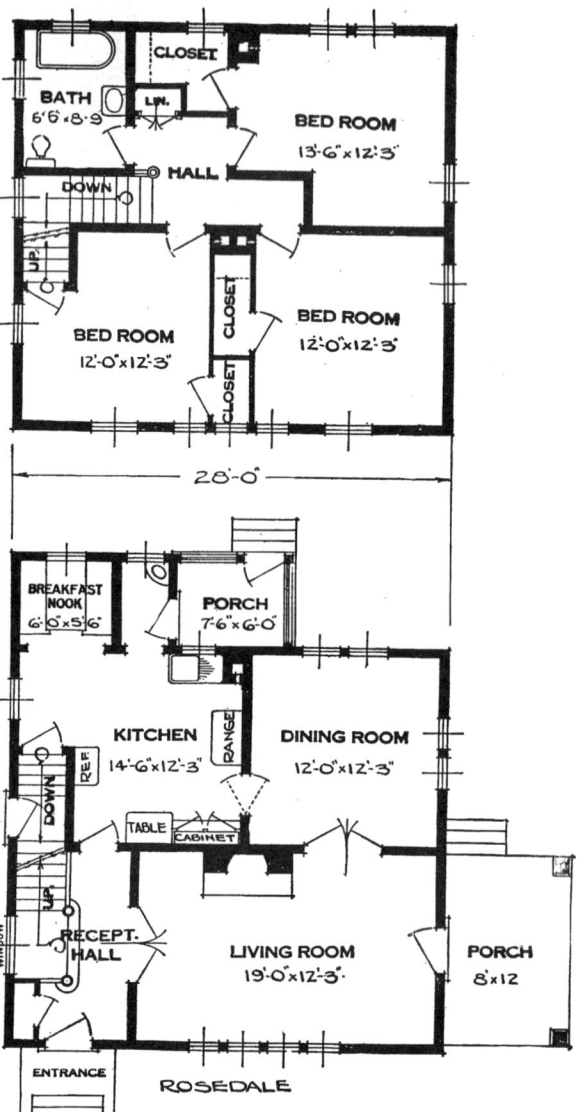

The ROSEDALE (Size 28x26')

The care of a family means responsibility, and responsibility in turn creates strength. Just as it is more economical to own a home in The Rosedale class than it is to pay rent, just so it is more economical for a man to support a family than to deny himself the breadth of vision which comes as the result of a happy union and a happy home life.

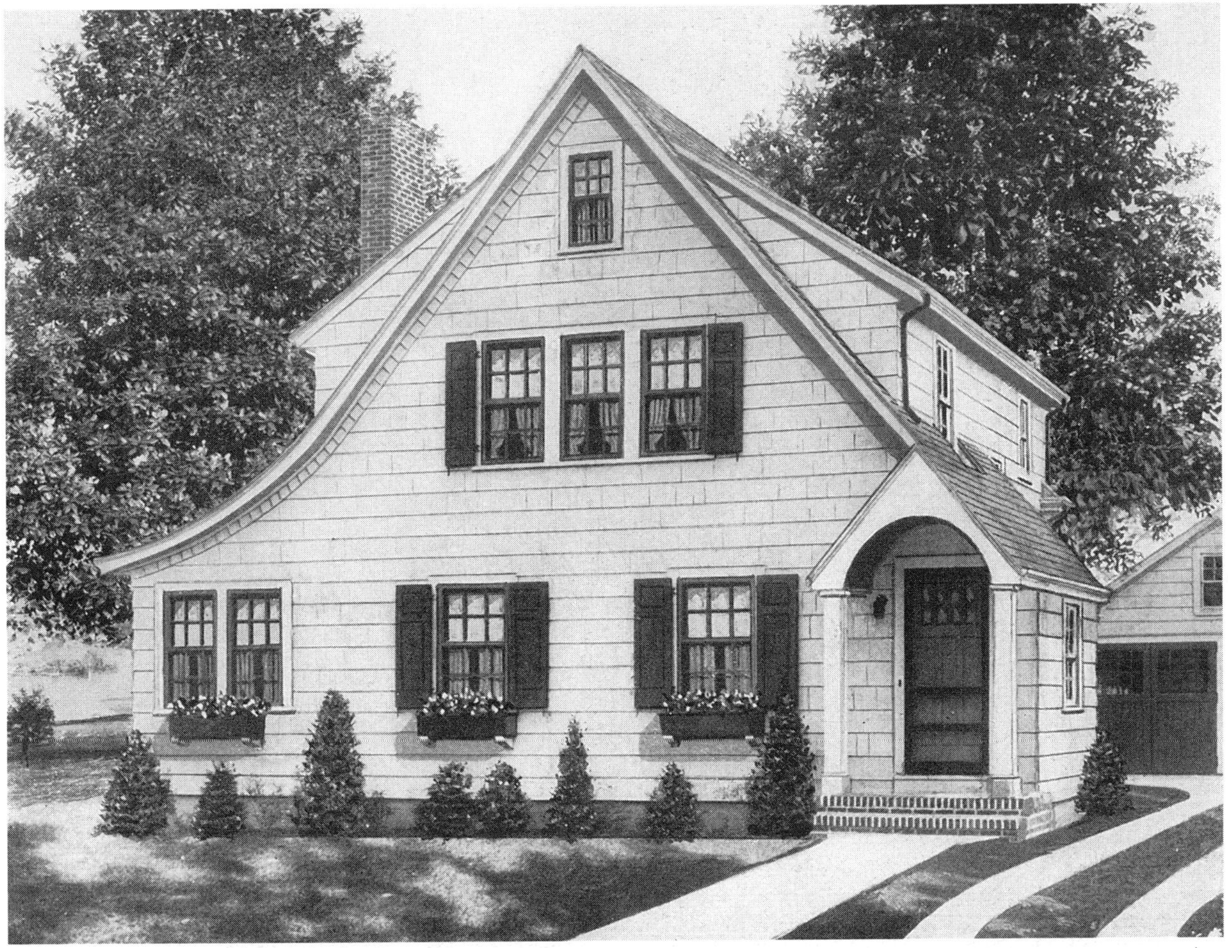

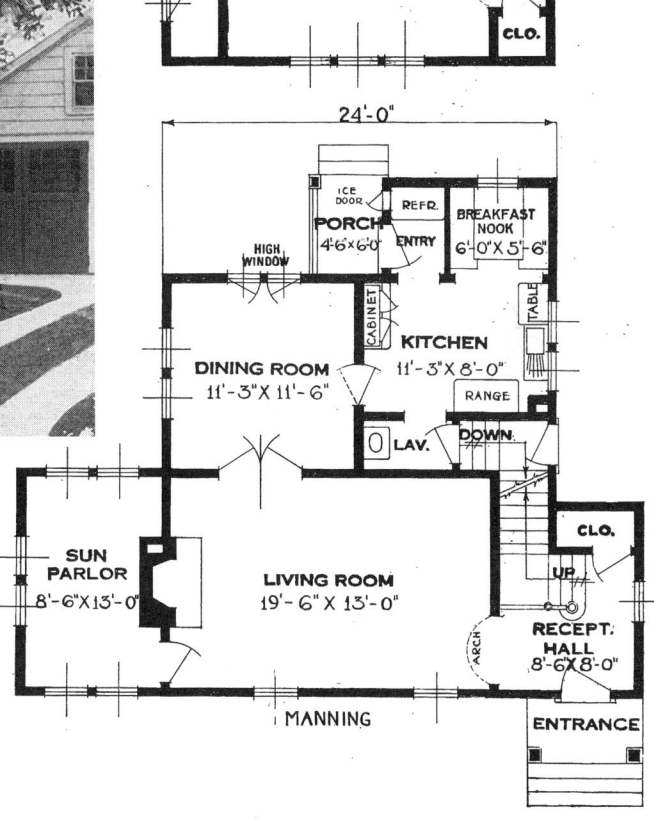

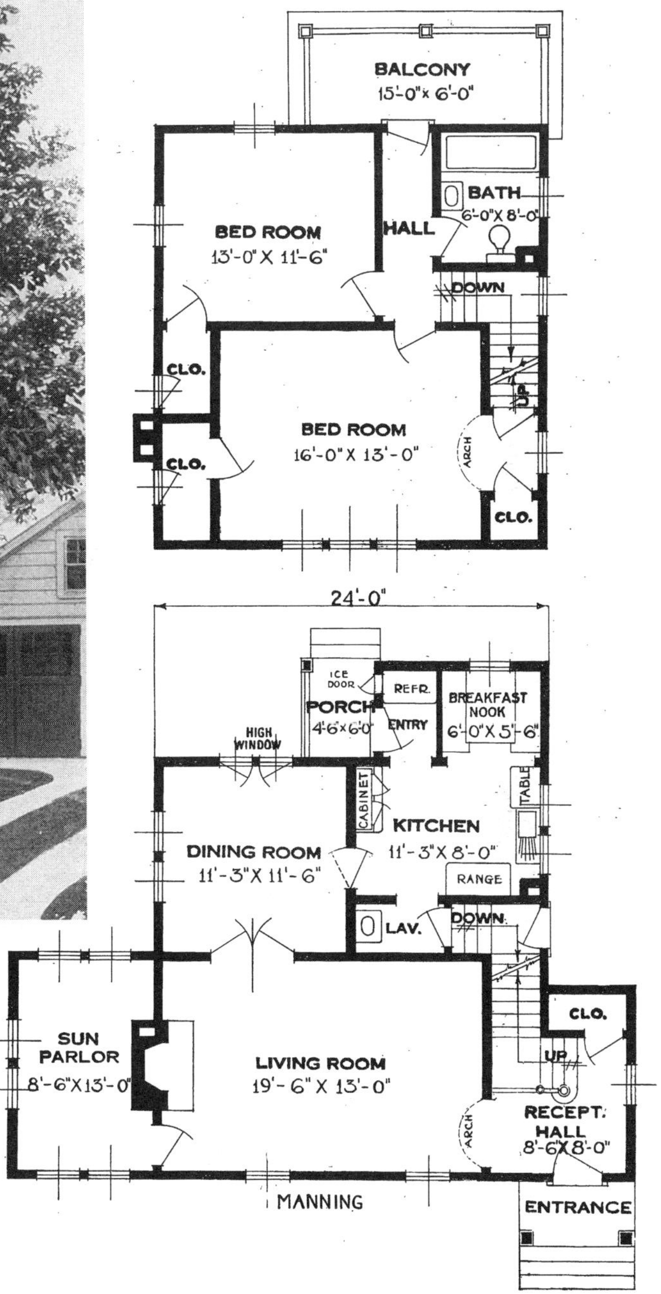

The MANNING (Size 24x26')

A good woman can make a cozy, comfortable home around any kind of a hearth, if her affections are satisfied. Single handed and alone, she cannot make the home joyful; she needs from her husband the multitudes of little courtesies and expressions of appreciation to which she is entitled. The Manning is the style of home many women will delight in making happy.

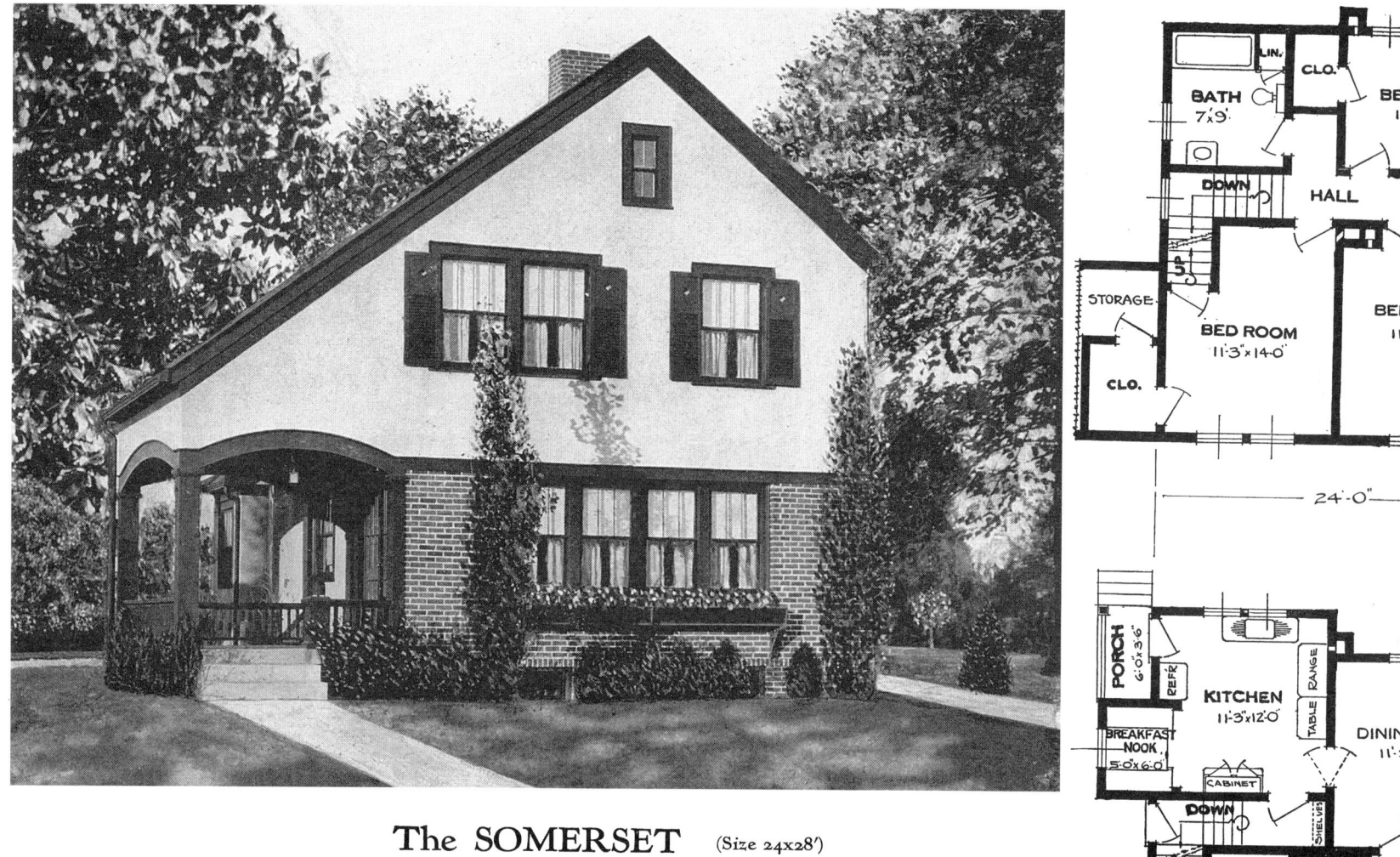

The SOMERSET (Size 24x28')

Homes founded on mutual interest are practically proof against the divorce evil. This is true because like attracts like, and when two individuals direct their hearts and efforts toward one single purpose, such, for instance, as the building and making happy a home, they daily learn to know each other better because they think each other's thoughts.

50

All plans are so prepared as to permit frame, stucco, brick or tile construction.

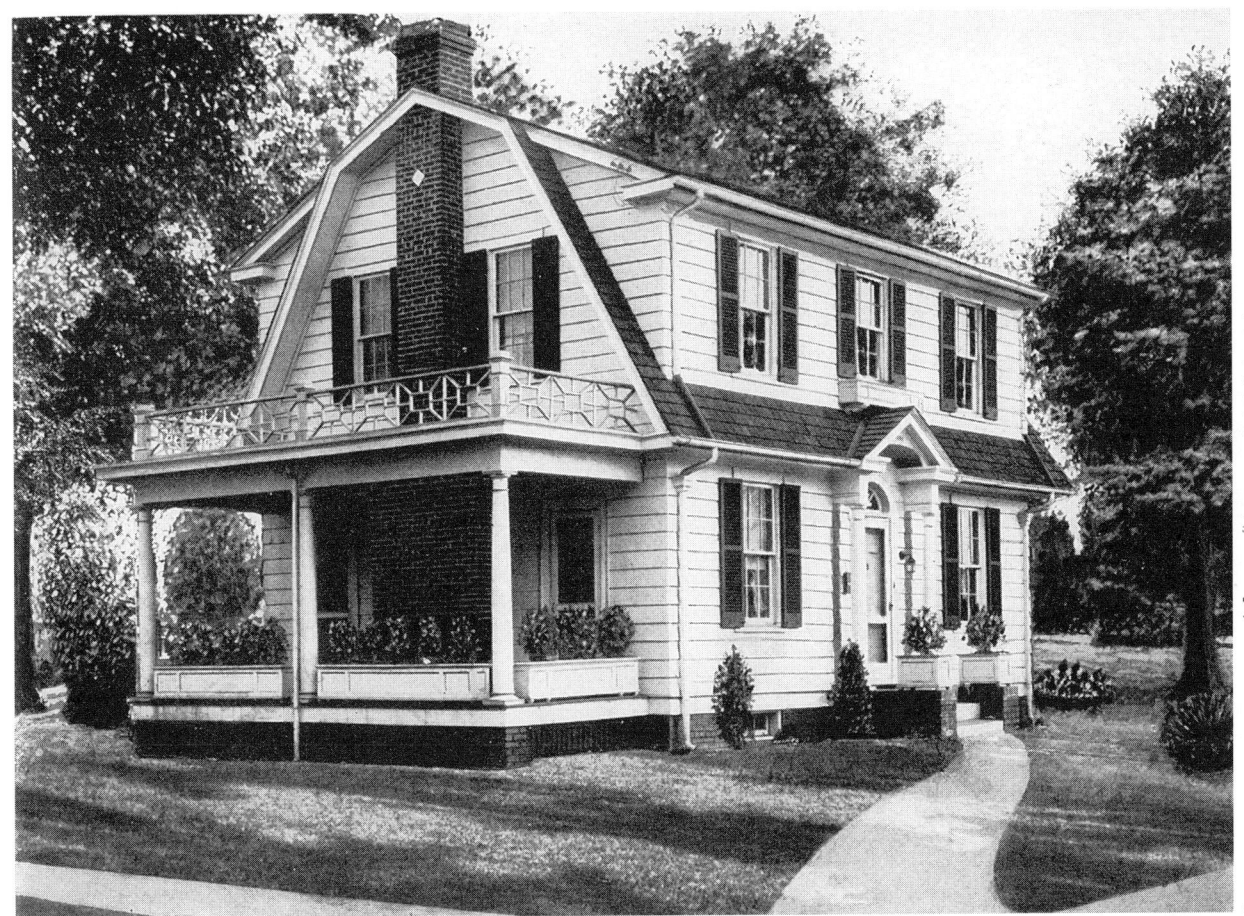

The OXFORD (Size 28x22')
(Also 30x24')

When freedom and joy are the wife's share in homes like The Oxford they become the child's heritage, and a happy childhood is an imperative preparation for a happy maturity. The sacred memories of a joyful home have kept many a man from losing his balance and self-respect. We would have little need for prisons if all children could enjoy the early home life to which they are entitled.

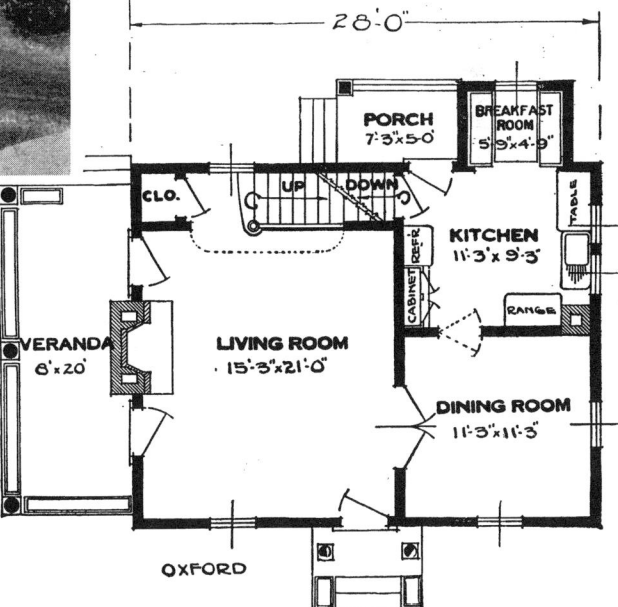

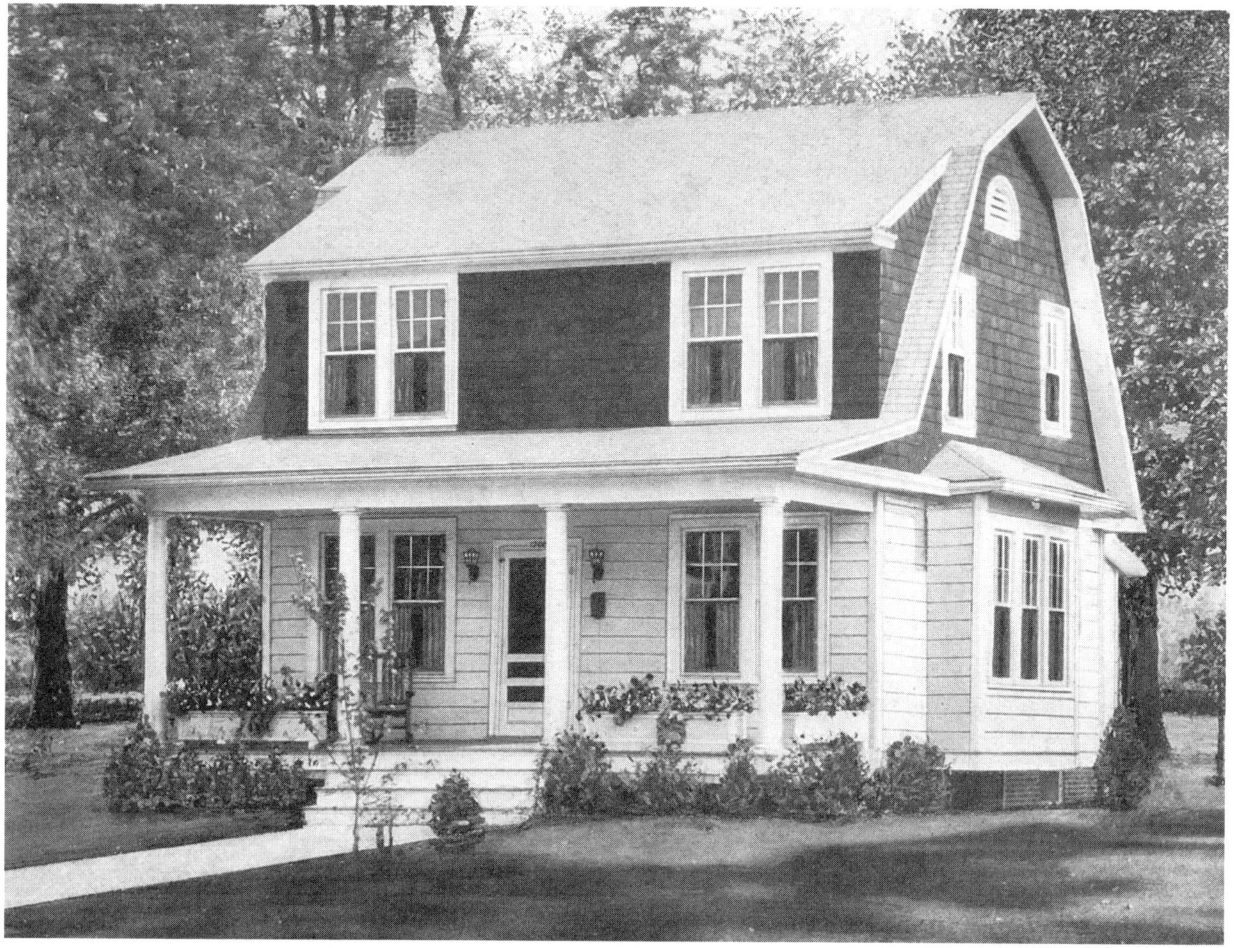

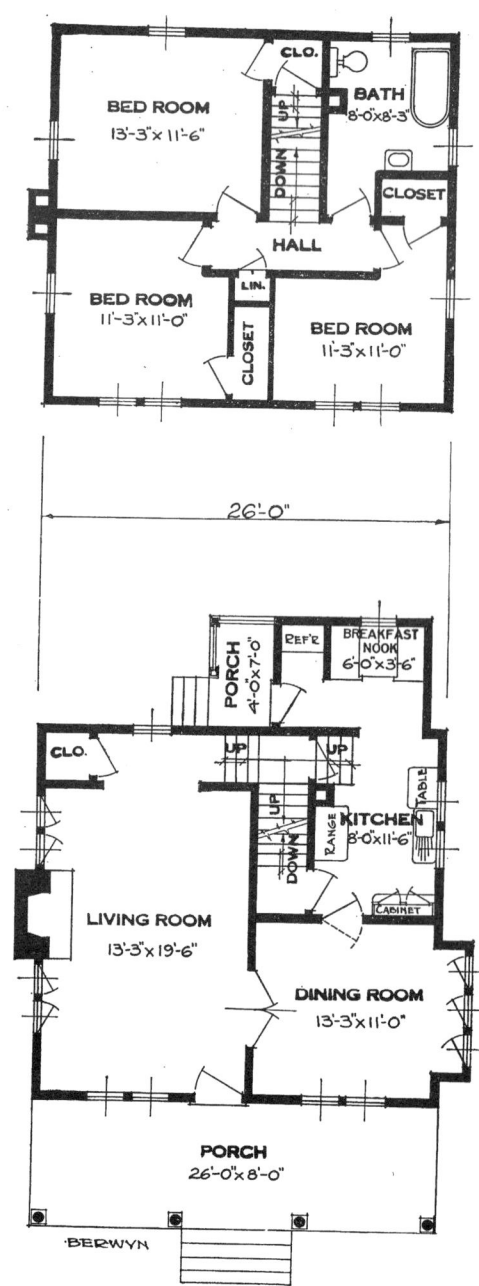

The BERWYN (Size 26x24')

Crowded tenements and apartment houses are the hotbeds of jealousy, disease and discord. It is hard for the heart to find room for expression when the mind is full of the cobwebs of gossip. Those who are earnestly seeking a purer atmosphere, where their children can be brought up in a better environment, will find The Berwyn an ideal house for a home.

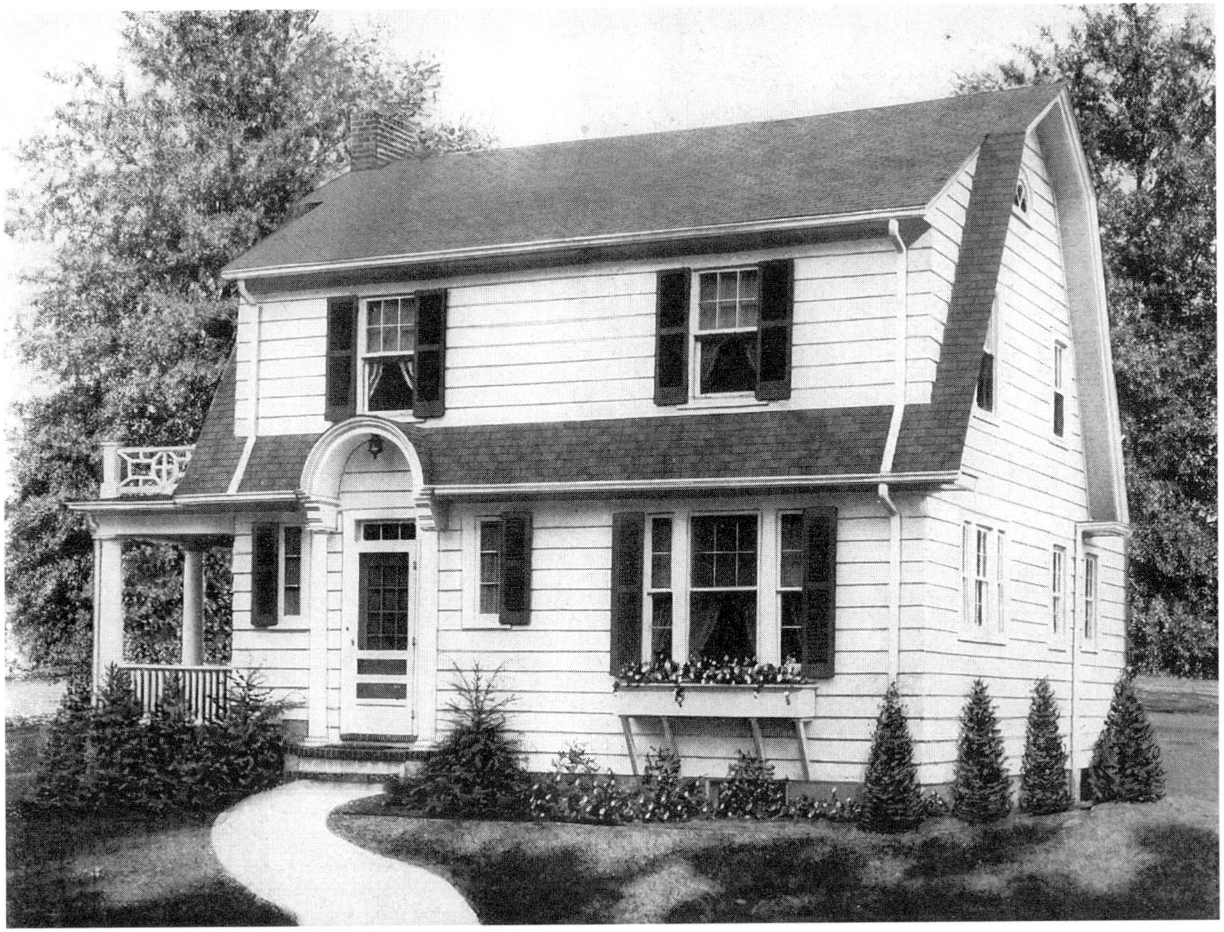

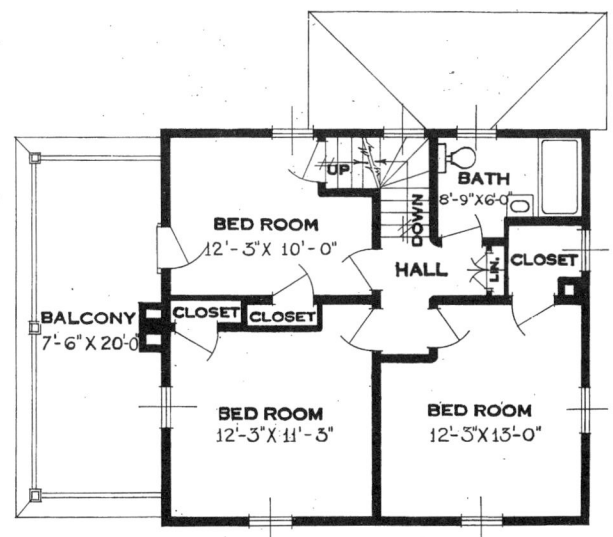

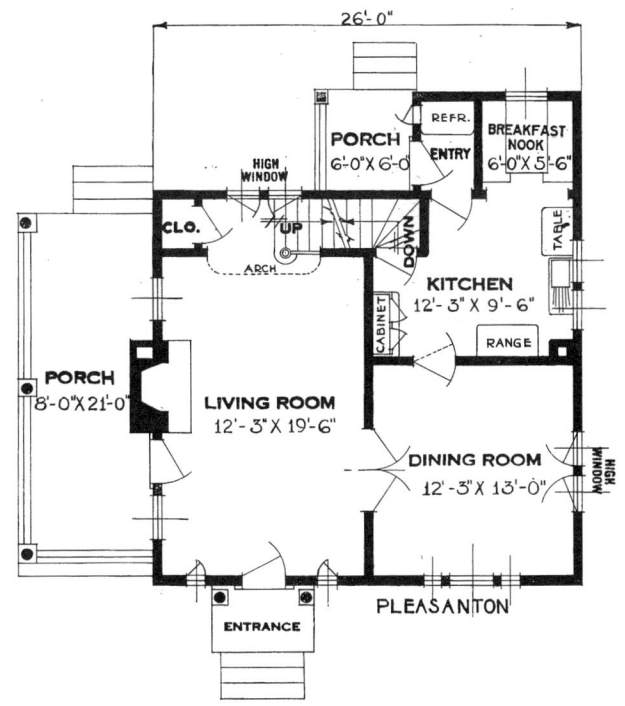

The PLEASANTON (Size 26x24′)

The price of a good woman's complete love is appreciation, affection, sympathy and a home—a home of her very own in which these virtues may be proudly and happily enjoyed. Happy will be the man who awakens to the importance of this vital fact and early makes the sacrifices necessary to realize his highest ambitions in a home like The Pleasanton.

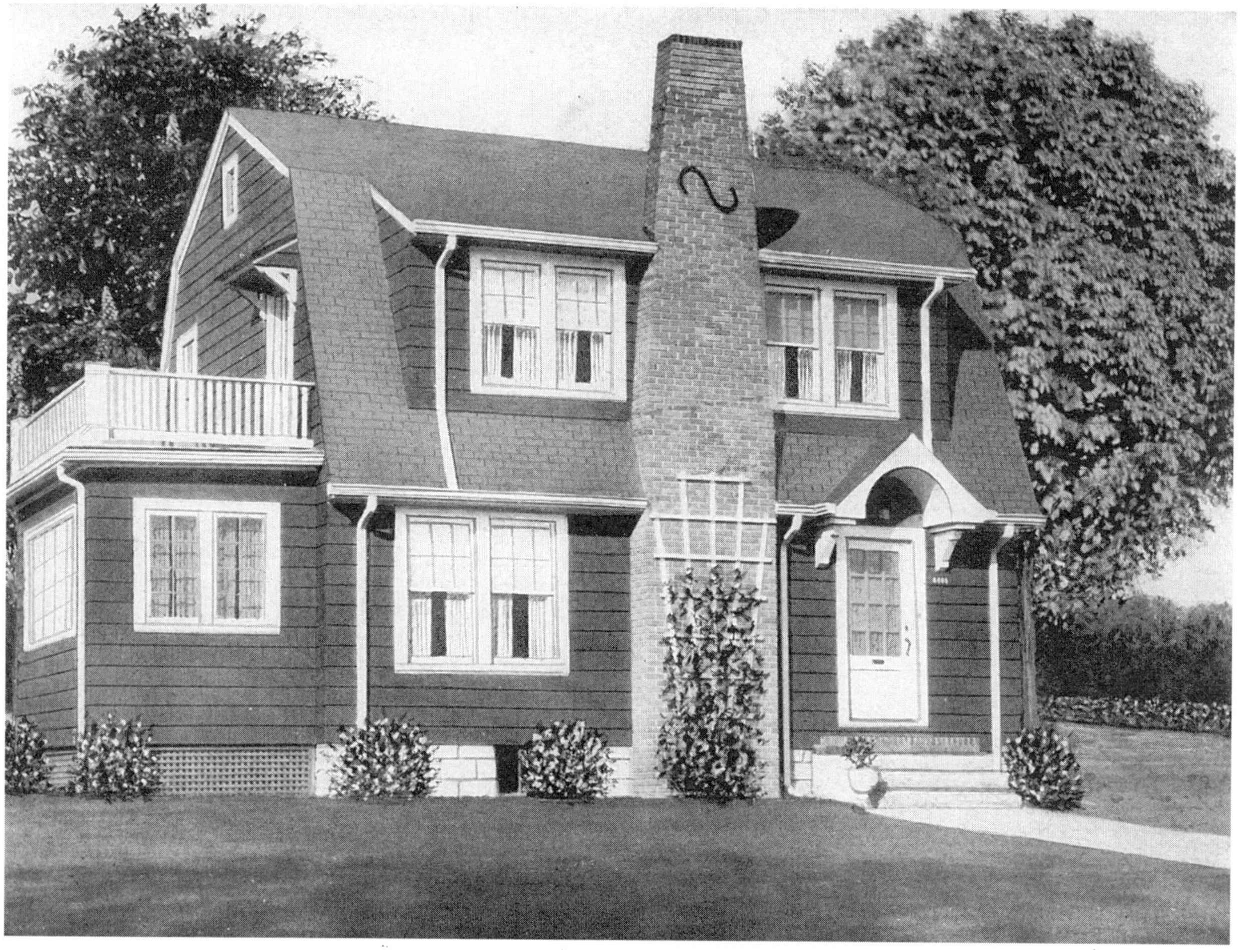

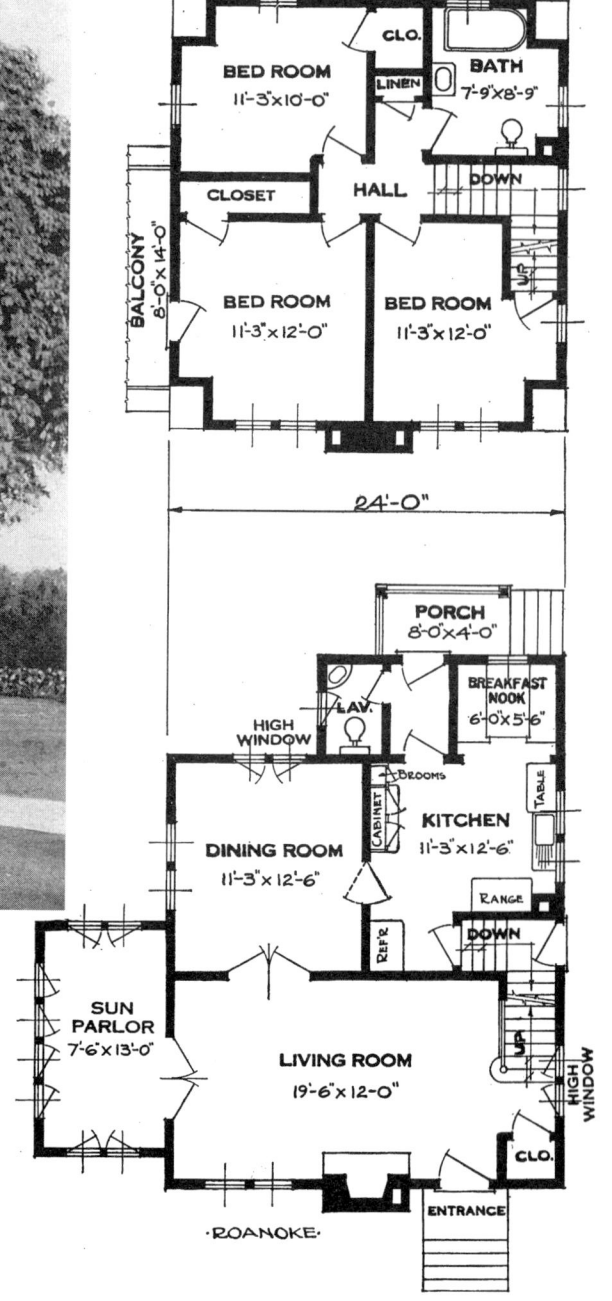

The ROANOKE (Size 24x26′)

In no other way can a man develop the respect of others for himself and his family as in the building of a home of his own. With home ownership comes fellowship and citizenship. One wins far more confidence by building a neat home on The Roanoke plan, to meet his requirements, than in burdening himself and his wife with a larger house than is needed.

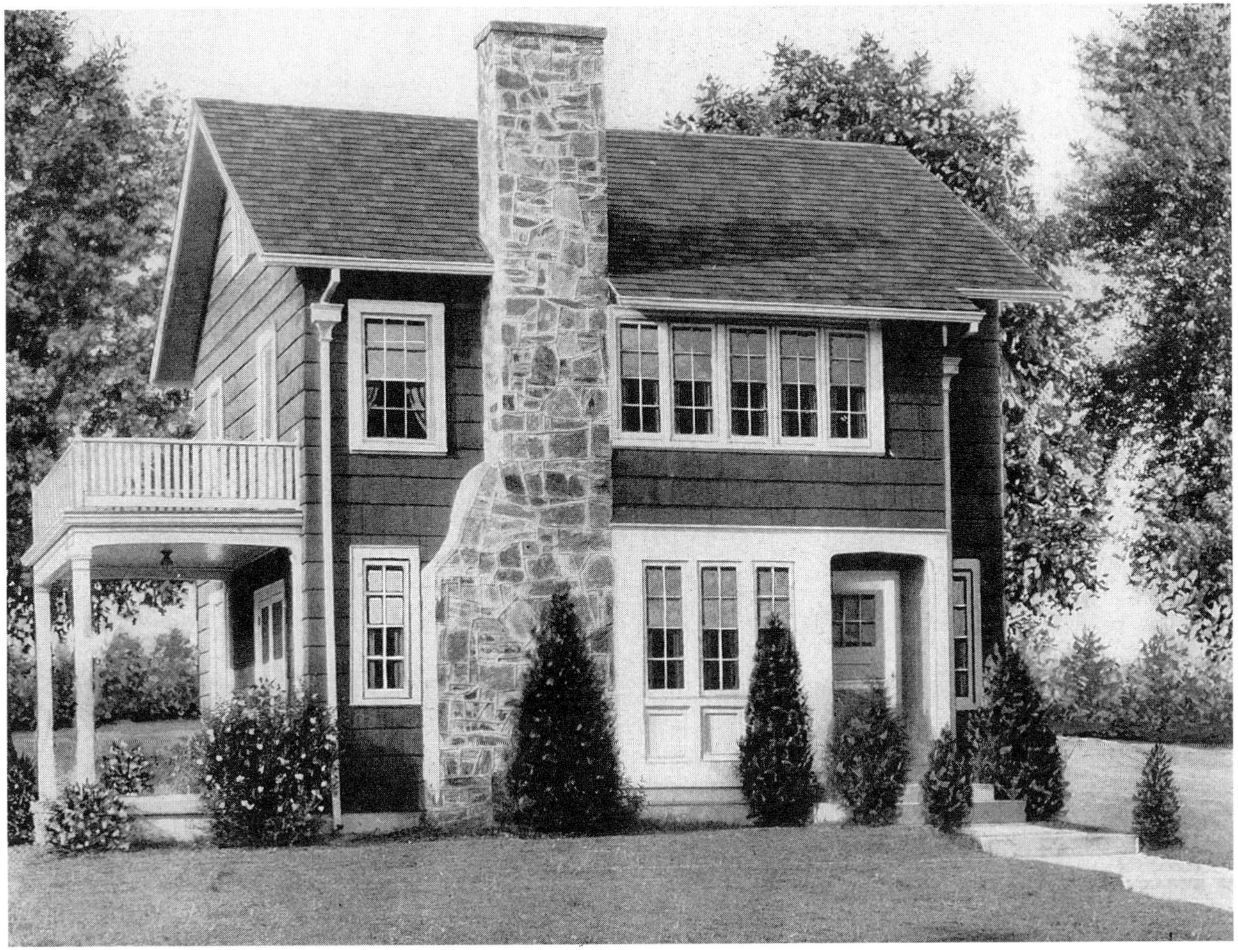

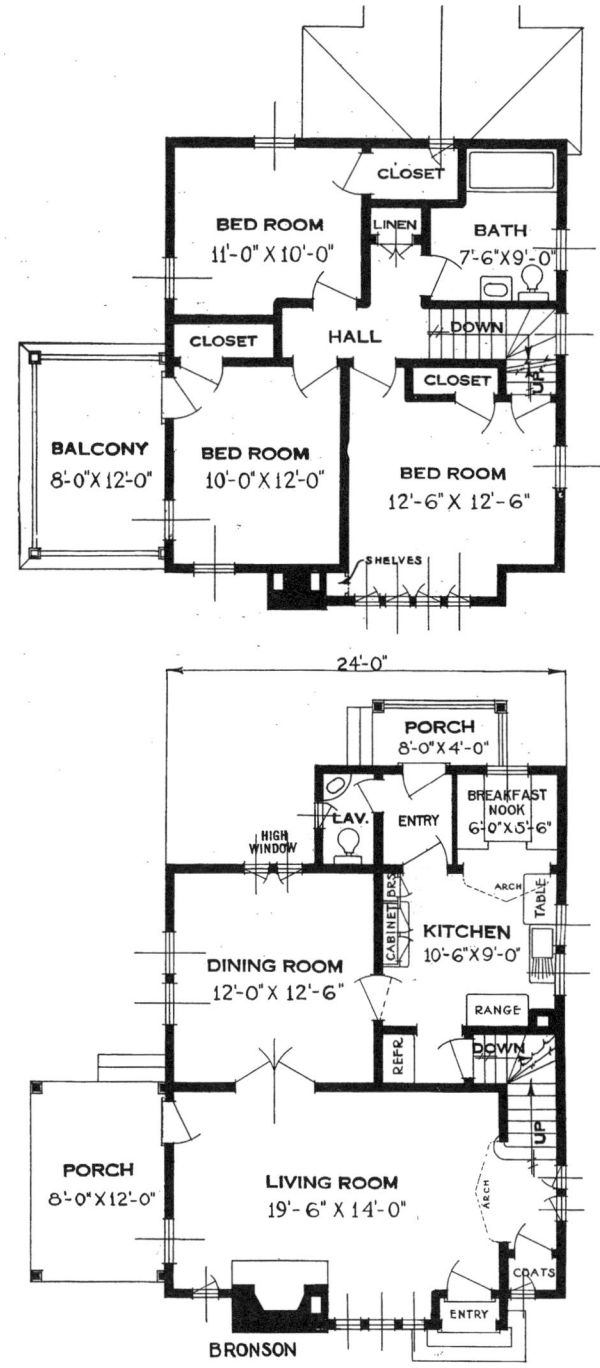

The BRONSON (Size 24x26')

Summer, winter, rain or shine, your home's your home. It is a permanent structure, yet consider how many comforts its walls contain, and what a wonderful refuge it is when shelter is sought from the world of chilly indifference. No home can be more secure against unwholesome influences than The Bronson, if it be reinforced by staunch purpose and unselfish love.

All plans are so prepared as to permit frame, stucco, brick or tile construction.

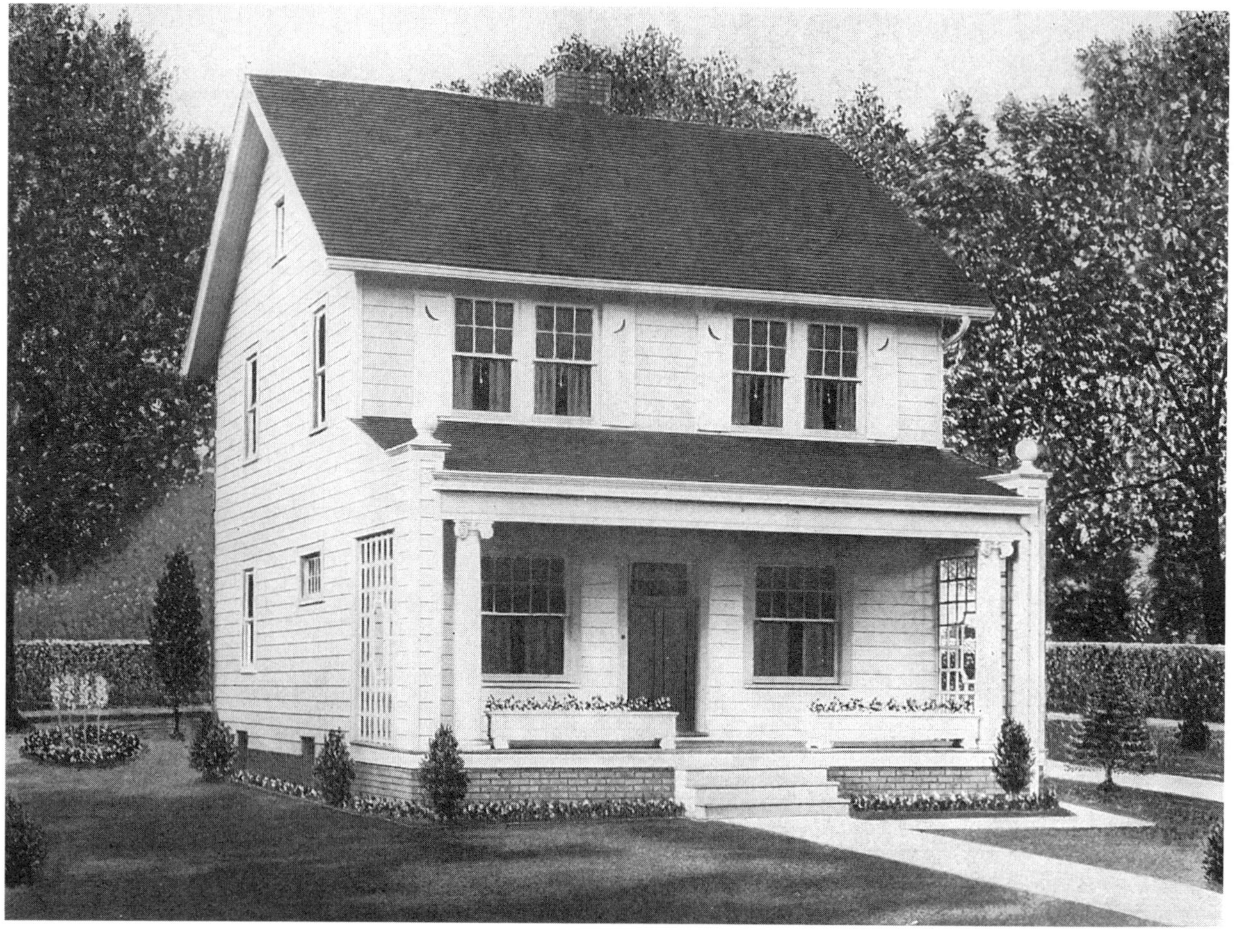

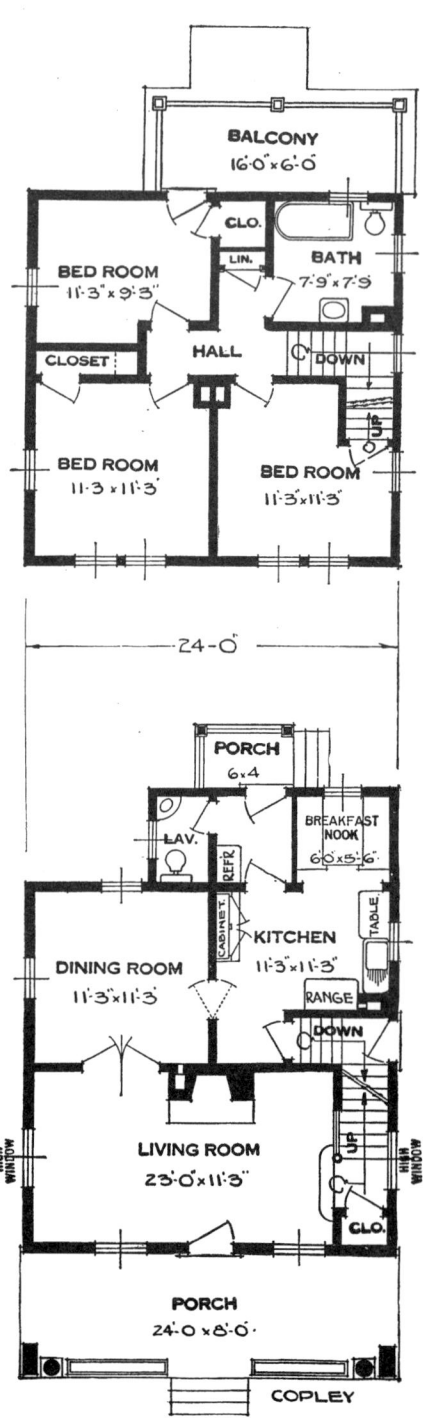

The COPELEY (Size 24x24′)

The money paid for rent will soon pay for the house rented, but it is still the landlord's, and the only thing of value which the renter has to show is a bundle of rent receipts. For those who resolve to spend their money more wisely, The Copeley will prove to be a permanent investment with daily dividends of independence beyond any monetary value.

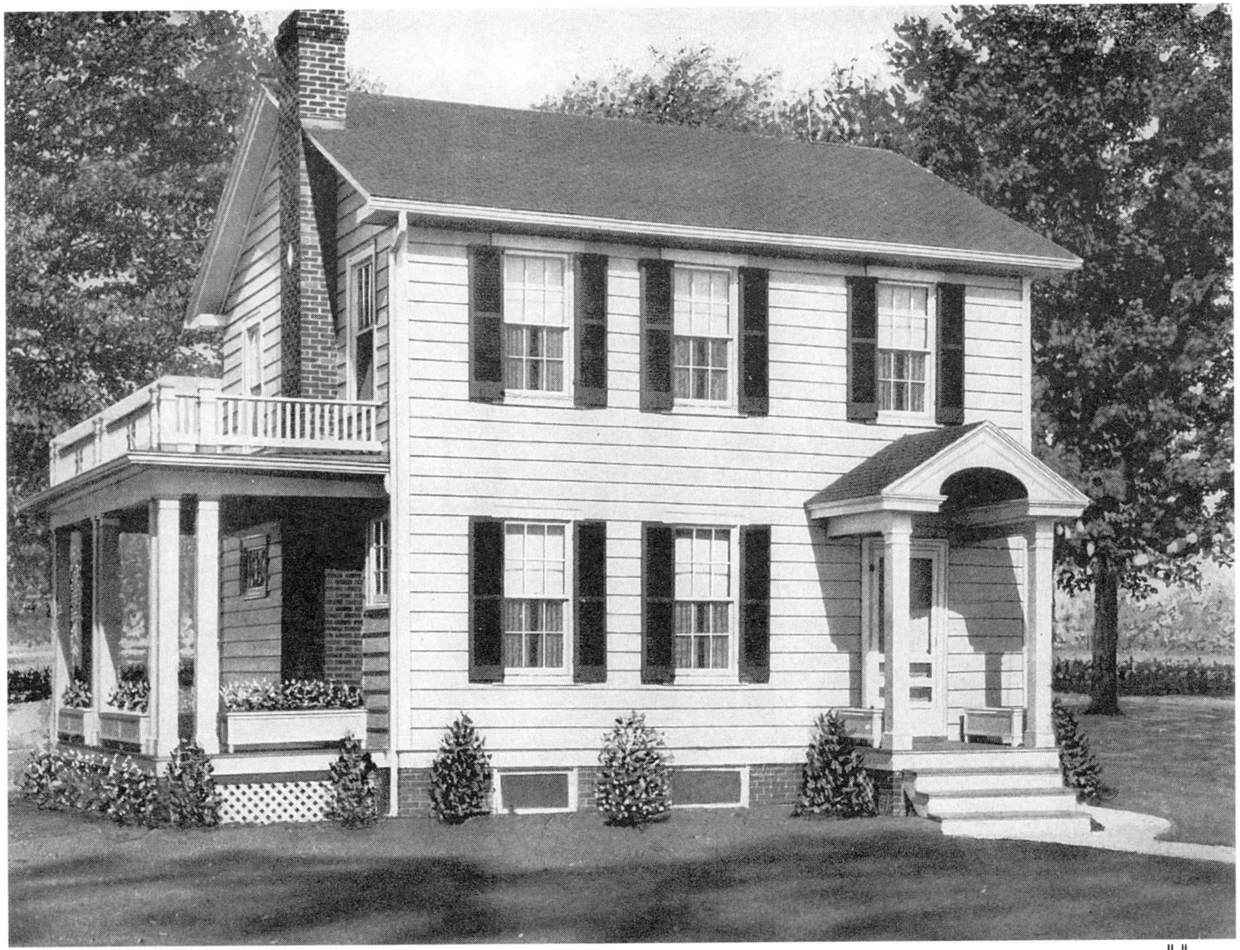

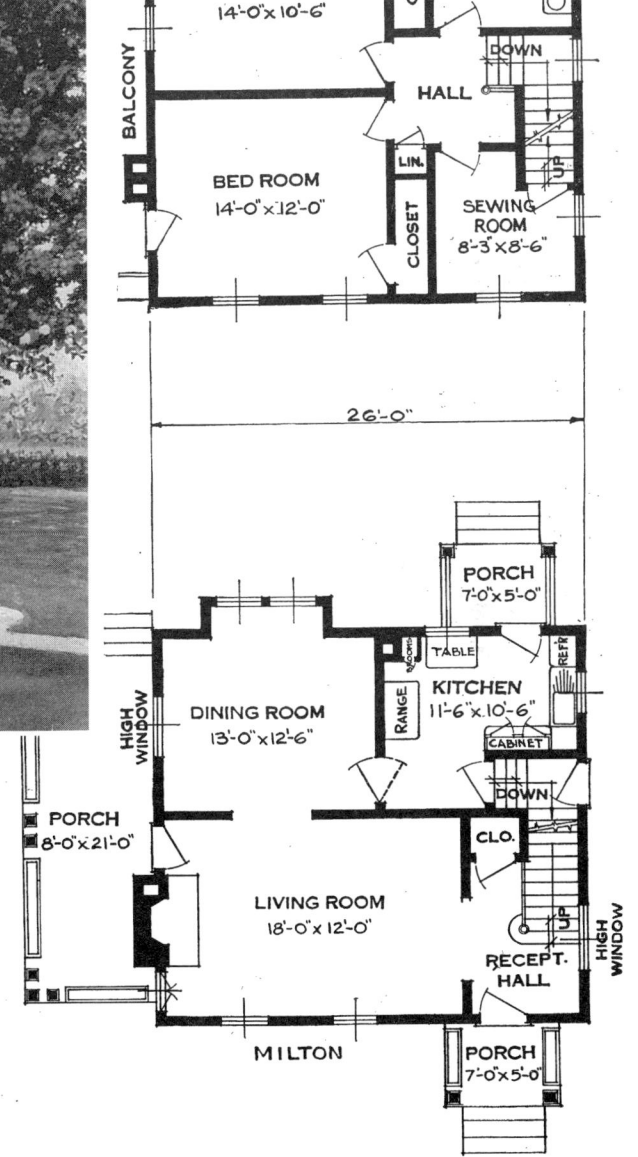

The MILTON (Size 26x24')

Had the laws of democracy been practiced in every land and country for the past ten centuries, such a thing as paying rent for a home would in this age be entirely out of the question. The unborn desire in every human heart for a home would at least prompt all to possess their place of habitation, even though it were not so attractive as The Milton.

57

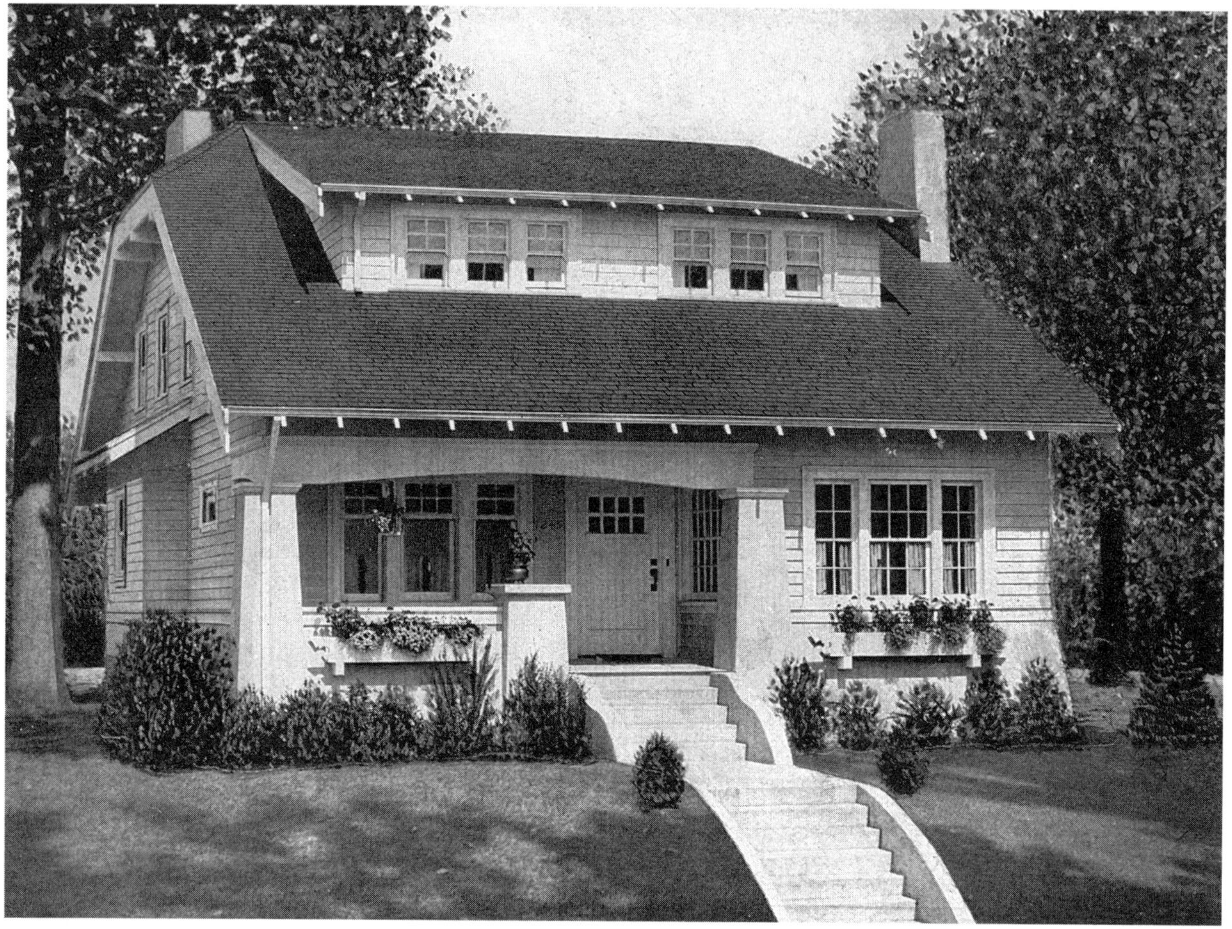

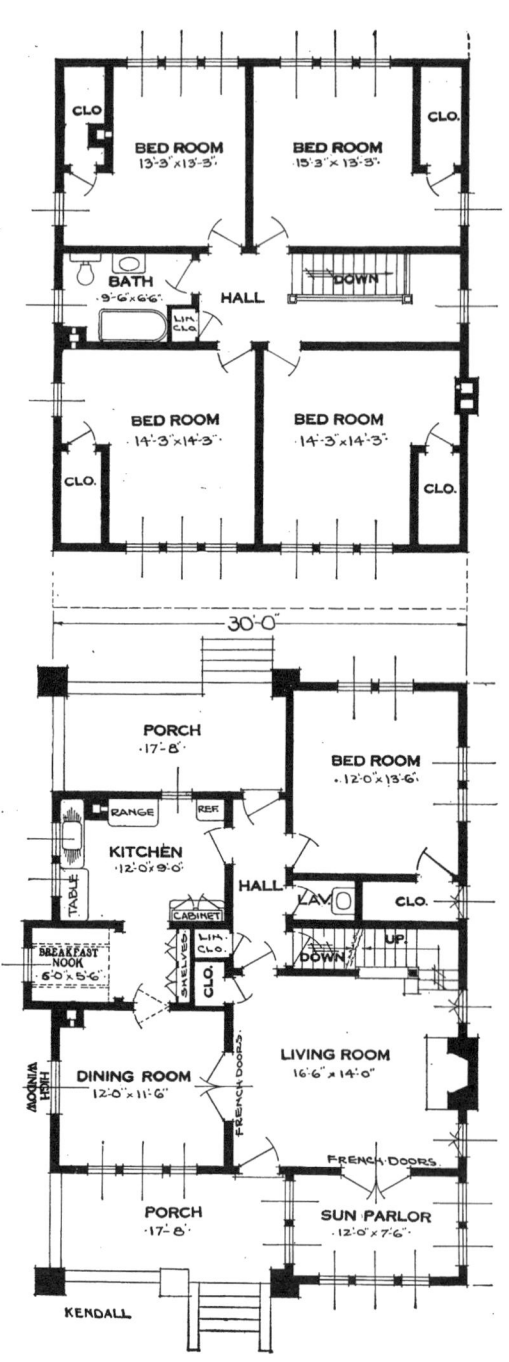

The KENDALL (Size 30x44')

Sunshine is to the physical body what joy is to the heart. Those frail of body should seek the sun porches of homes of The Kendall plan, and those frail of heart can find inimitable balm in the building and making complete a new home and a new environment. Health and home joy come to those who prepare expectantly for them.

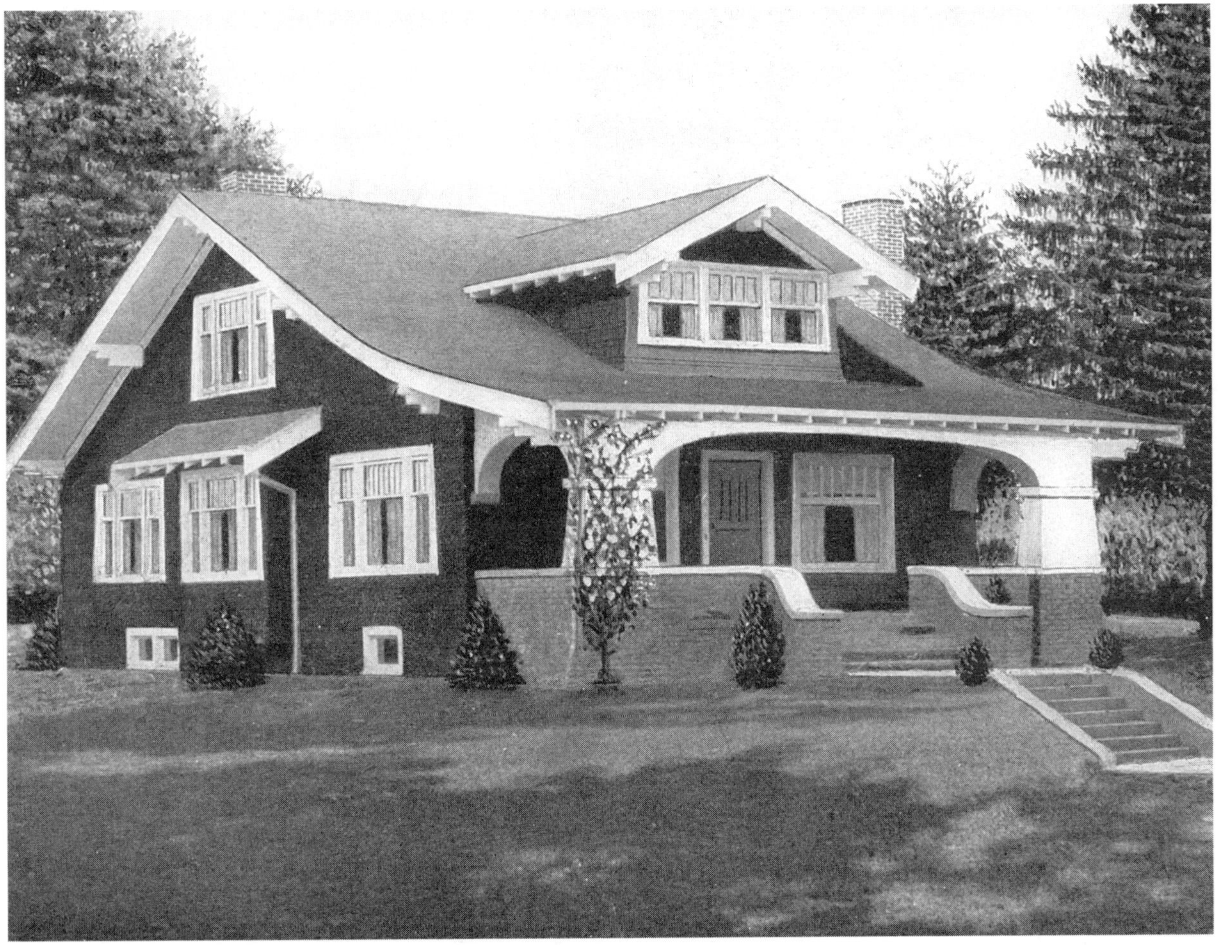

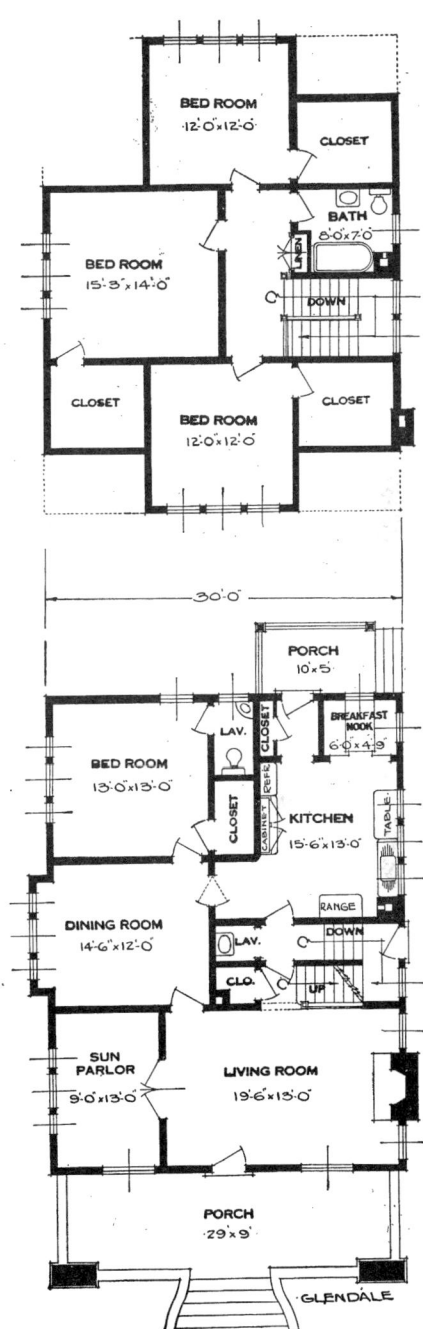

The GLENDALE (Size 30x40')

The human mind is a most powerful magnet, and never fails to attract to us those things and conditions on which our hearts are earnestly and constantly centered. The Glendale is within reach of him who wills and fears not the petty thorns of sacrifice, knowing that these will be forgotten or remembered with delight when the goal is finally realized.

All plans are so prepared as to permit frame, stucco, brick or tile construction.

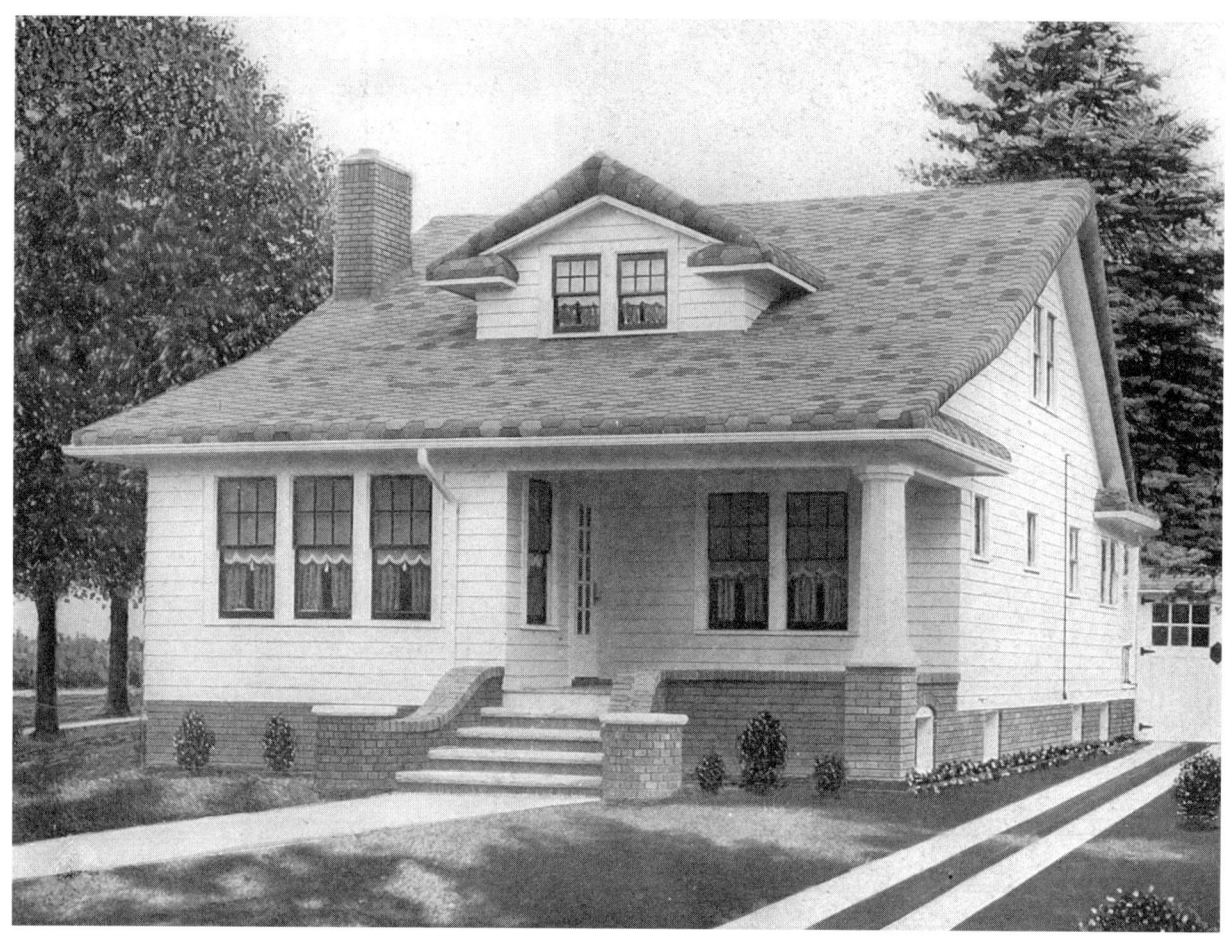
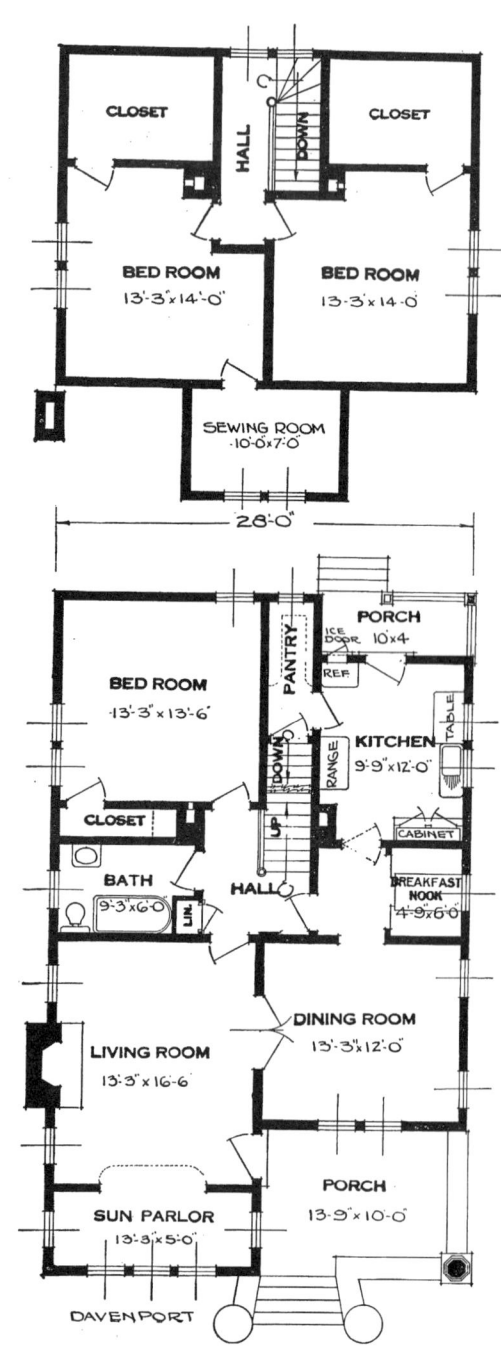

The DAVENPORT (Size 28x36')

One of the greatest possible assets a man can plan and develop for the future safety of his wife and children is a home. If all men had the backbone and stamina to build for their family substantial homes similar to The Davenport, charitable institutions and orphan asylums would soon go out of business for the lack of inmates.

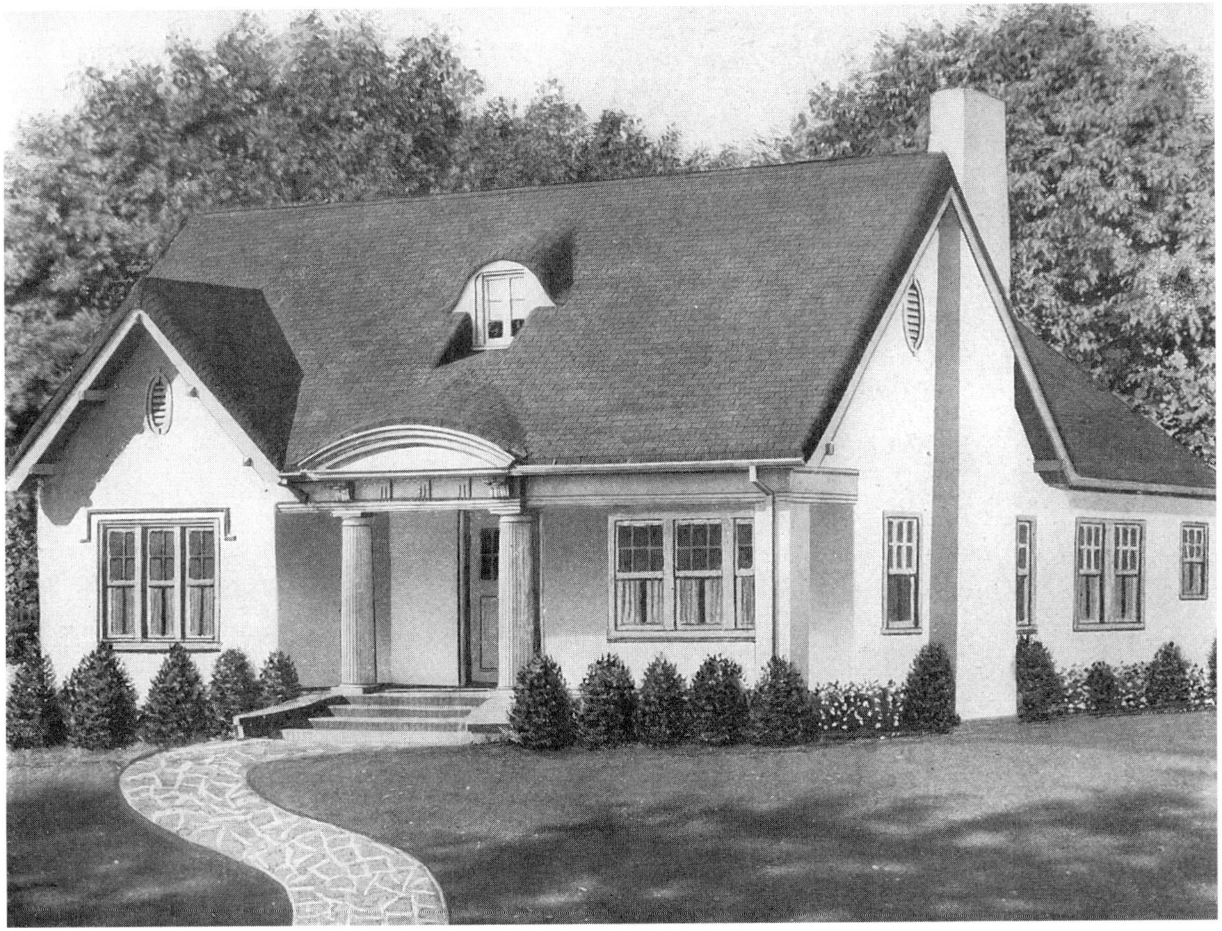

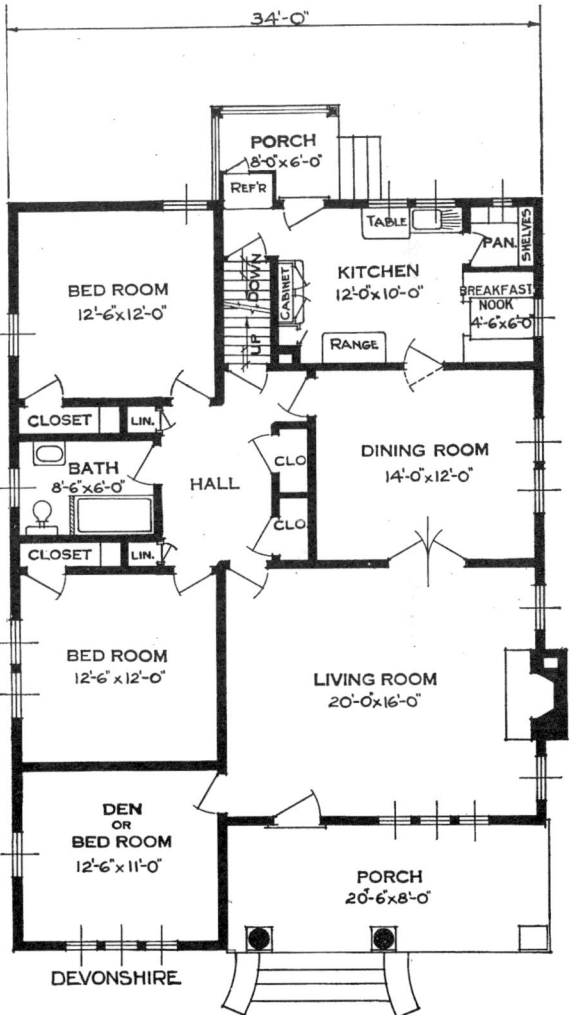

The DEVONSHIRE (Size 34x48')

All the creative, uplifting forces of nature conspire to help those who unselfishly seek a home of comfort and refinement where the finer qualities of their natures may be cultivated and their field of endeavor broadened. Those whose honest efforts enable them to build The Devonshire for a home may confidently expect the peace of mind to which they are justly entitled.

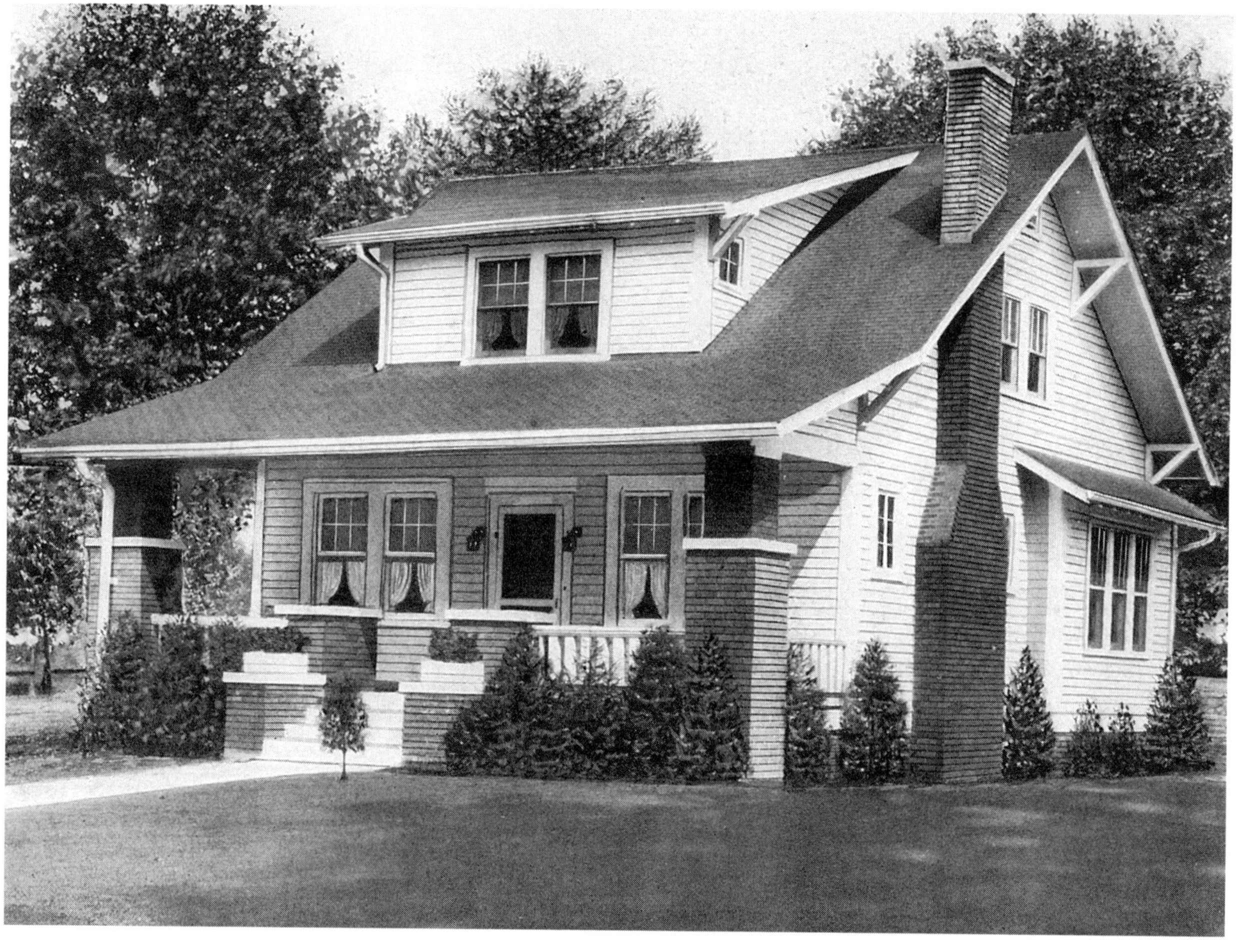

The ALLENDALE (Size 26x30′)

The reward for a thing well done is to have done it. Homes built by others can never give us the inner satisfaction which comes as the reward for hours and weeks spent in the careful planning of a home of our own. In erecting The Allendale in accordance with their ideals, many will learn with peculiar delight the care-joy of home building.

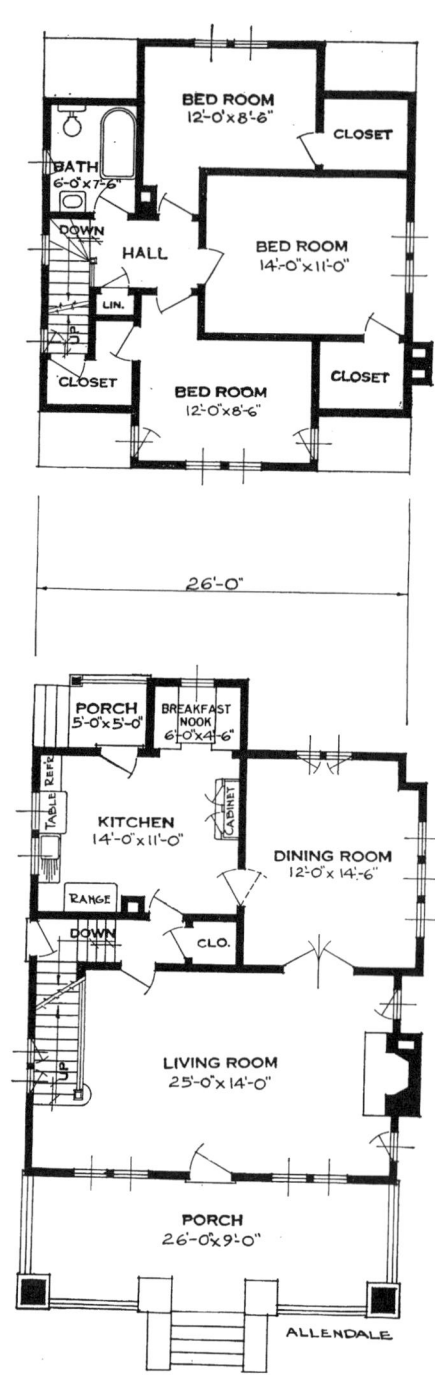

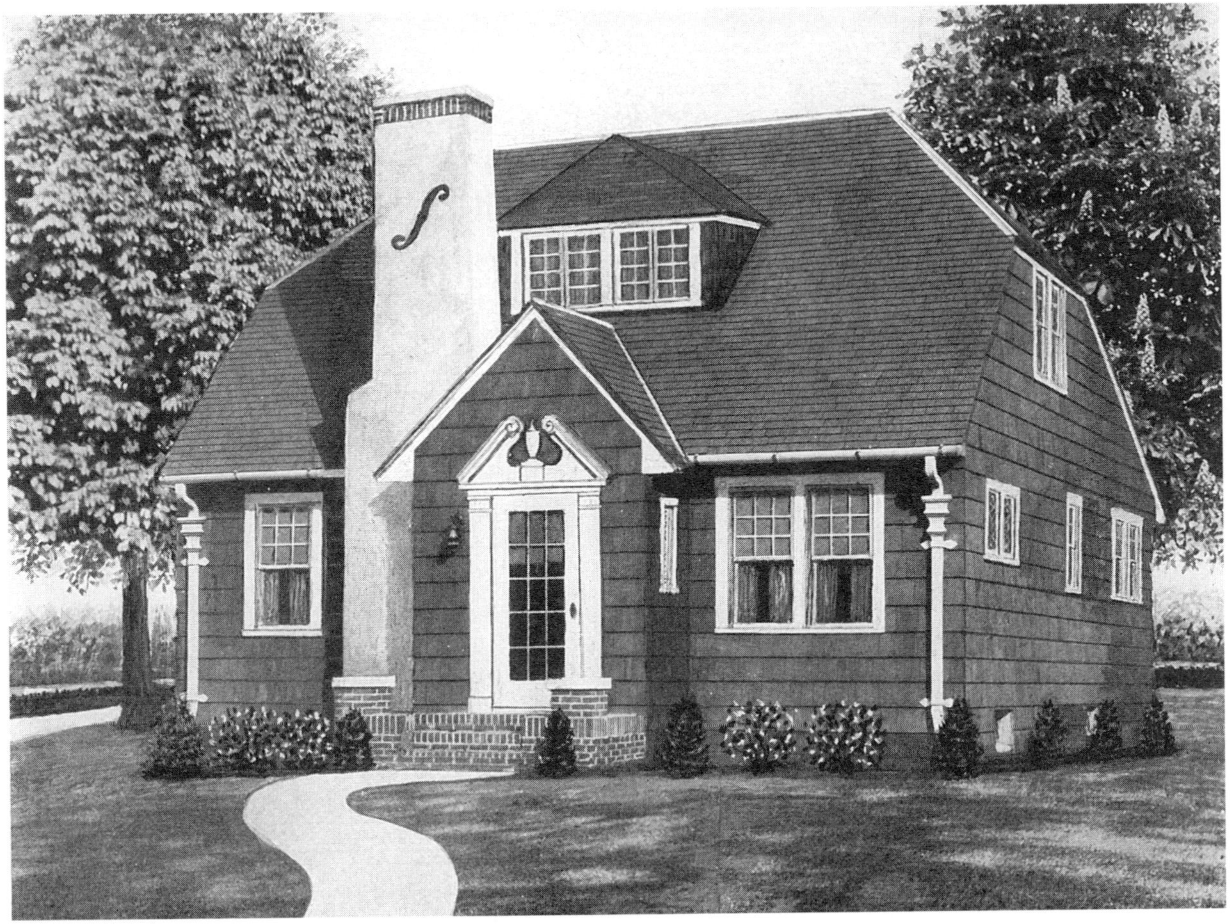

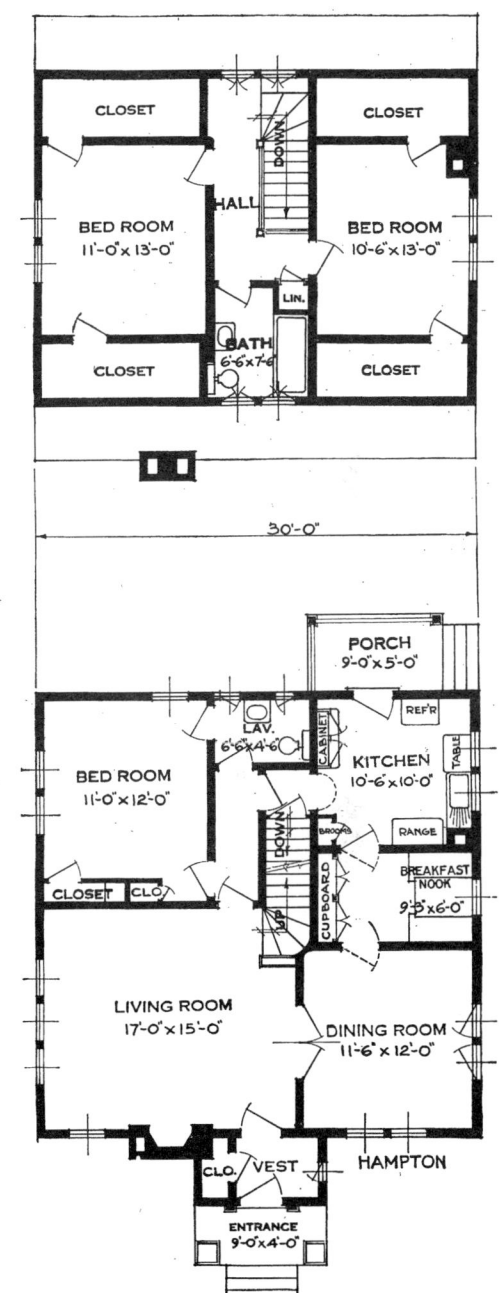

The HAMPTON (Size 30x30')

There is something in the nature of a woman that calls for seclusion in the home life. Presumably it is the maternal instinct that instinctively leads to privacy for protection. The woman whose inner self calls for a freer life in a private home, will obey the most sacred impulse if she patiently persists until such call is answered by the possession of The Hampton.

All plans are so prepared as to permit frame, stucco, brick or tile construction.

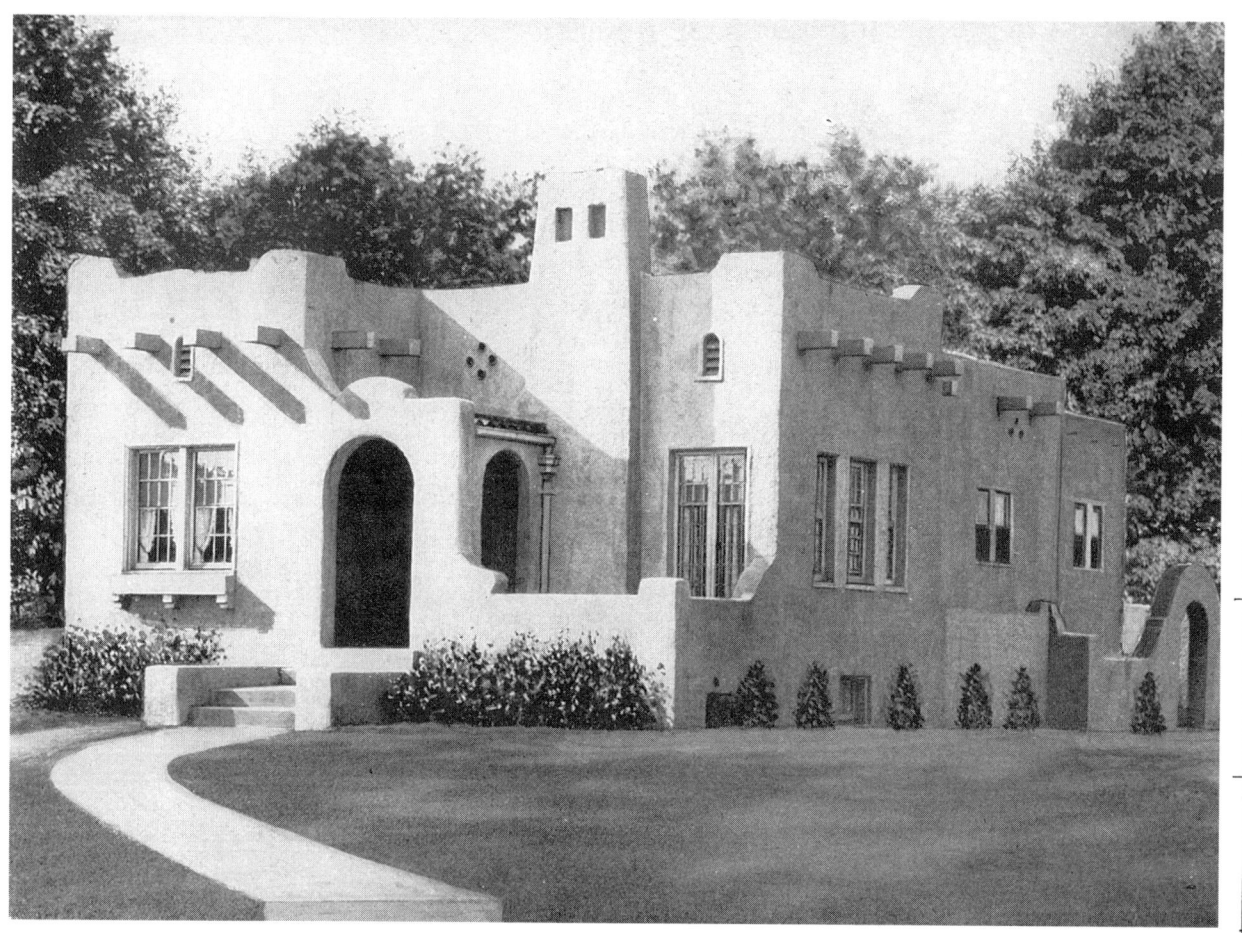

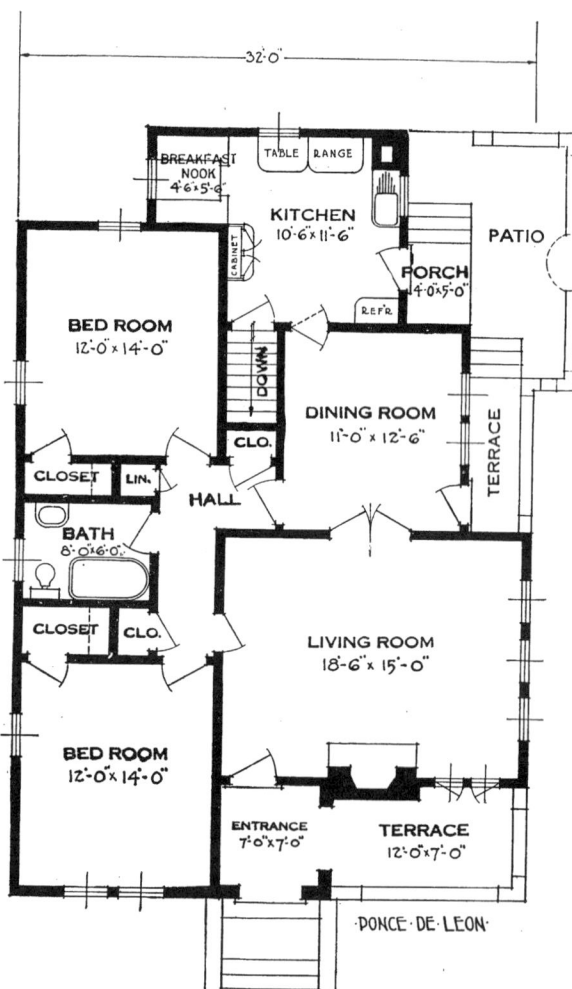

Men are what their thoughts and home life make them.

The PONCE DE LEON (Size 32x42')

This beautiful Spanish bungalow is one of the most attractive five-room designs so far offered to lovers of Spanish architecture. It can be constructed at low cost, due to the simplicity of the exterior design and the practical floor plan, yet it will stand on any street anywhere as a home of distinction.

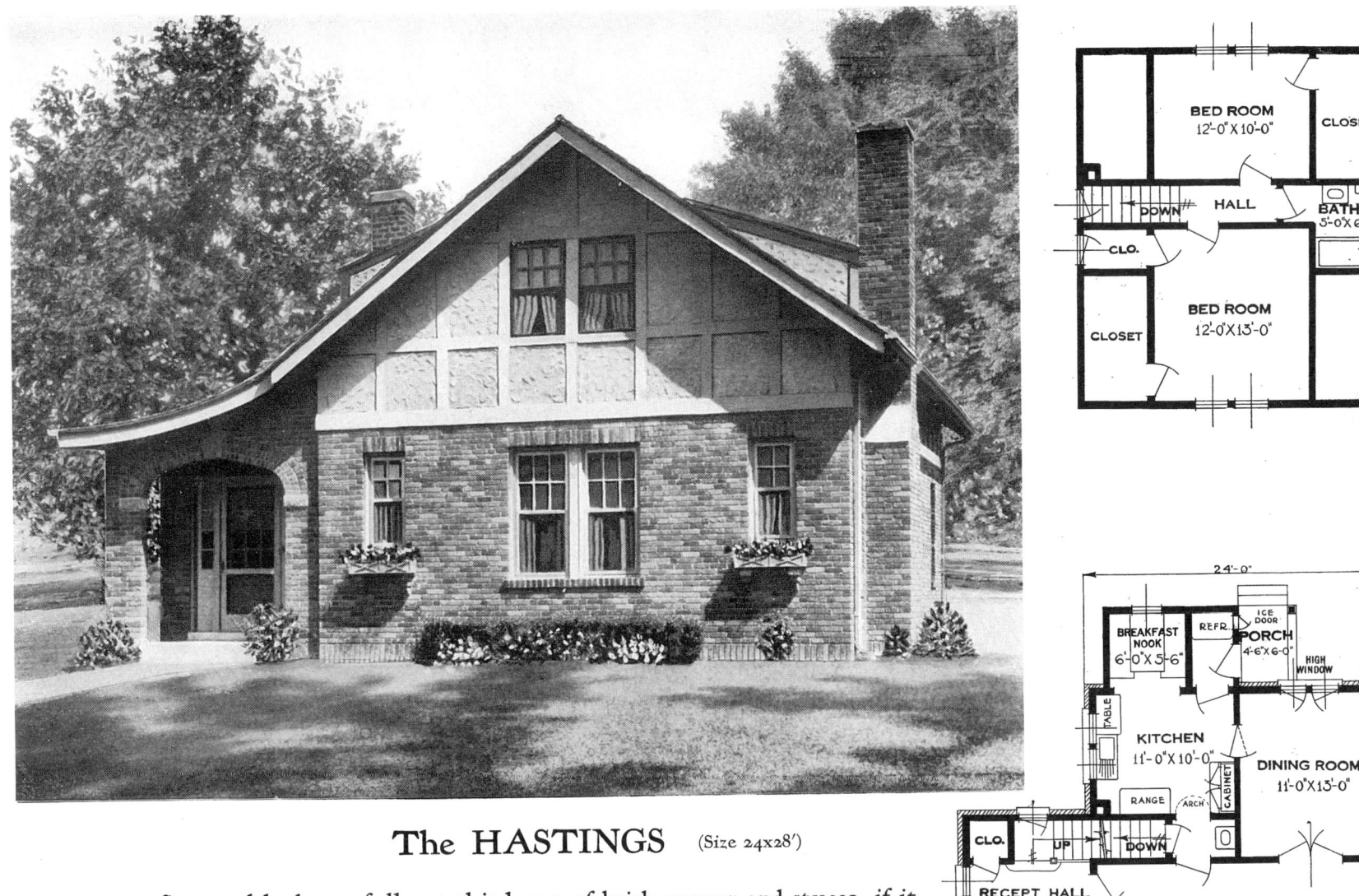

The HASTINGS (Size 24x28′)

Stop and look carefully at this home of brick veneer and stucco, if it is a cottage of five rooms that is wanted. It is correct in every detail, both as to exterior and interior, and every homey idea has been added that can be found in homes that sell at figures twice to three times its cost.

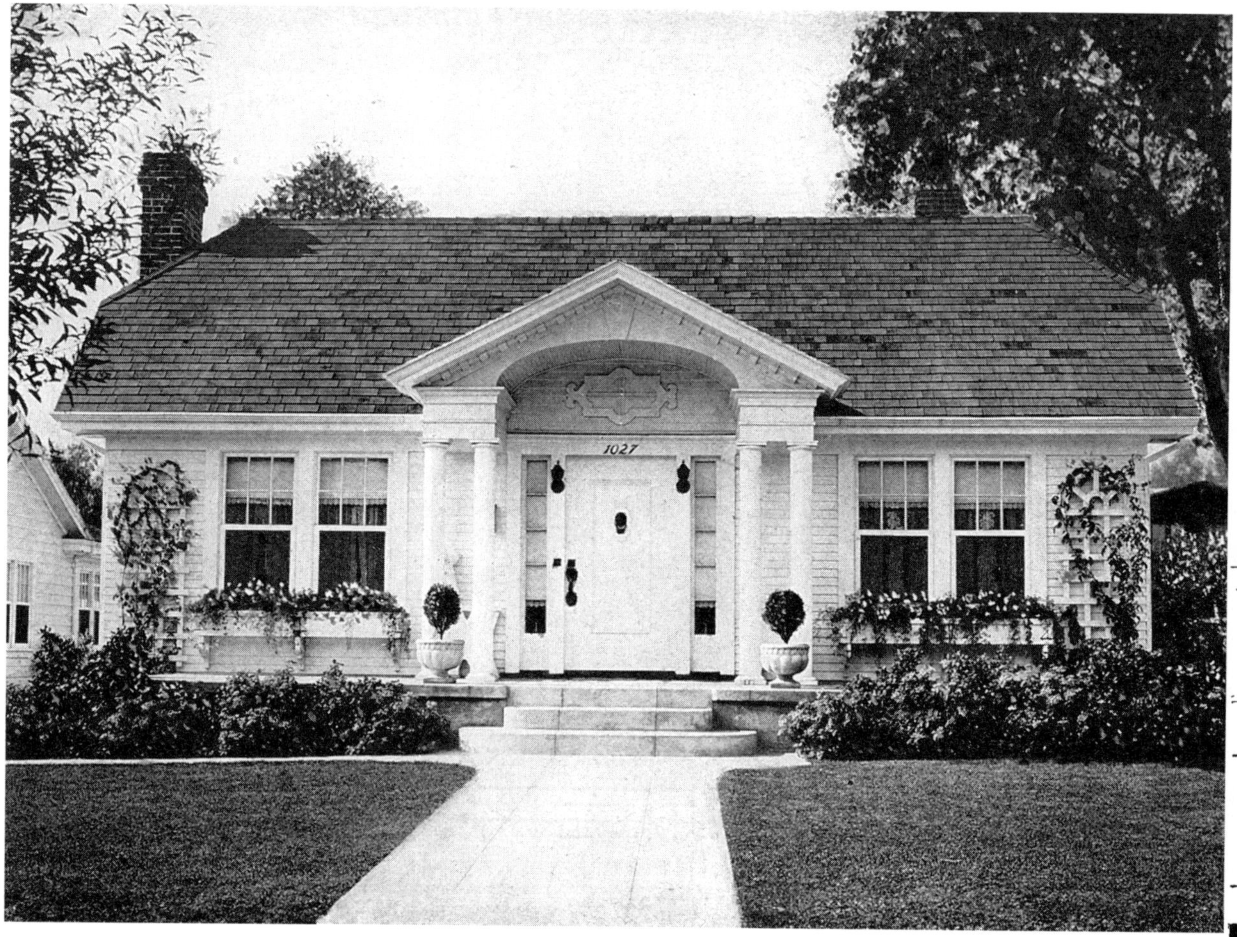

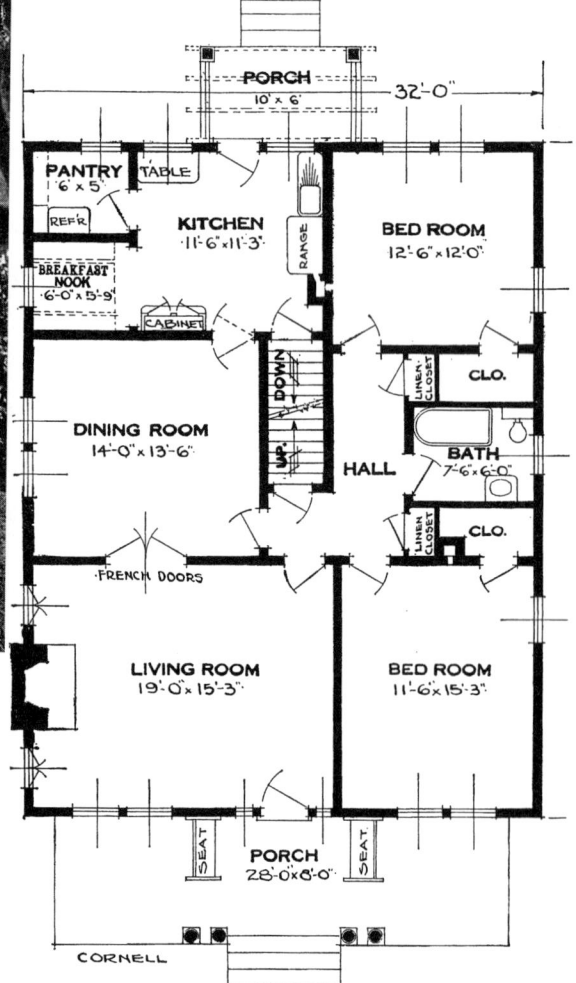

The CORNELL (Size 32x42′)

True peace and enduring happiness are found only by those who unselfishly seek to develop the best in themselves and in others. The most natural place for such growth and influence is in the individual home where inner strength is constantly developed by conscious freedom, and fear is shut out and destroyed by a sacred purpose.

The "guess and cut" way of constructing homes is fast giving way to more modern methods.

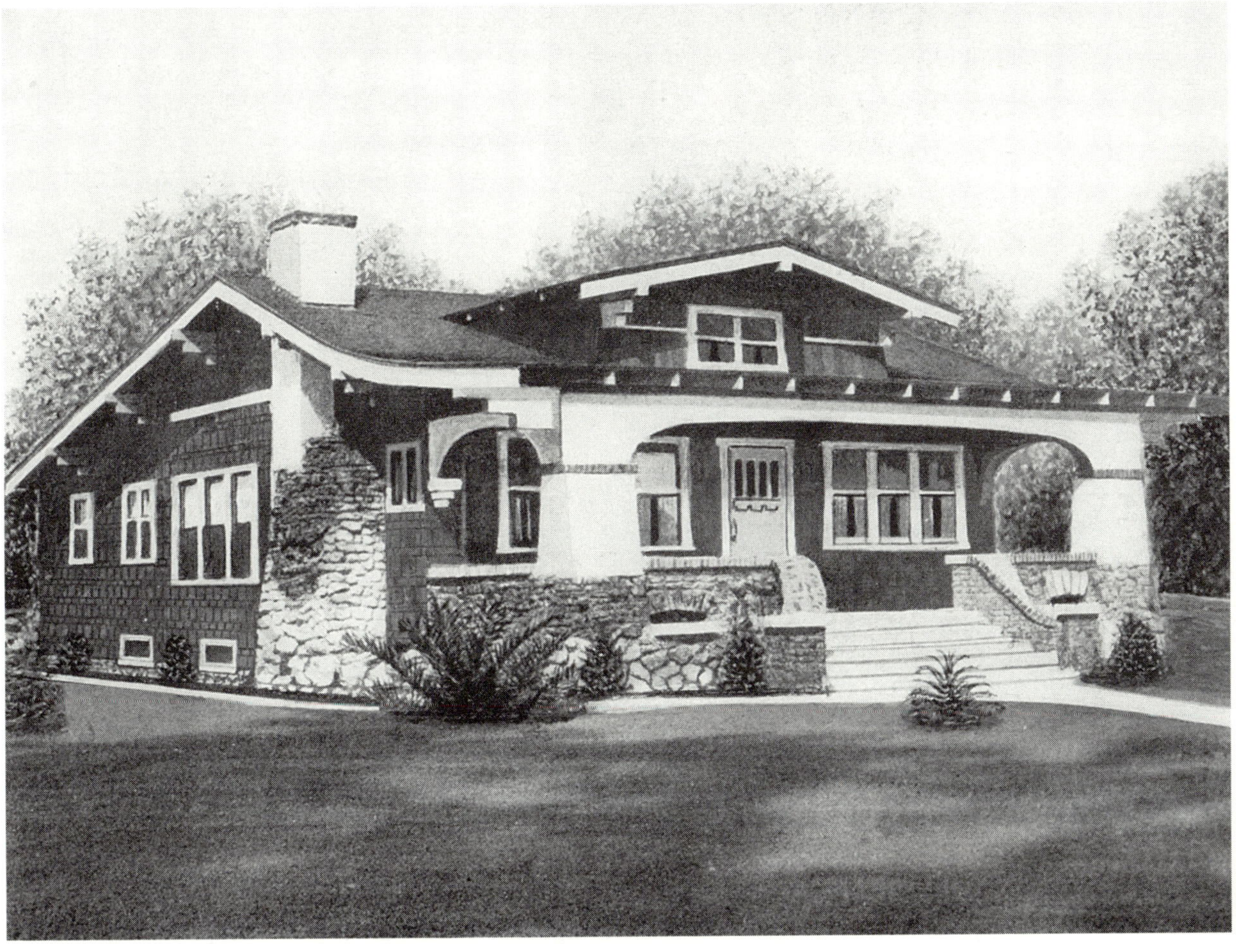

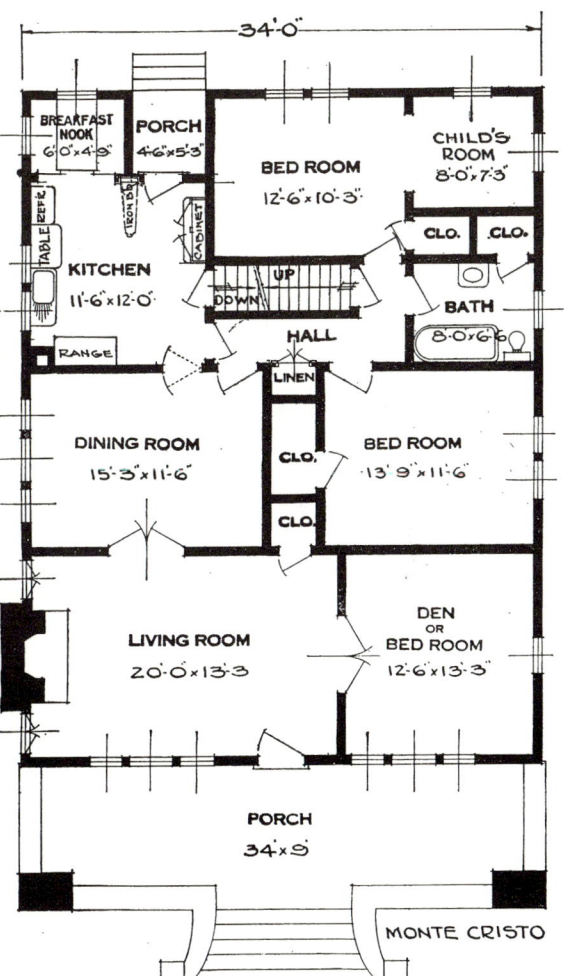

> In the selection of a home woman's intuition is often worth more than man's reason.

The MONTE CRISTO (Size 34x44')

Those who plan a home for a place of rest and contentment and in the planning think not of children and their comforts and joys, know little of the law of love and the underlying principles of happiness and mental growth. In The Monte Cristo the child's room is most thoughtfully arranged, and happy will be the occupants of this home if they are blessed with the care of children.

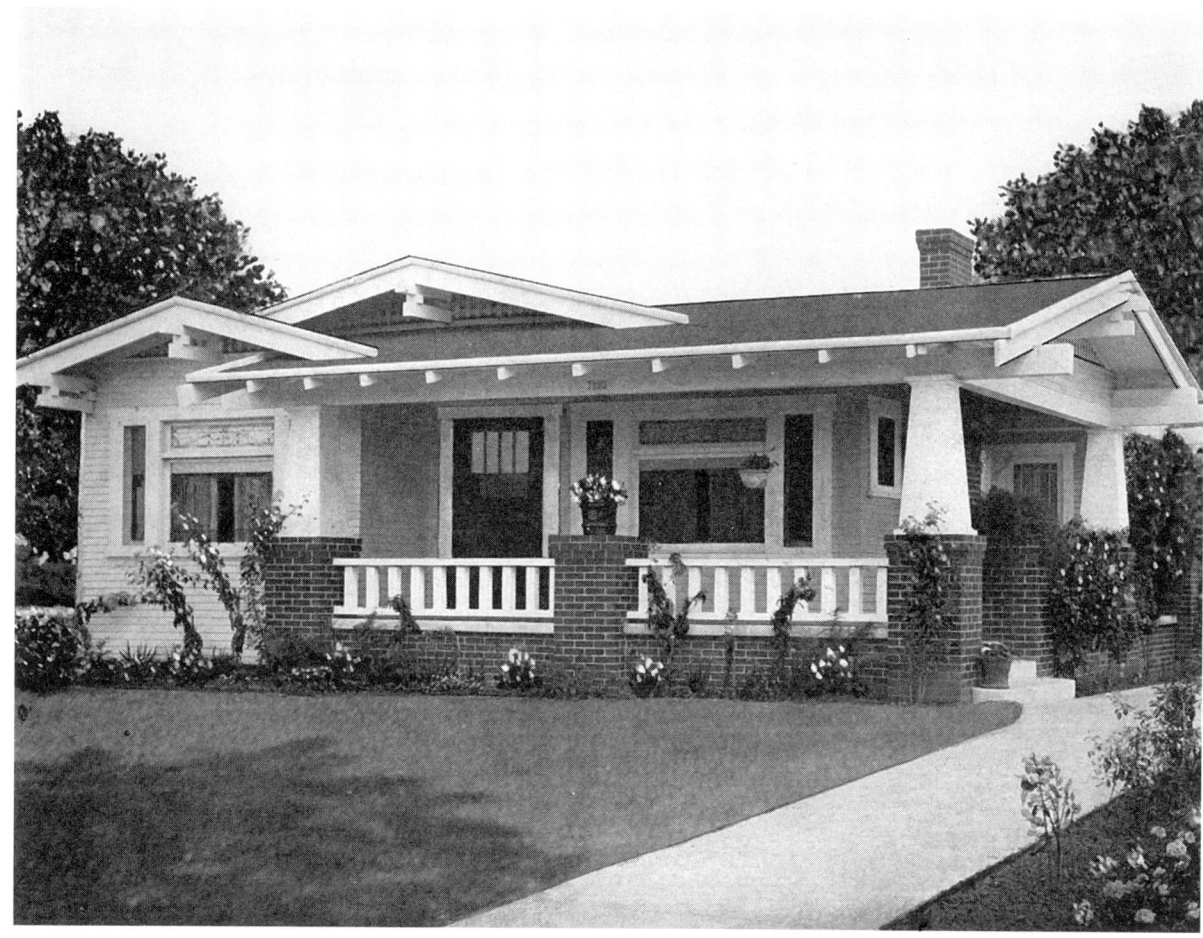

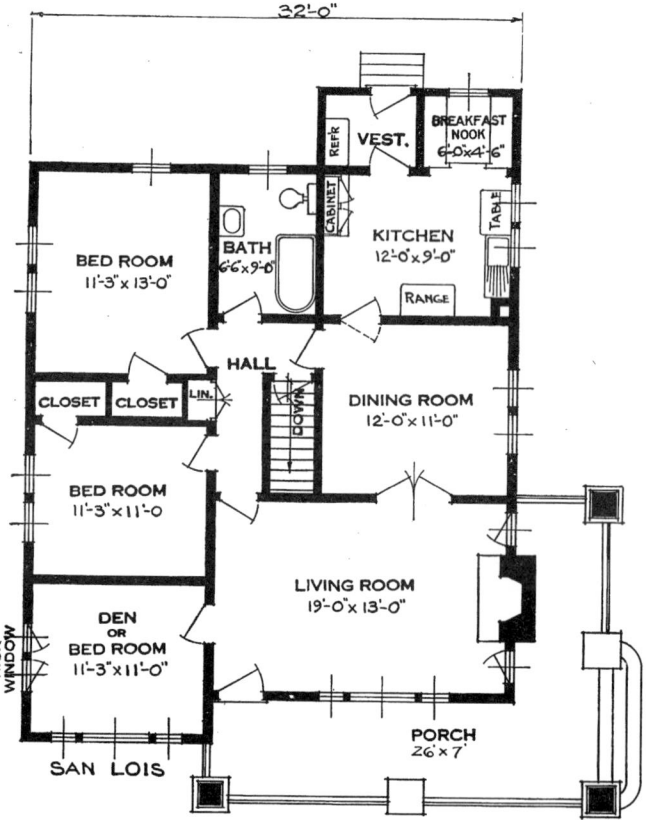

In the happiness of the home lies the health and strength of the whole family.

The SAN LOIS (Size 32x40')

There can be no freedom nor peace of mind in mature life for those who do not pay the price in youth. The price of freedom and peace is independence gained through sacrifice. Those who make the sacrifices necessary to enable them to own The San Lois will turn the present seeming desert into the paradise of their early dreams.

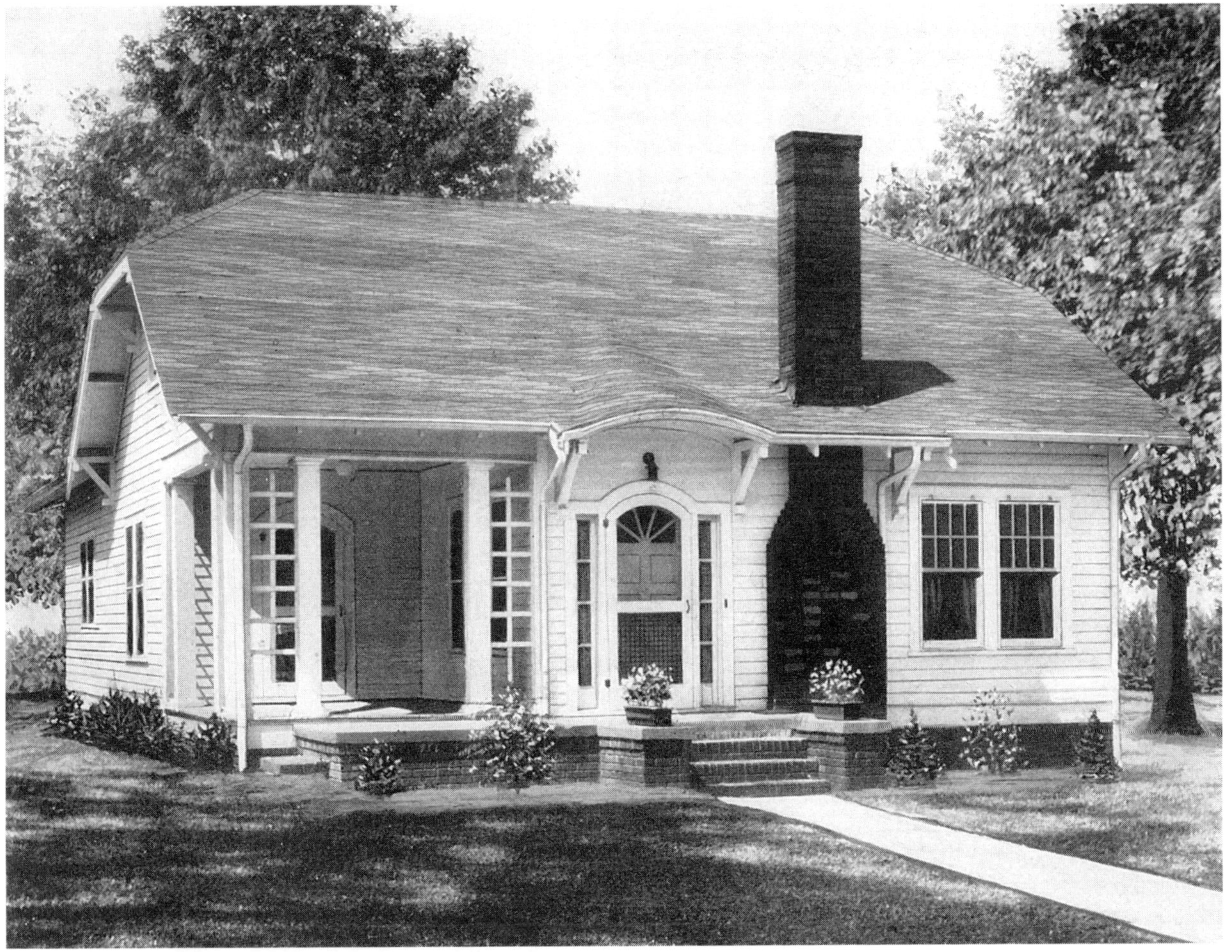

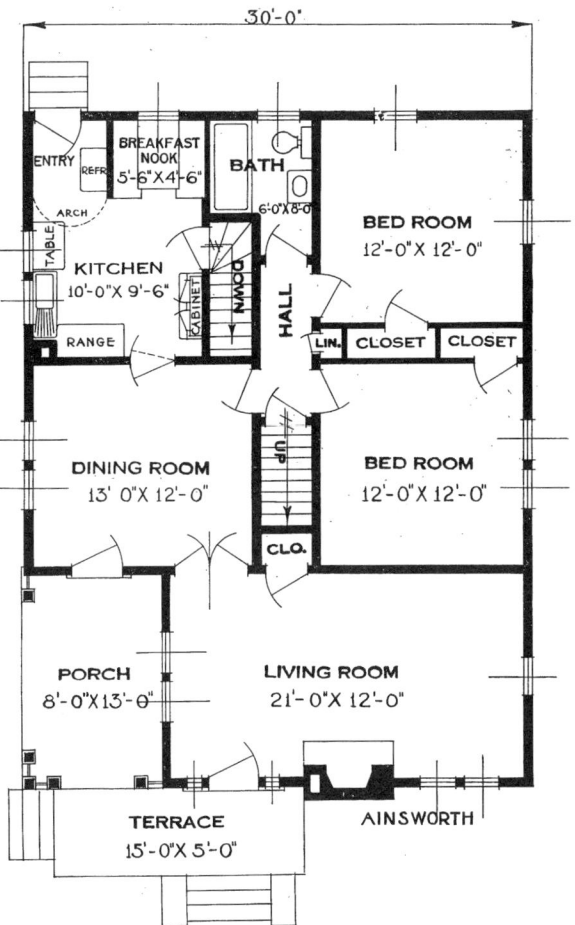

The AINSWORTH (Size 30x40′)

Becoming dissatisfied with unpleasant home surroundings is the sign of growth, and, if considered in this light rather than a complaint against fate, one should take courage and make greater effort, knowing that it is possible that The Ainsworth may soon become his home by the operation of the natural law of persistent purpose.

It is just as important to economize in home construction as it is to economize in current expenses later.

All plans are so prepared as to permit frame, stucco, brick or tile construction.

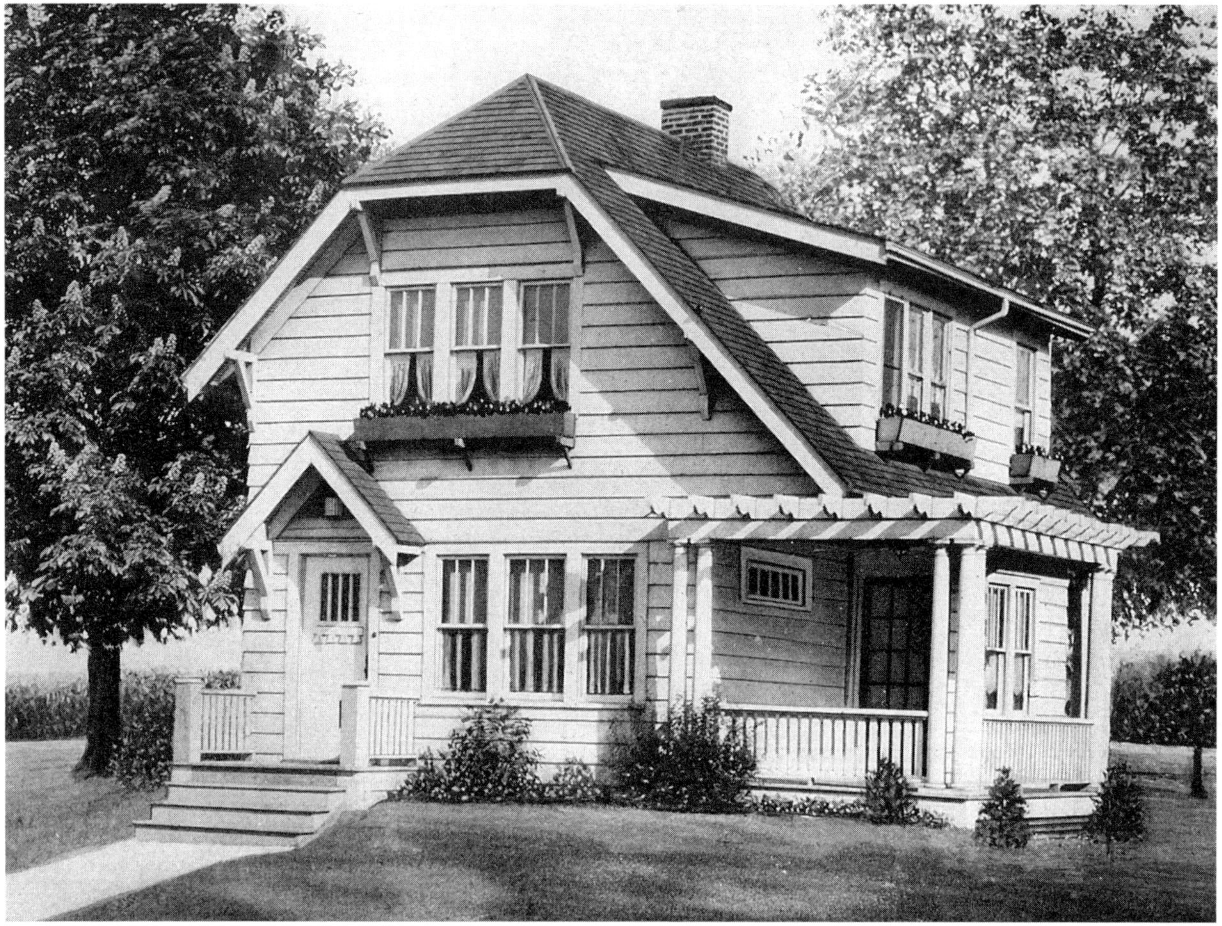

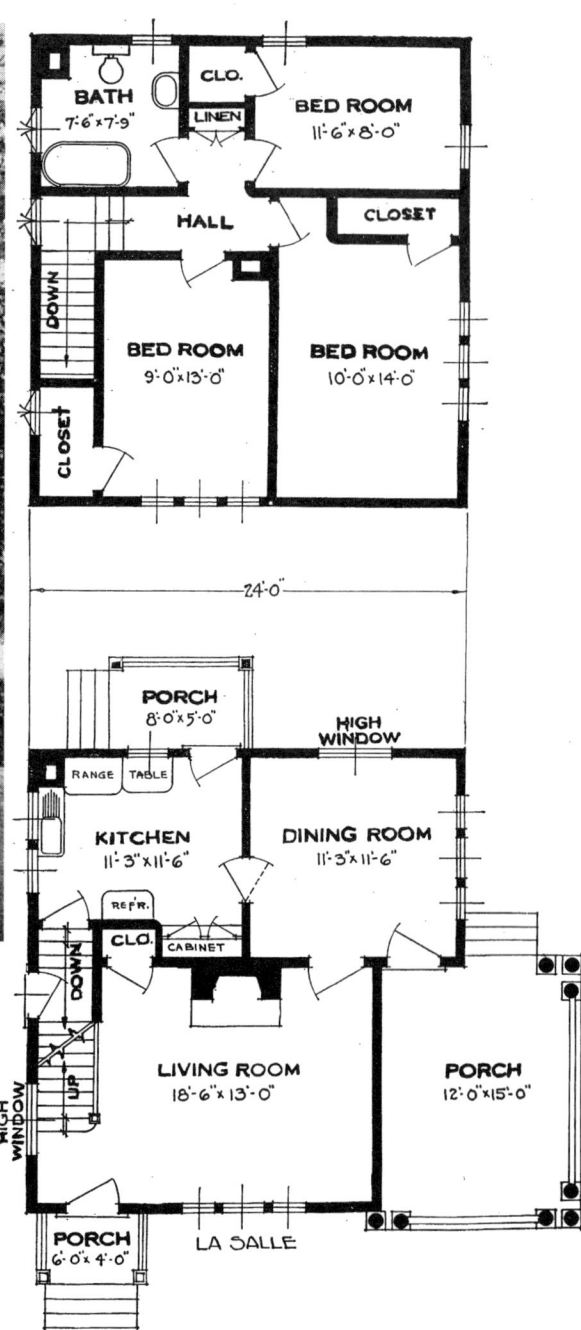

The LA SALLE (Size 24x26′)

One takes little interest in beautifying a home and garden which belong to another, and which may be sold without notice. There is a feeling of inappreciation and uncertainty which deeply affects his love for home. Those who build The La Salle, and know that every improvement added increases its value, will find both their time and money well and joyfully spent.

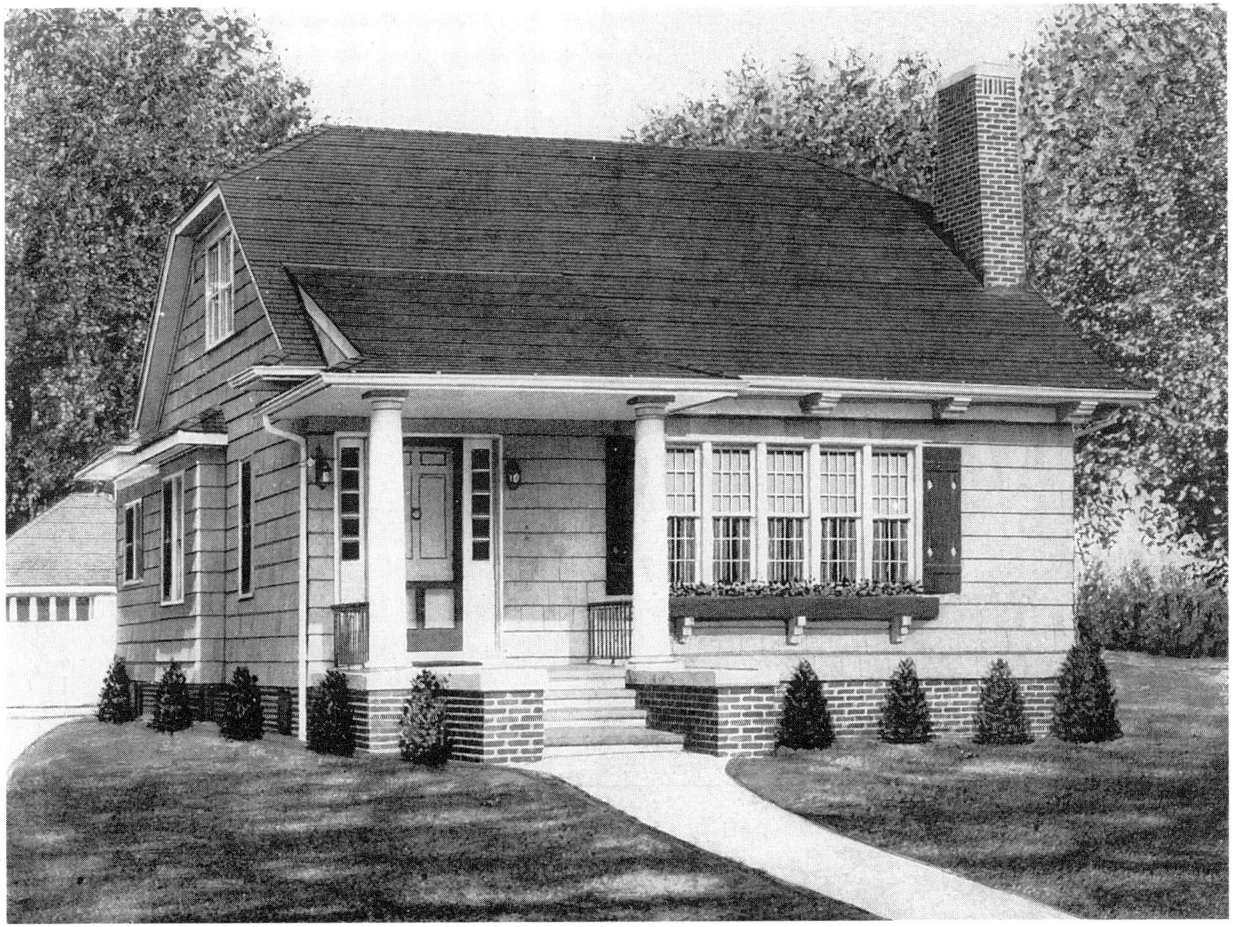

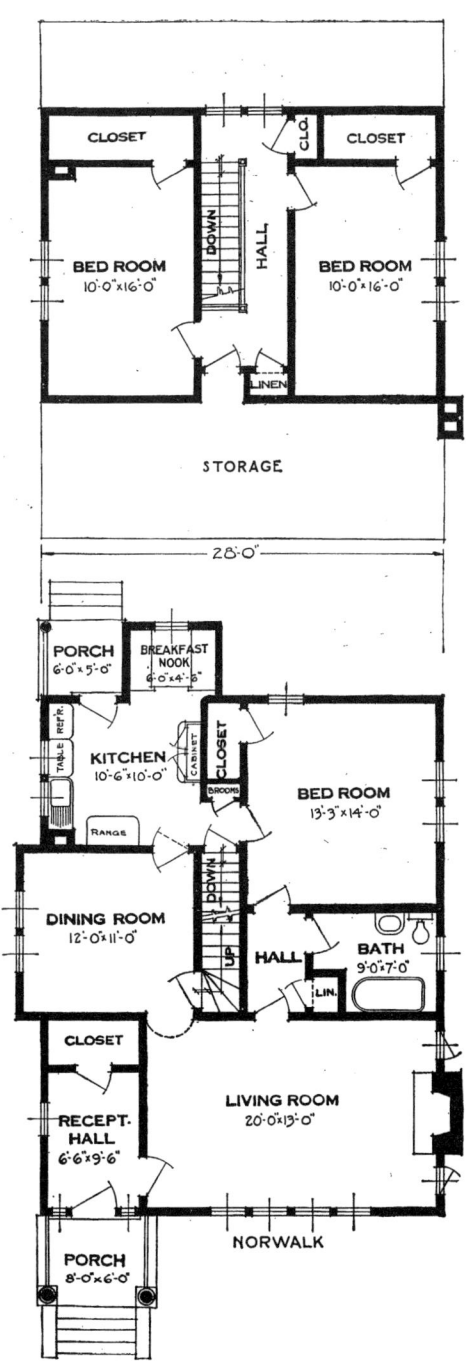

The NORWALK (Size 28x36')

Forming a habit of placing in a Building and Loan Association all earnings which one does not need for immediate use, is the surest road to the ownership of The Norwalk for a home.

The sacrifices made in the saving of a home are the highly prized diary notes in one's record of accomplishment.

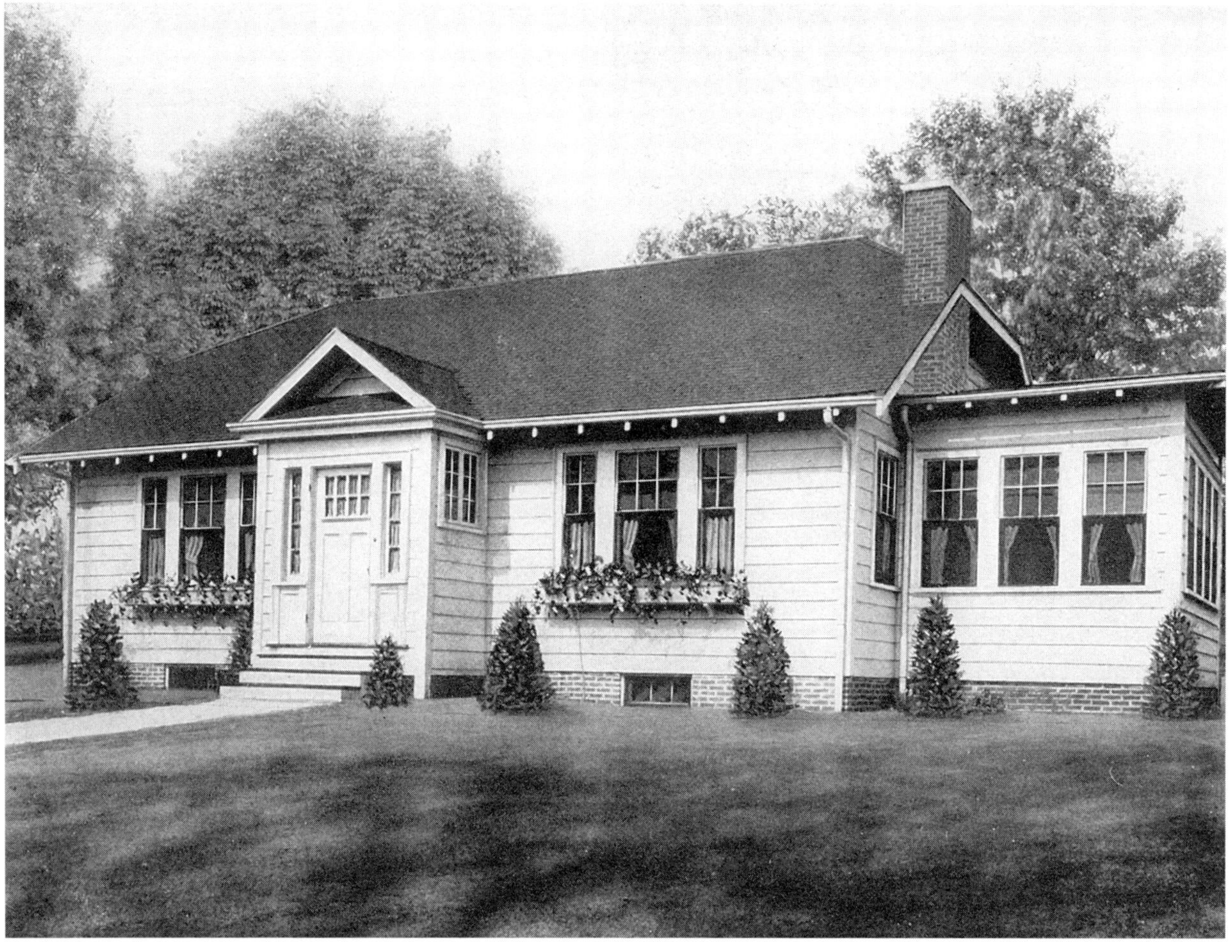

> Keeping young is simply a question of keeping joy and sunshine in the heart.

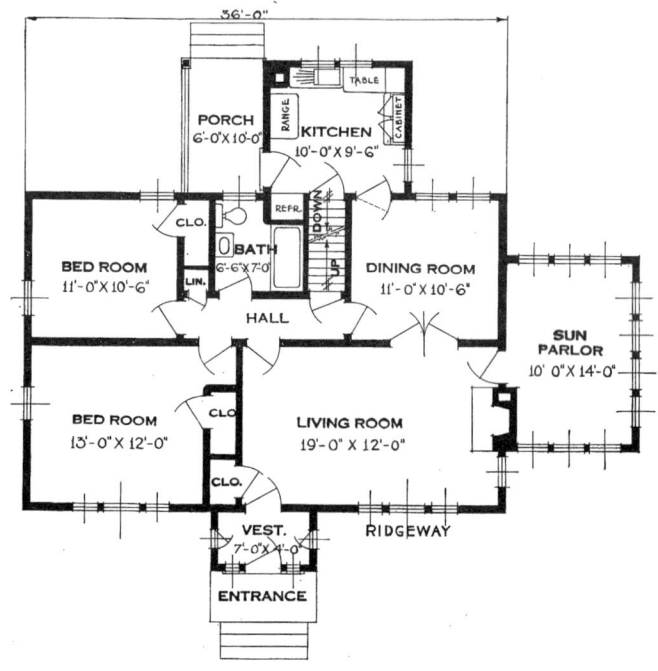

The RIDGEWAY (Size 36x24')

In all parts of the country the demand for small bungalows is growing, and The Ridgeway is offered as typical of the inexpensive type being constructed in many sections. The coziness of the exterior effect is at once admitted by all, and the construction is such as to provide coolness in summer and warmth in winter.

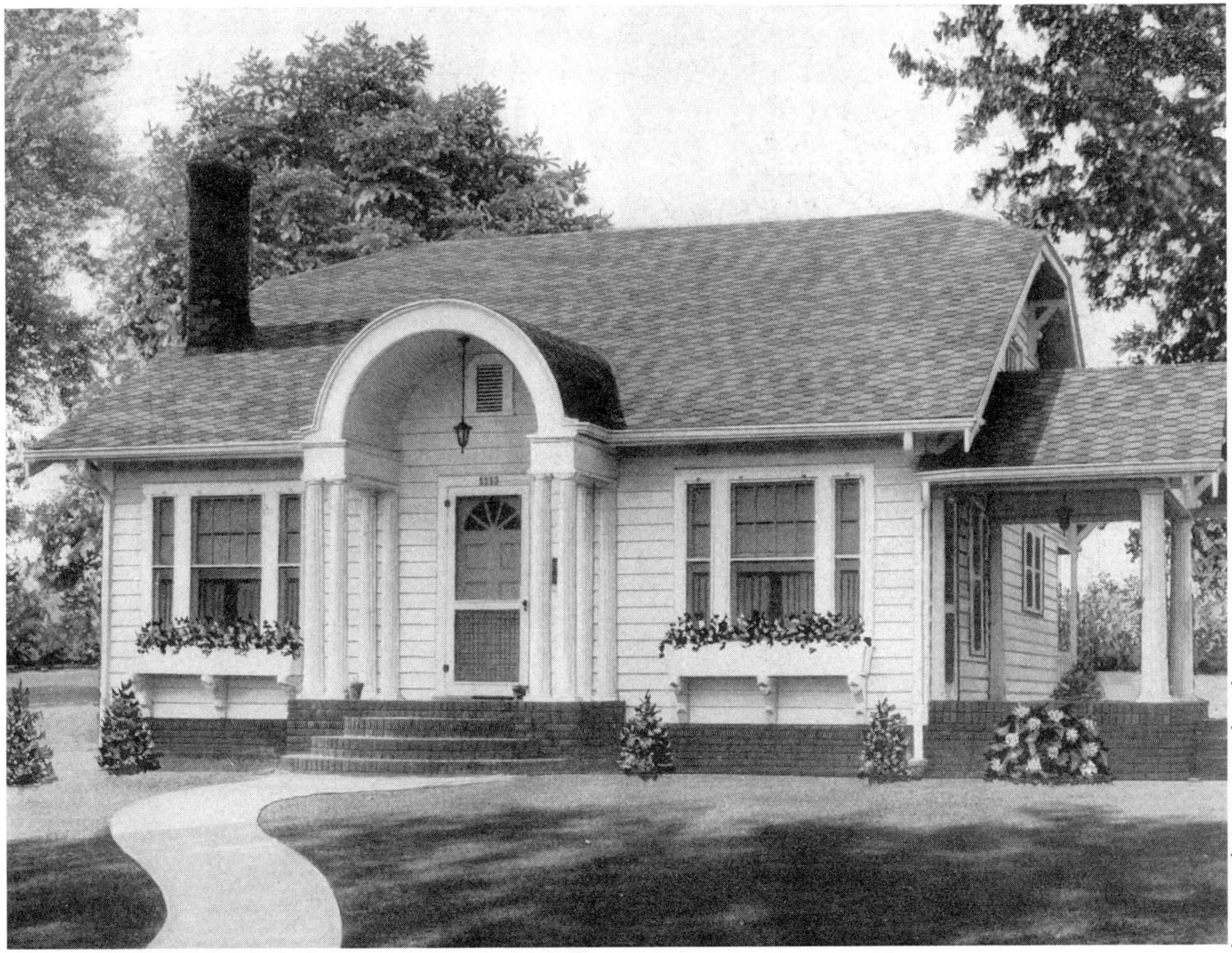

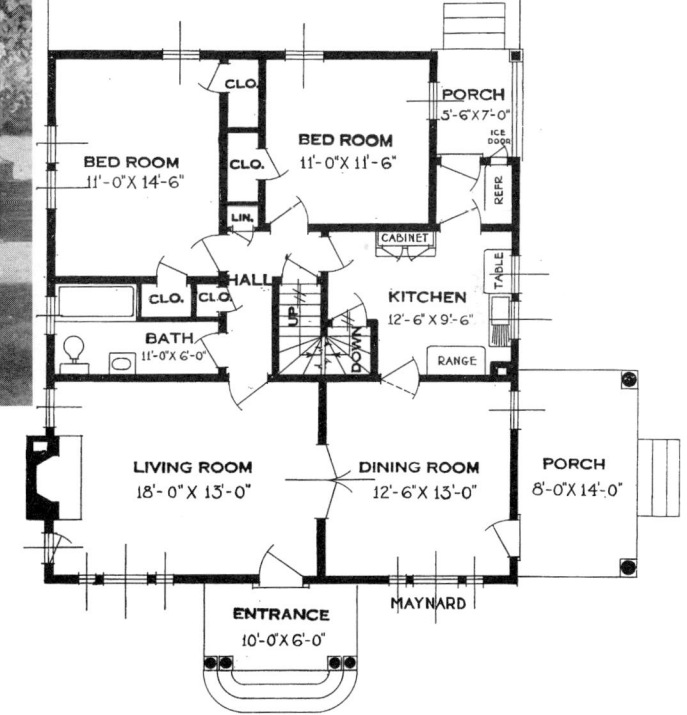

> Applying efficiency methods to the business of housekeeping enables the housewife to be fair to herself and thereby keep fair in the eyes of her husband.

The MAYWOOD (Size 32x36')

Upon every face is written the record of the life the man or woman has lived, and present thoughts and conditions are clearly shown in the voice and manner. Careworn faces and voices with discordant notes seldom emerge from happy new homes like The Maywood, in which the very walls are respondent with mutual interest and sympathy.

73

All plans are so prepared as to permit frame, stucco, brick or tile construction.

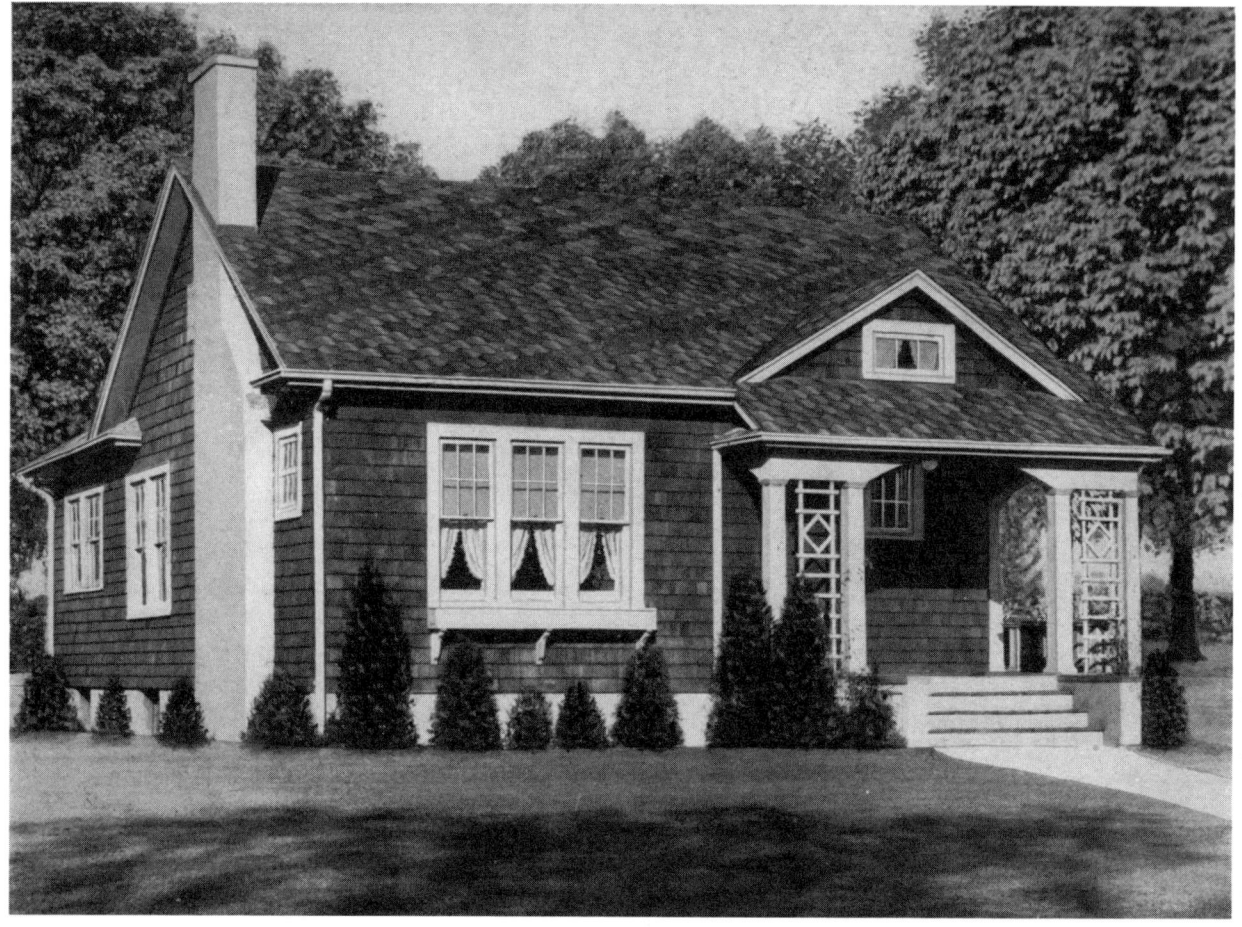

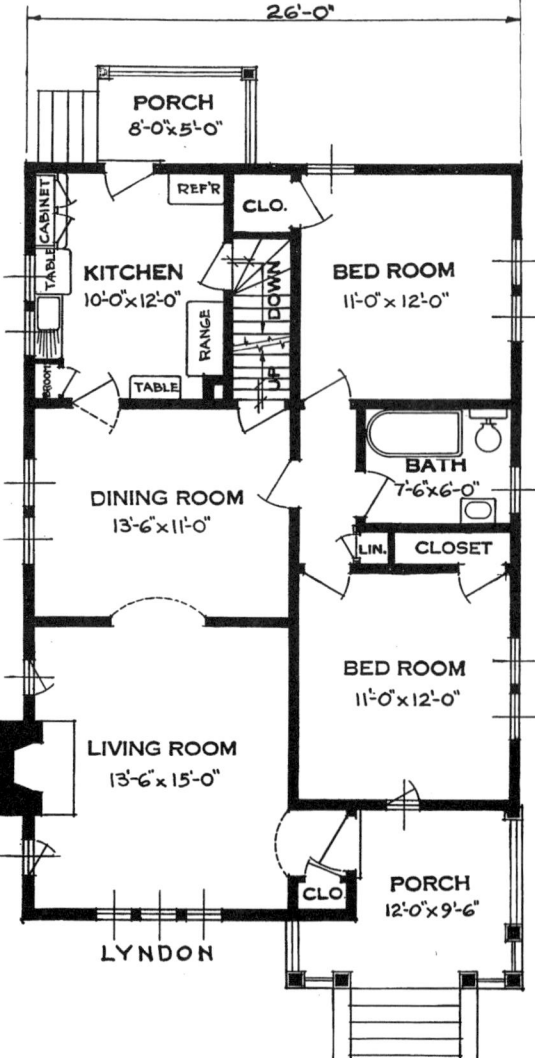

"The greatest asset a man can have is a family and a home of his own."

The LYNDON (Size 26x40')

Unnecessary work is always unfair work. It is unfair for the housewife to be forced to take hundreds of unnecessary steps in the daily routine of housekeeping because she was not considered in the planning of the home. In arranging the floor plan for The Lyndon, the architect considered first practical economy for the wife who does her own housework.

All plans are so prepared as to permit frame, stucco, brick or tile construction.

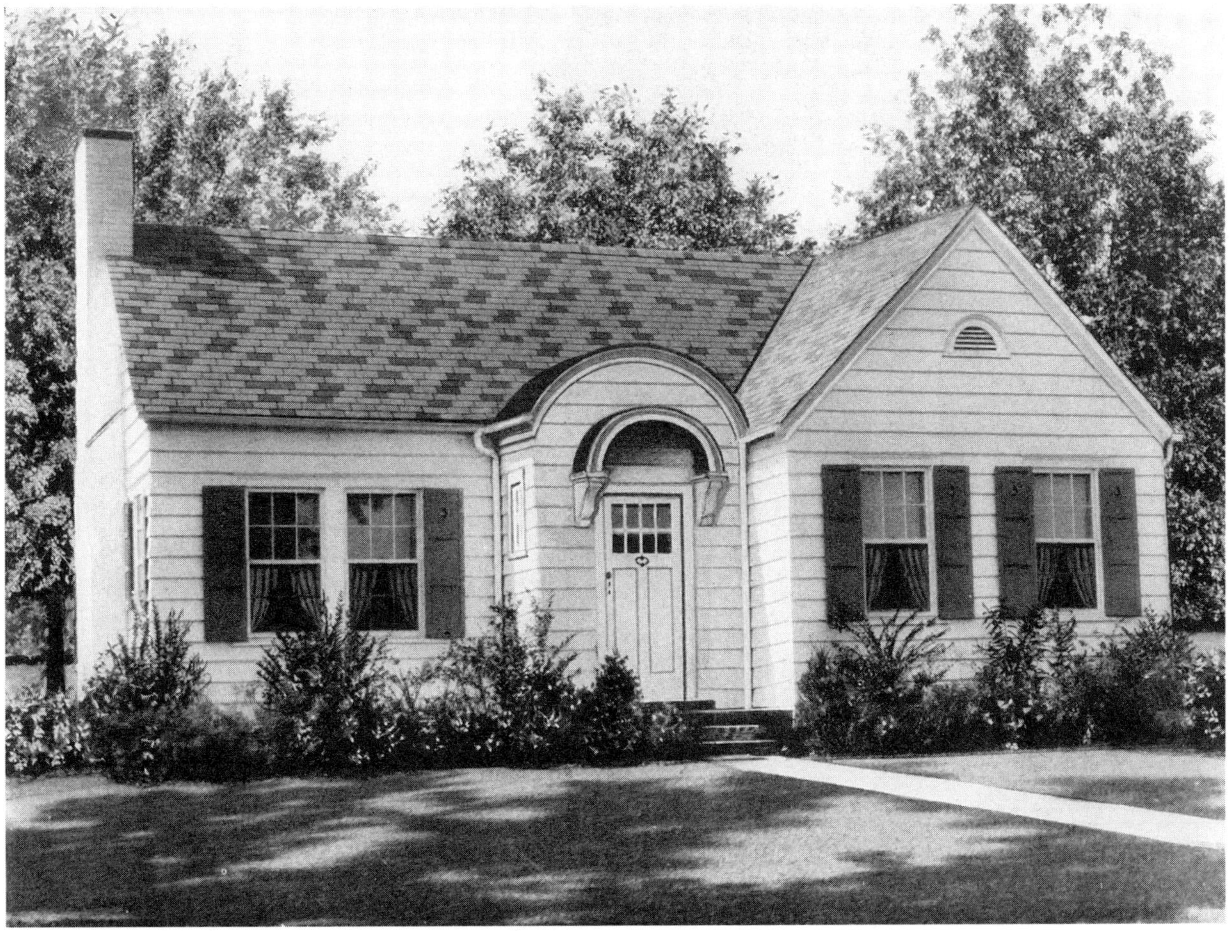

> Every child has the right to be well born and well reared in a permanent home.

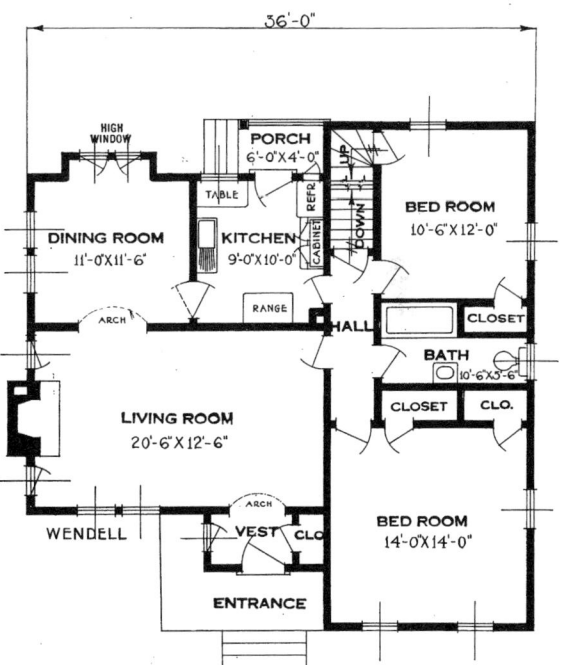

The WENDELL (Size 36x24')

The feeling of aloneness is almost entirely unknown in small, comfortable homes like The Wendell. Mental depression comes, as a rule, from tired nerves and unsightly surroundings. In the small new home which has been provided with an abundance of light, life is more cheerful and housekeeping is cut to the minimum.

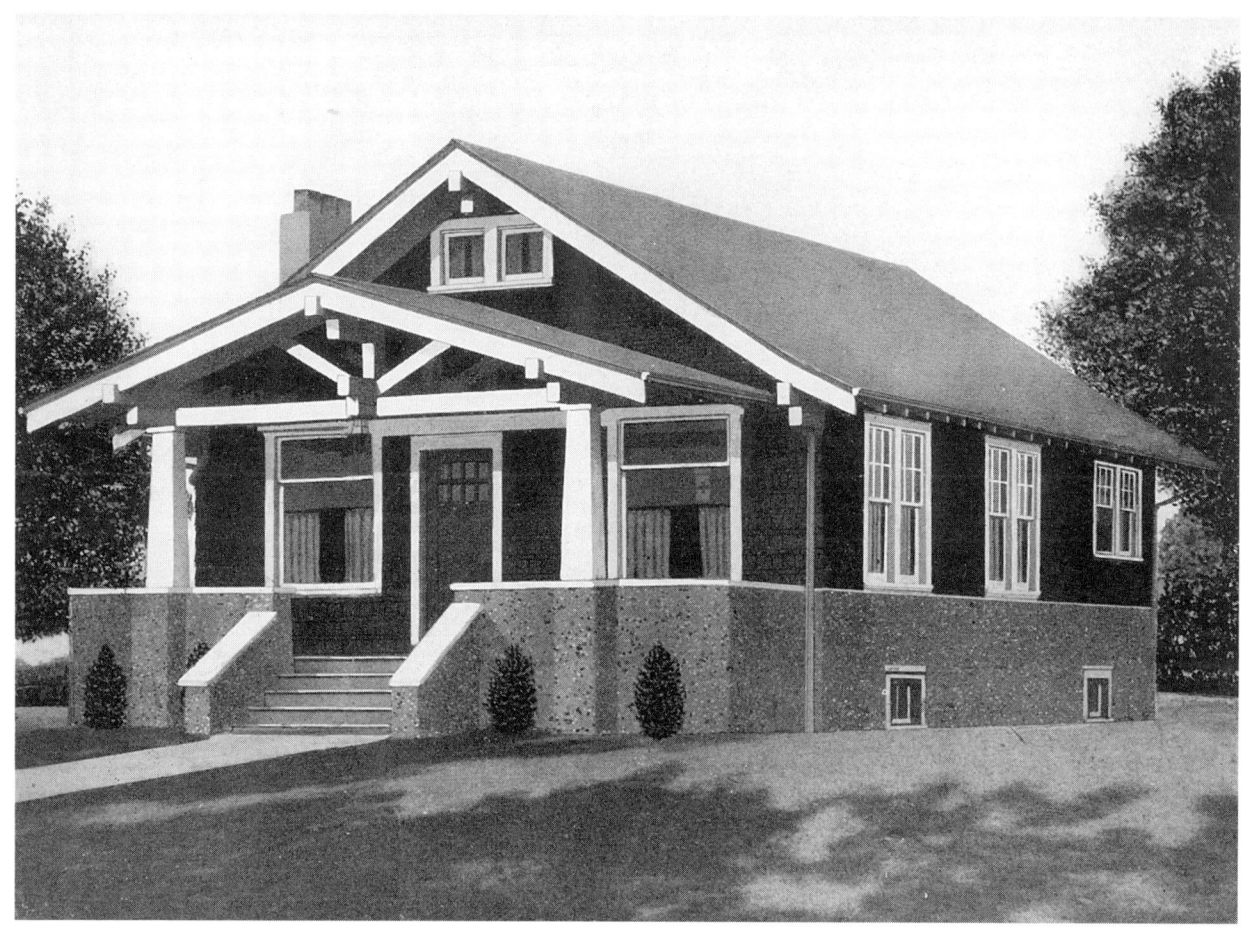
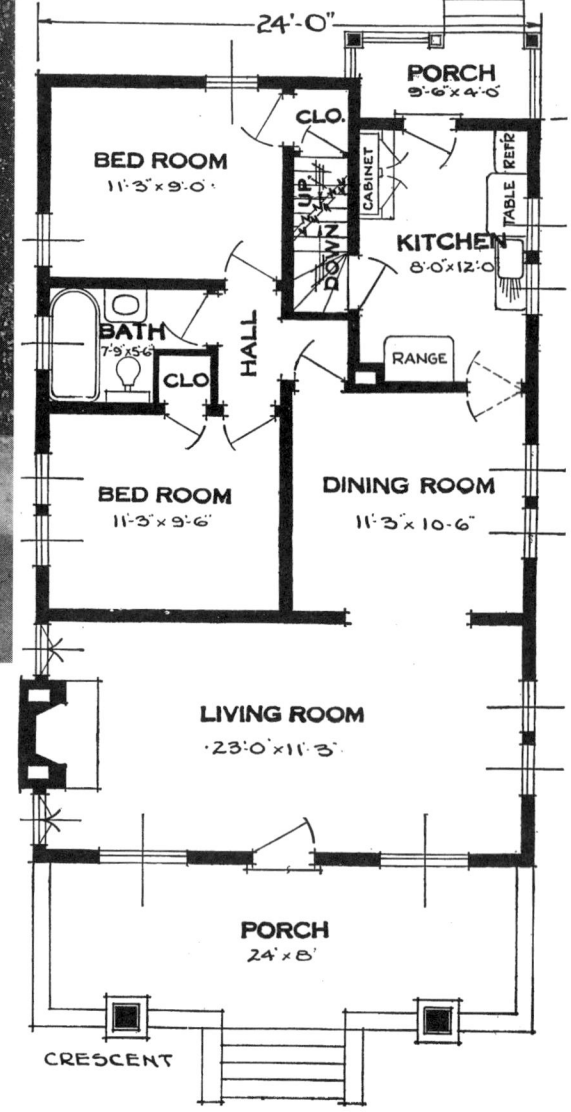

The CRESCENT (Size 24x36')

Practically all renters pay one-fourth of their earnings to landlords. This means that millions are monthly invested in worthless rent receipts. But this does not compare with the vast amount of home joy which the masses are missing. There is an inner joy and satisfaction in owning a convenient home of The Crescent plan which nothing else can give.

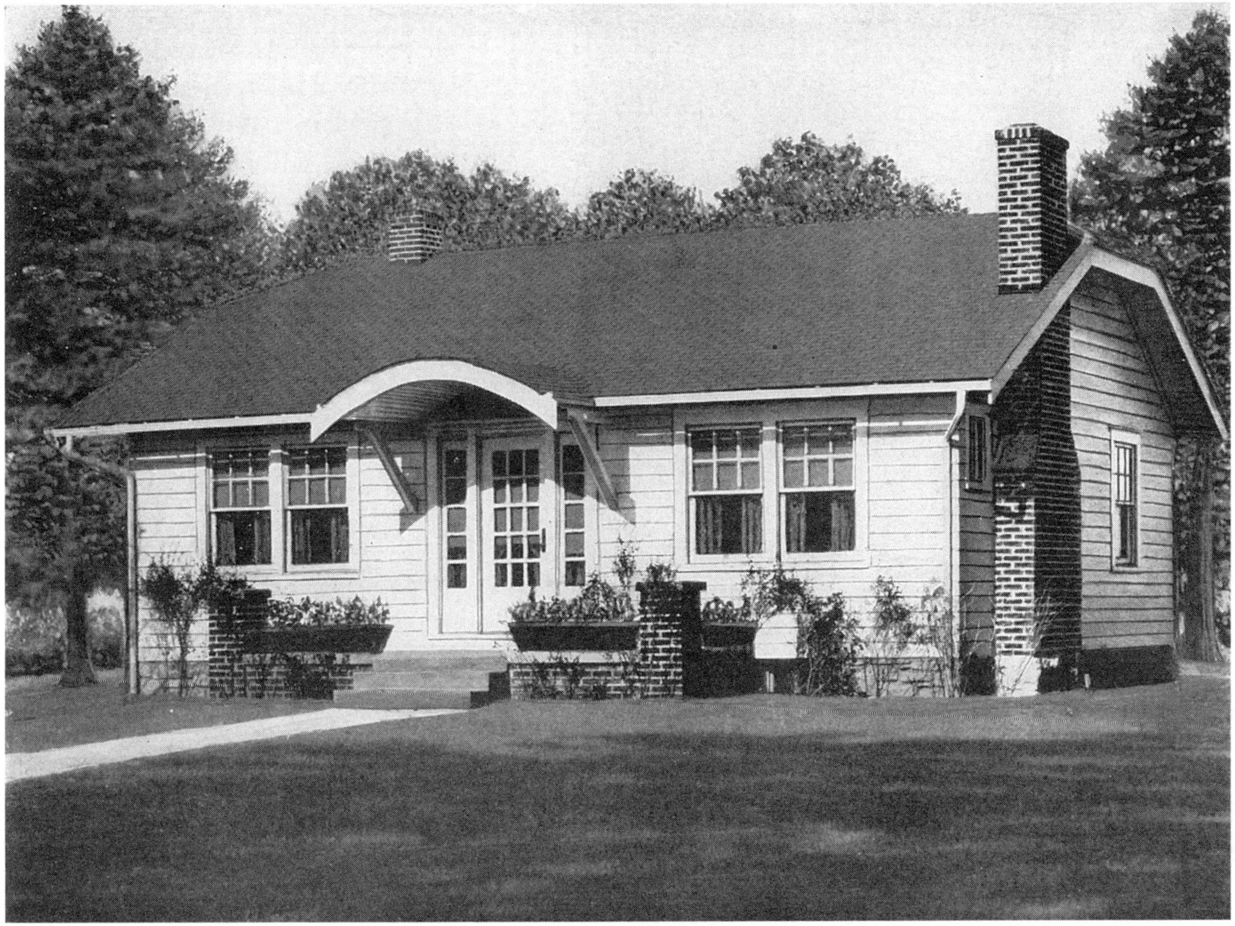

> The happiest families are not those that rest in the lap of luxury, but rather those who express mutual sympathy in homes of simplicity.

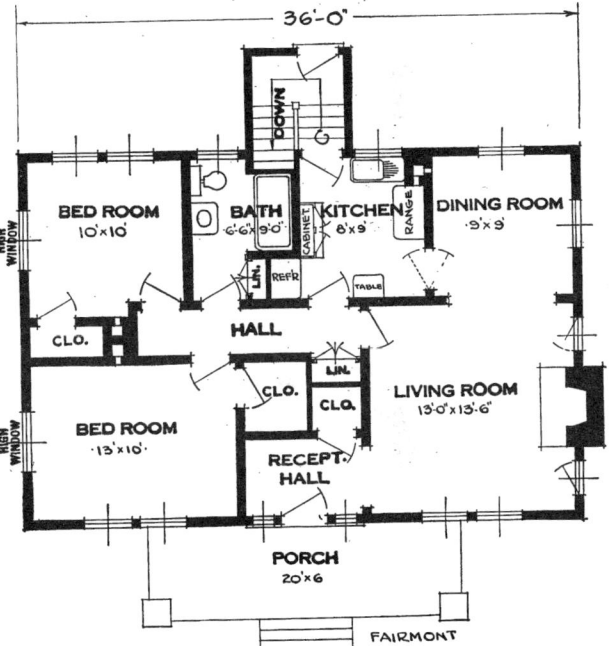

The FAIRMONT (Size 36x24')

Hundreds of hearts yearn for a fuller, freer life in a beautiful little bungalow like The Fairmont. In small, convenient homes, life is longer, because there is less labor and the hearts are lighter. Dodging unnecessary drudgery in housework is simply applying twentieth-century efficiency methods to the business of housekeeping.

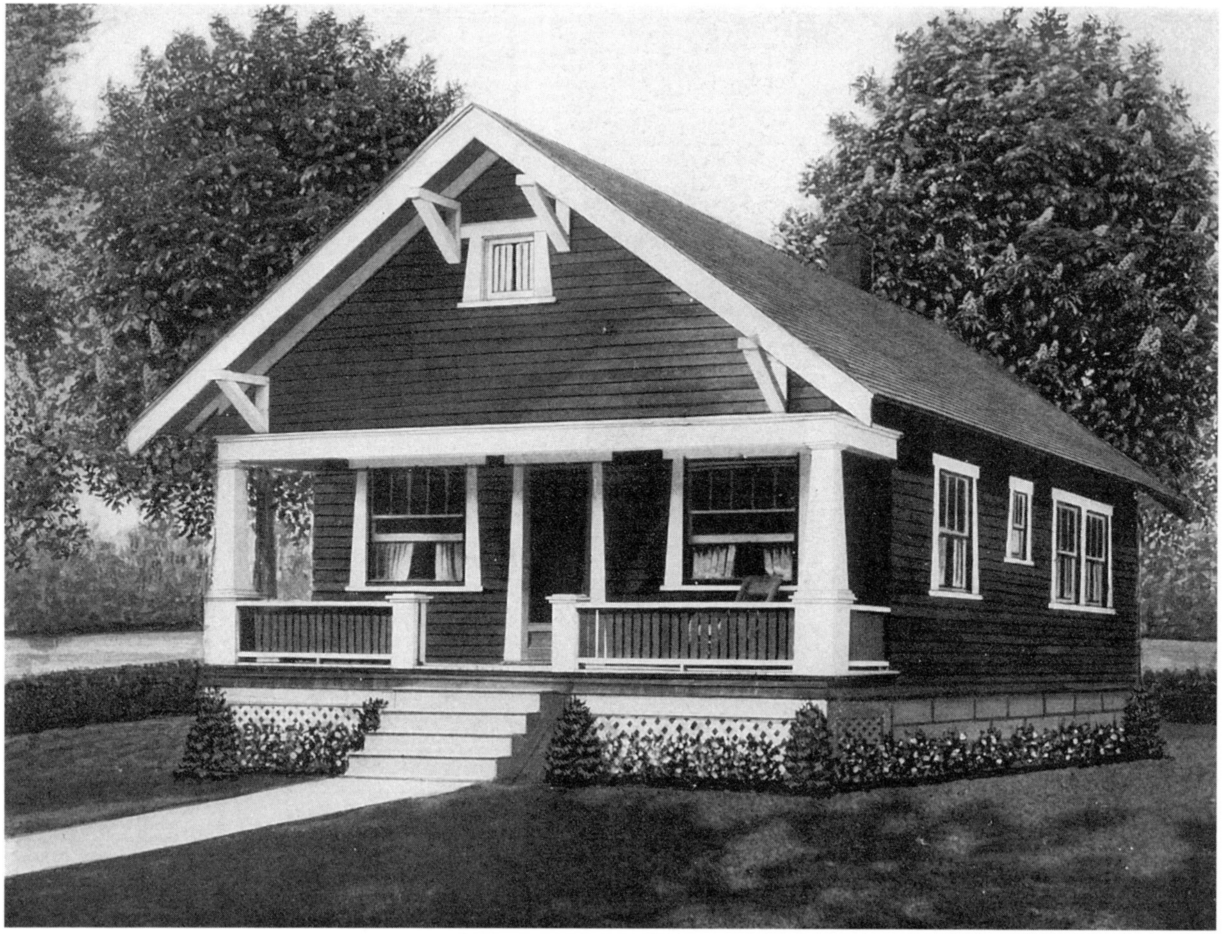

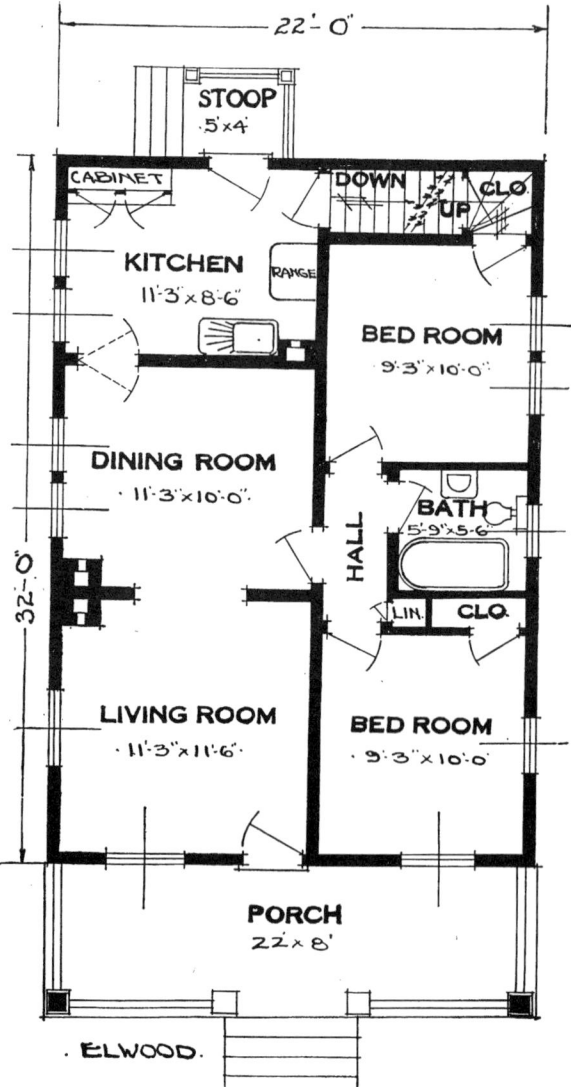

The ELWOOD (Size 22x32')

It is when a man's earnings are paying for a home like The Elwood for himself and family that he is willing to work overtime and on holidays. There is a resolute note in his voice and a pride in his step seldom found in the man whose desire for a home has found no chance for expression in an undesirable and unsightly rented house.

> Doctors have but few calls from happy new homes that are provided with an abundance of light.

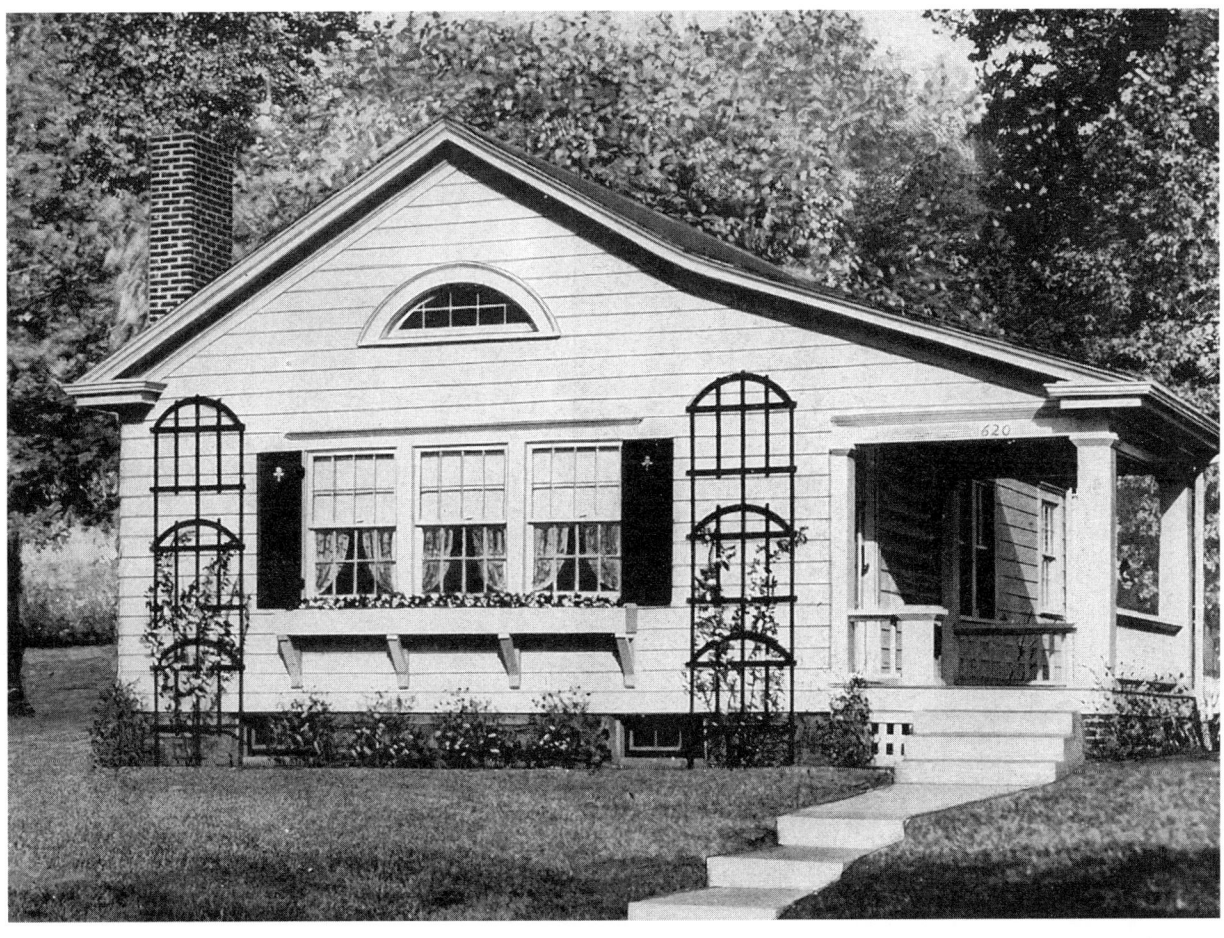

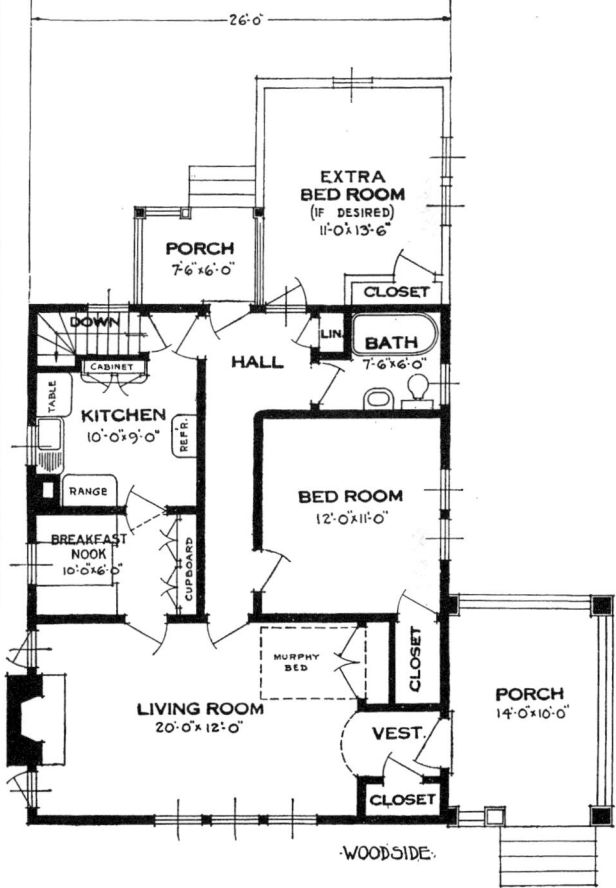

> The nickels and dimes that go down in drink and up in smoke could easily solve the housing problem.

The WOODSIDE (Size 26x32')

If more floor space per dollar is wanted in a home, without the sacrifice of architectural correctness, The Woodside will meet with much favor, for not only is it spacious, but unusually attractive as well, and a study of its floor plan will convince one readily of its many time and labor-saving features.

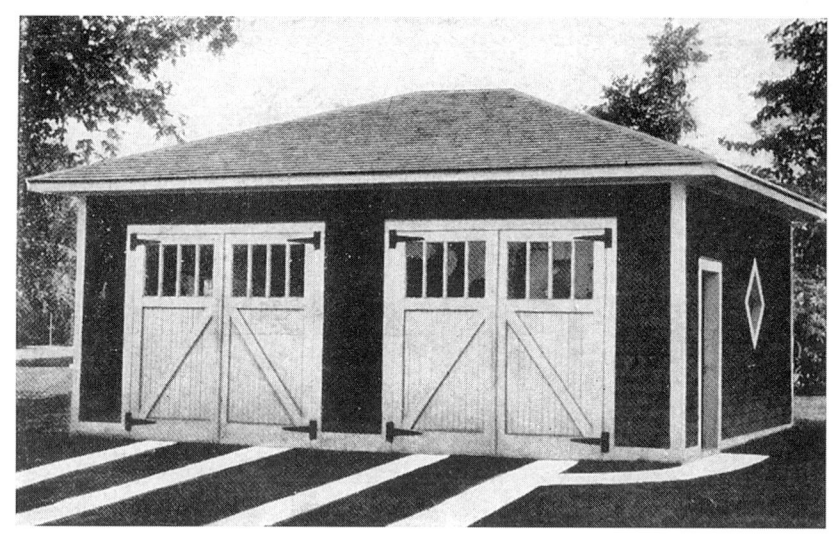
E-22

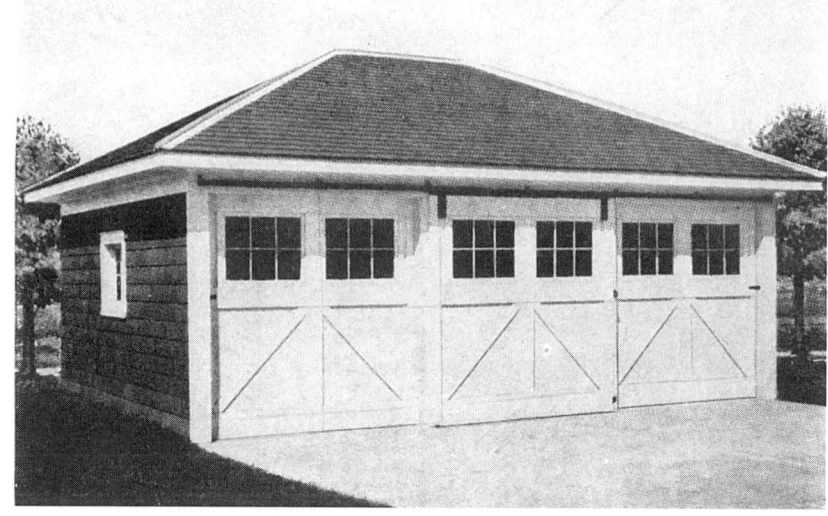
D-26

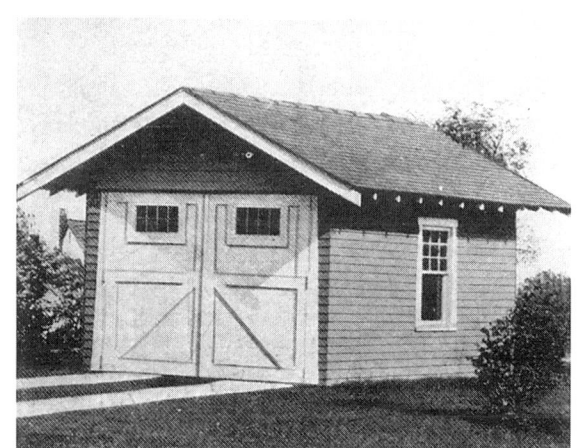
B-10

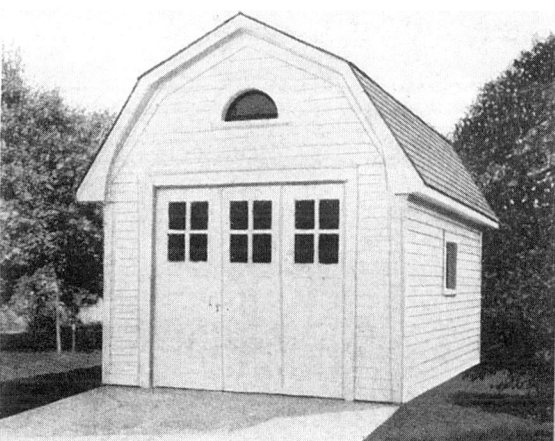
A-12

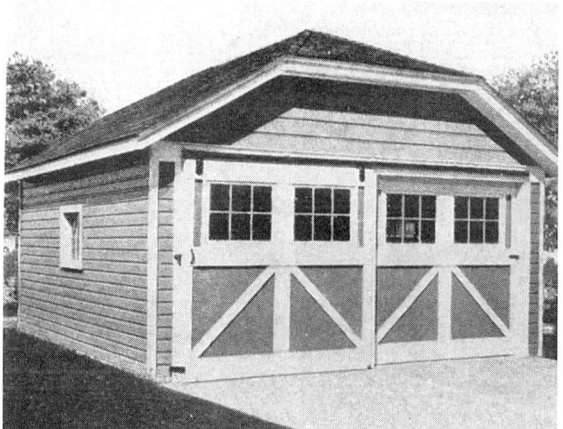
C-18